MW01405162

Monographs of the Hebrew Union College Number 21

Ideals Face Reality
Jewish Law and Life in Poland
1550–1655

An I. Edward Kiev Library Foundation Book

Monographs of the Hebrew Union College

1. *Lewis M. Barth,* An Analysis of Vatican 30
2. *Samson H. Levey,* The Messiah: An Aramaic Interpretation
3. *Ben Zion Wacholder,* Eupolemus: A Study of Judaeo-Greek Literature
4. *Richard Victor Bergren,* The Prophets and the Law
5. *Benny Kraut,* From Reform Judaism to Ethical Culture: The Religious Evolution of Felix Adler
6. *David B. Ruderman,* The World of a Renaissance Jew: The Life and Thought of Abraham ben Mordecai Farrisol
7. *Alan Mendelson,* Secular Education in Philo of Alexandria
8. *Ben Zion Wacholder,* The Dawn of Qumran: the Sectarian Torah and the Teacher of Righteousness
9. *Stephen M. Passamaneck,* The Traditional Jewish Law of Sale: Shulḥan Arukh, Ḥoshen Mishpat, Chapters 189–240
10. *Yael S. Feldman,* Modernism and Cultural Transfer: Gabriel Preil and the Tradition of Jewish Literary Bilingualism
11. *Raphael Jospe,* Torah and Sophia: The Life and Thought of Shem Tov ibn Falaquera
12. *Richard Kalmin,* The Redaction of the Babylonian Talmud: Amoraic or Saboraic?
13. *Shuly Rubin Schwartz,* The Emergence of Jewish Scholarship in America: The Publication of the *Jewish Encyclopedia*
14. *John C. Reeves,* Jewish Lore in Manichaean Cosmogony: Studies in the *Book of Giants* Traditions
15. Robert Kirschner, *Baraita De Melekhet Ha-Mishkan*: A Critical Edition with Introduction and Translation
16. *Philip E. Miller,* Karaite Separatism in Nineteenth-Century Russia: Joseph Solomon Lutski's *Epistle of Israel's Deliverance*
17. *Warren Bargad,* "To Write the Lips of Sleepers": The Poetry of Amir Gilboa
18. *Marc Saperstein,* "Your Voice Like a Ram's Horn": Themes and Texts in Traditional Jewish Preaching
19. *Emanuel Melzer,* No Way Out: The Politics of Polish Jewry, 1935–1939
20. *Eric L. Friedland,* "Were Our Mouths Filled With Song": Studies in Liberal Jewish Liturgy
21. *Edward Fram,* Ideals Face Reality: Jewish Law and Life in Poland 1550–1655

Ideals Face Reality

Jewish Law and Life in Poland 1550–1655

EDWARD FRAM

HEBREW UNION COLLEGE PRESS
CINCINNATI

© Copyright 1997 by the Hebrew Union College Press
Hebrew Union College-Jewish Institute of Religion

Library of Congress Cataloging-in-Publication Data

Fram Edward.

Ideals face reality : Jewish law and life in Poland, 1550–1655 / Edward Fram.
p. cm.—(Monographs of the Hebrew Union College ; no. 21)
Includes bibliographical references and index.

ISBN 0-87820-420-2

1. Jews—Poland—History—16th century. 2. Jews—Poland—History—17th century. 3. Jews—Poland—Politics and government. 4. Jewish law—Cases. 5. Jews—Legal status, laws, etc.—Poland. 6. Poland—Ethnic relations. I. Title. II. Series.

DS135.P6F676 1997
943.8'004924—dc21

97-2538
CIP
r97

Printed on acid free paper
Manufactured in the United States of America

DR. I. EDWARD KIEV

1905–1975

Distinguished Rabbi, Chaplain, and Librarian

In September 1976, Dr. Kiev's family and friends established a Library Foundation bearing his name to support and encourage the knowledge, understanding, and appreciation of scholarship in Judaica and Hebraica.

In cooperation with the Hebrew Union College Press, the foundation presents this study by Edward Fram as an I. Edward Kiev Library Foundation volume.

For my wife and friend

Liane

Contents

xi Acknowledgments

xiii Abbreviations and Style

1 Introduction

JEWISH LIFE IN EARLY MODERN POLAND

Chapter One
15 Jews Among Poles

Chapter Two
38 The Jewish Community

Chapter Three
48 Personal Piety

SOCIAL AND ECONOMIC REALITIES AND THE LAW

Chapter Four
67 Social Issues as Halakhic Determinants

Chapter Five
106 The Acquisition of Leases

Chapter Six
129 Bills Payable to Bearers

Chapter Seven
144 Bankruptcy and Those who Fled their Creditors

165 Bibliography

179 General Index

183 Index of Medieval and Pre-Modern Rabbinic Sources Cited

Acknowledgments

The publication of this book allows me to thank those whose assistance has made the study possible. Fellowships from Columbia University and its Center for Israel and Jewish Studies allowed me to attend the university, where this work began as a doctoral dissertation, and benefit from its rich human and scholarly resources. Financial support provided by the Social Sciences and Humanities Research Council of Canada, the National Foundation for Jewish Culture, the Memorial Foundation for Jewish Culture, the Woodrow Wilson National Fellowship Foundation (Charlotte W. Newcombe Fellowship), and a Fulbright-Hays Doctoral Fellowship allowed for ongoing full-time study and research during graduate school. Corrections and reworking of the original manuscript were made during a Ray D. Wolfe Post-Doctoral Fellowship at the University of Toronto and after my arrival at the Department of History of Ben-Gurion University of the Negev.

Nothing has been more important in creating this work than fine teachers and perceptive readers. At various stages I have benefited from the advice of Professors Robert Somerville, Dwight Van Horn, David Weiss Halivni, and the late John Gilchrist. Each taught me skills while gently guiding me away from numerous pitfalls. The chair of the Hebrew Union College Publications Committee, Michael A. Meyer, has also made many helpful comments.

Professor Haym Soloveitchik introduced me to the often unappreciated treasures that lay in medieval rabbinic legal texts. His ability to make texts "talk history" remains the benchmark for me and, I know, for many others. His comments on this manuscript were but some of his many kindnesses to me over the years. Professor Yosef Hayim Yerushalmi gave sage counsel in many spheres and urged me to introduce comparative dimensions into the study. Finally, Professor Michael Stanislawski not only initiated me into the study of eastern European Jewry but guided me through many of its complexities. In reviewing this work he again and again forced me to restate sometimes complicated rabbinic arguments in a clearer, more concise fashion. I am now thankful for his prodding. Needless to say, as good teachers, all three offered their suggestions and comments but left me to chart my own course, for which they do not bear responsibility.

The patience and tireless efforts of numerous librarians enabled me to locate many of the works used in this book. The reference staffs of Butler Library of Columbia University, the Jewish Theological Seminary Library, the New York Public Library's Jewish and Slavonic divisions, the Mendel Gottesman Library of Yeshiva University, the Jagellonian University Library, and the Ben-Gurion University of the Negev Library have shown great dedication and even greater abilities. In particular, Rabbi Jerry Schwarzbard, Special Collections Librarian of the Jewish Theological Seminary, was ever willing to provide friendship as well as expert practical help regarding rare books and manuscripts.

The process of editing has been almost painless due to the efforts of Barbara Selya, managing editor of the Hebrew Union College Press. Her wise suggestions have made the text more accurate and easier to read. A grant from the Publications Committee of the Faculty of Humanities of Ben-Gurion University has facilitated the indexing of the volume.

While many people leave their work at the office each night, this endeavor has been ever with me for many years. As a result, my children, Ayala and David, and even more so my wife, Liane, have been cheated of much time and attention. Their unstinting love and support cannot be adequately acknowledged but only returned in kind.

Abbreviations and Style

B.T.	Babylonian Talmud
BZIH	*Biuletyn żydowskiego instytutu historycznego*
J.T.	Jerusalem Talmud
PH	*Pinqas ha-medinah o pinqas shel va'ad ha-qehillot ha-ro'shiyyot be-medinat Liṭa'.* Edited by Simon Dubnow. Berlin: Ajanoth, 1925.
PVAA	*Pinqas va'ad arba' araẓot.* Edited by Israel Halperin. Revised and edited by Israel Bartal. With an Introduction by Shmuel Ettinger. Jerusalem: Mossad Bialik, 1990. (References to the index are to the first edition of 1945.)
TMM	*Taqqanot medinat Ma'hareyn.* Edited by Israel Halperin. Jerusalem: Mekize Nirdamim, 1952.
YSS	*Yam shel Shelomoh*

Books of the Bible are abbreviated according to the guidelines of *The Chicago Manual of Style*, 14th ed. (Chicago: University of Chicago Press, 1993). Names of publishers have been provided for works published since 1900.

Place names have been spelled according to *Webster's New Geographical Dictionary* (Springfield, Mass.: Meriam-Webster, 1984) following English forms. Thus "Kraków" is spelled "Cracow" and "Lwów," "Lvov." Towns that do not appear in this reference work have been spelled according to Polish orthography. Hebrew names that appear in the Bible have been written in their standard English form (e.g., "Jacob" not "Ya'aqob") while non-biblical names and all other Hebrew terms have been transliterated following the rules found in *The Jewish Encyclopedia* (New York: Funk and Wagnalls, 1907) although the *quf* is represented here as a "q" instead of a "ḳ" and the *vav* as "v" in place of a "w." The object of the transliteration has been to allow the reader who so desires to recreate the original Hebrew as accurately and easily as possible rather than obtaining a close modern vocalization.

Readers may cringe with each use of "sixteenth and seventeenth centuries" as a code to refer to approximately the second half of the sixteenth century and the first fifty-five years of the seventeenth century. If so, I apologize but I have found it a convenient matter of style.

Introduction

Jewish life in early modern Poland was characterized by an adherence to the rabbinic law (halakhah) that Polish Jewry had inherited from medieval Franco-German Jewry. Almost all aspects of Jewish activity, even the most personal of matters, fell within its purview. Some areas, such as that prohibiting adultery and consanguineous sexual relationships, remained constant throughout the ages. Yet, as had always been the case, in other areas, particularly commerce, rabbis were constantly forced to grapple with the complexities of contemporary life and reinterpret the law.

This study attempts to analyze how sixteenth- and seventeenth-century Polish jurists, responding to those complexities and applying particular legal principles to novel situations, adapted the halakhah to the evolving sensibilities of Jewish society. Through an examination of cases in which the law confronted unfamiliar circumstances or the special needs of individuals or groups within the community, not only do the dynamics of the halakhah come under scrutiny but, perhaps more importantly, a greater understanding of the attitudes of rabbis of the period toward changes in certain communal values is possible. These changes became apparent, for example, when families attempted to insure inheritances for daughters even though the Torah (Pentateuch) appears to prohibit them; or when letters of credit enjoyed wide popularity even though they were halakhicly invalid. Such situations posed difficult problems for rabbis committed to the preservation of a tradition perceived to represent divine law.

Rabbis were not the sole source of Jewish legal authority. The halakhah also recognized the right of the community to issue legally binding enactments on residents. Most such rulings were in complete harmony with the halakhah; occasionally, however, particularly in areas of commerce, they were not. The very existence of those few public laws calls the centrality of the halakhah and the place of the rabbinate in daily life in sixteenth- and seventeenth-century Poland into question.

In this study, rabbinic legal decisions (responsa), talmudic and legal exegesis, the ordinances of Polish Jewry's political leadership, and Polish legal records all serve as tools to define the role and limits of the halakhah in Polish-Jewish society and to delineate rabbinic responses to its nonobservance.

The relationship of Jewish law and Jewish life in early modern Poland has generally not been treated by scholars. Some of the legal issues faced by Polish halakhists have been discussed by historians and students of Jewish law, including Philip Bloch and Paltiel Dickstein, but their work deals only with the legal issues at hand and does not analyze the character of the legal discussions or place them in social or historical context. Other scholars, most notably Majer Bałaban, P. H. Wettstein, and Israel Halperin, have transcribed or collected communal ordinances of the Polish-Jewish community without considering their relationship to the halakhah. Only Jacob Katz has explored the tensions imposed by Jewish law on Jewish life in Poland, although his most detailed study of the subject is limited to a particular aspect of Sabbath law and does not concern itself with the dynamics of the legal process.[1]

In contrast to the popes who headed the Catholic church, rabbis in the post-talmudic age could not simply alter rules found in Scripture or change talmudic decrees to meet the needs of their day.[2] Jewish laws were considered binding even if the factors that had motivated their enactment had vanished. Rabbis and laymen in subsequent periods had the right to enact statutes to meet the needs of their age but could not openly disregard any aspect of the law or take legal precedent lightly. At the same time, if rabbis failed to integrate modern life into the framework of the law, they threatened to render the latter irrelevant and undermine its authority. Thus in each generation and in every locale rabbis had to interpret the law in light of the needs of those who lived by it.[3] Some of their decisions were informed not only by the law itself but by a host of variables, among them

---

1. See Jacob Katz, *Goy shel Shabbat* (Jerusalem: Zalman Shazar Center, 1984), pp. 70–83. Also see Katz's *Masoret u-mashber* (Jerusalem: Mossad Bialik, 1958), pp. 78–87.

2. On the extent of the medieval papacy's legal power see Kenneth Pennington, *Pope and Bishops* (Philadelphia: University of Pennsylvania Press, 1984), pp. 28–29.

3. See, however, Samuel Morell, *Precedent and Judicial Discretion: The Case of Joseph Ibn Lev*, South Florida Studies in the History of Judaism, no. 26 (Atlanta: Scholars Press, 1991), who writes that "it is doubtful whether the rabbinic authorities knowingly recognized this type of tendentiousness as legitimate in most areas of halakha and utilized it consciously and openly in judicial methodology" (p. 96). Elsewhere in his work, Morell cites a number of examples in which practical considerations appear to have shaped the legist's legal conclusions quite consciously (pp. 136, 146). A blatant example of a jurist allowing practical considerations and communal pressure to convince him to alter his legal judgment can be found in Isaac ben Abraham of Poznań, *She'elot u-teshubot Rabbeynu Yiẓḥaq me-Pozna'*, Ya'aqob Aharonfeld, et al., eds., (Jerusalem: Machon Yerushalayim, 1982), no. 93, p. 199, a responsum from a decade or two beyond the period under discussion here.

public policy considerations, social and economic concerns—indeed, even by the temperament of the *poseq* (a rabbinic scholar who decides issues of law).[4]

A number of exegetical methods were available for expanding the parameters of the law while respecting the integrity of authoritative sources. Practical or inductive reasoning, or simply conjecture, could be used to reinterpret a talmudic passage and to suggest that the text was discussing something other than what it seemed. The provenance of a troublesome legal text could be limited to circumstances dissimilar to what a jurist faced, effectively neutralizing the legal impact of the original case. Precedents could be narrowed or broadened to afford much greater flexibility in dealing with a problem. If the present situation was extreme, a text could even be deliberately misinterpreted in the course of developing a line of thought. A jurist had to separate contemporary cases from previous legal thought if he was to follow an independent approach. Hermeneutical methods, however, did not tell Jewish legists when to attempt a reinterpretation of the law.[5]

Admittedly, the notion that law is shaped by external forces, if pursued too vigorously, can lead to reductionism. Yet halakhists remained bound to both custom (*minhag*) and to canonical legal texts such as the Talmud and the commentaries of the medieval Franco-German legists. Polish rabbis could only interpret texts; they could not forsake them. Interpretation, much of which involves meanings added by the reader, ultimately had to fit texts, whether well or poorly. And since Polish rabbis also believed that Polish Jewry was descended from the thirteenth-century German Jewish pietists, Ḥasidey Ashkenaz, for at least one Polish rabbi, Joel Sirkes (1561–1640), this meant not accepting leniency in legal matters where a tradition of lenience did not exist.[6]

---

4. While such forces pressured and shaped halakhic thought, it is unlikely that one can arrive at an overarching concept of justice that explains all judicial decision making on the basis of these concerns. At best one can use case studies to demonstrate the nature of the process.

5. Examples of some of the legal methods used by a sixteenth-century Ottoman decisor to gain greater legal flexibility are analyzed in Morell, *Precedent and Judicial Discretion.*

6. See Joel Sirkes, *She'elot u-teshubot ha-bayit ḥadash* (Frankfurt, 1697), no. 79. Sirkes was, however, the only one to record such a position in the name of Ḥasidey Ashkenaz. He grounded the idea of stringency in the concepts of holiness and piety (see *Responsa,* nos. 110, 139; Joel Sirkes, *She'elot u-teshubot ha-bayit ḥadash ha-ḥadashot* [Koretz, 1785], no. 32, 43, 51, 89).

The authority to rule in halakhic matters had been imparted to rabbis from earlier generations in a chain that was ultimately traced back to the Talmud and Mount Sinai. No one else was similarly authorized. While philosophers may have been intimately familiar with the values of Judaism, ethical thought was not inextricably bound up with revelation. Moreover, philosophers, unlike halakhists, owed no particular allegiance to the legal precedents of earlier authorities.[7] And while the law is not a closed logical system, philosophers and others used sources of knowledge that the Franco-German halakhic tradition did not admit. And while Jewish mysticism had a limited role in the halakhic process among a number of Polish halakhists, the halakhah remained the supreme legal source among Polish jurists of the age.[8]

When deciding matters of law, rabbis were generally not required to provide the basis for their decisions, many of which were given as they were asked, orally. However, in written responses to the inquiries of colleagues, jurists were obliged to justify their conclusions. Rarely did rabbis articulate their nonhalakhic concerns in the course of their legal arguments; a nontextual approach would leave a rabbi's view unmoored in classical sources and with diminished claims to obedience.[9] Generally, then, traces of nonlegal concerns in halakhic thought must be sought in a jurist's interpretation of texts. One must examine to what extent a legist reinterpreted his sources, endowing them with new meaning.[10] When a number of such reinterpretations are combined and analyzed in light of the realities of contemporary society, they may suggest a marked concern for something other than a purely objective reading of the law.

Thus the *poseq* straddled a fine line between tradition and innovation. The very purpose of his quoting earlier sources was to anchor his decisions

---

7. See Frank Easterbrook, "Method, Result, and Authority: A Reply," *Harvard Law Review* 98.3 (January 1985): 627–29.

8. On the role of both Jewish mysticism and philosophy in the halakhic thought of contemporary Polish jurists, see my "Jewish Law and Social and Economic Realities in Sixteenth and Seventeenth Century Poland" (Ph.D. diss., Columbia University, 1991), pp. 129–74.

9. See Frank Easterbrook, "Legal Interpretation and the Power of the Judiciary," *Harvard Journal of Law and Public Policy* 7.1 (Winter 1984): 97–98.

10. Not every reinterpretation is a sign of change. Care must be taken to determine whether texts take on a new meaning simply because words convey different meanings to people in different times and places. Exegetes also produce novel ideas while trying to harmonize seemingly contradictory texts.

in tradition and halakhic authority and make it appear as if he were conservatively following the Mosaic tradition. Yet these highly sophisticated and intelligent men surely knew that all their prooftexts and sources did not always address head-on the questions they were discussing. On the other hand, they never stated that they were trying to intuit what the Torah, or rabbis of the Talmud, or even God Himself, would have wanted in any given situation.[11] Legislative intent had little, if any, place in Jewish jurisprudence. Rabbis were propagators of an ancient legal tradition that was characterized by specific legal rules and assumptions. They tried to deal with the evolving needs of their societies within the rubric of this legal system. So long as they respected the legitimacy (i.e., authority) of canonical texts, legal fictions and textual reinterpretations were valuable tools in reshaping the law. Even the boldest jurists couched innovation in the language of tradition.

The time frame of this study encompasses approximately the years between 1550 and 1655, a period of exceptional creativity in the annals of Polish Jewry, particularly in the fields of self-government and halakhah. The cultural blossoming of Polish Jewry was in part a reflection of the personalities of the day. Rabbinic intellectual activity came to life in Poland with the arrival of Rabbi Jacob Pollak (1460/70–after 1522) and flourished in the talmudic academy of Rabbi Shalom Shakna (d. 1558). Although both Pollak and Shakna left little written material, Shakna's students, such as Rabbis Moses Isserles (d. 1572) and Solomon Luria (ca. 1510–1574), evidenced little literary reticence. Not only did they leave volumes of halakhic thought, but they produced students who themselves produced students who continued their exegetical and legal activities. It was only the combination of the Cossack rebellions in the eastern lands of the Polish-Lithuanian Commonwealth in 1648–1649, the Swedish invasions that rocked the western half of the country and reached Poznań and Cracow in 1655, and the Muscovite attacks in the east that saw slaughters in Vilnius, Lvov, and Lublin in the same year, that caused a serious, albeit temporary, rupture in the development of talmudic scholarship in Poland. While Polish yeshivot

11. Some authorities did attribute Divine inspiration (*ruaḥ ha-qodesh*) to works that eventually gained universal acceptance such as the Mishnah, Moses Maimonides' *Code of Law*, and Joseph Karo and Moses Isserles's *Shulḥan 'aruk*. See Jacob Spiegel, "Derek qeẓarah bi-lshon tanna'im ve-'al peshat ve-derash ba-mishnah," *Asufot* 4 (1990): 23–26, and particularly n. 58. But, as Spiegel points out, contemporaries of the authors of these works hardly thought of them in such terms.

(talmudic academies) continued to attract students from western Europe even after the events of the mid-seventeenth century,[12] many Jews, including leading scholars such as Rabbi Shabbetay ben Me'ir ha-Kohen (1621–1662), fled their homes in the wake of the devastation and epidemics that follow war.[13]

The extended period of peace enjoyed by Poland in the sixteenth and first half of the seventeenth century afforded teachers the opportunity to transmit their values from one generation to the next. Perhaps even more important than the establishment of schools of higher learning for spreading rabbinic culture during this period was the development of printing.[14] With printed books readers could spend time studying texts instead of copying them and learn about a wide range of material without a teacher.[15] More Jews had access to rabbinic texts at the beginning of the seventeenth century than at any time in the age of manuscripts, although their numbers should not be exaggerated—printed books remained relatively expensive and few people owned more than a handful.[16]

---

12. Although many assume that talmudic academies in Poland declined after 1648, M. Rosman has cogently argued that while Polish yeshivot did not reach the scholarly heights that they occupied during the sixteenth century, the country remained a center for Torah study until the mid-eighteenth century. See Mosheh Rosman, "Dimmuyav shel beyt Yisra'el be-Polin ke-merkaz Torah aḥarey gezerot Ta"Ḥ—Ta"Ṭ," *Zion* 51.4 (1986): 442–48.

13. Many Jews had left Poland for western centers before 1648 but Jewish emigration from Poland intensified after the Cossack rebellion. See Moses Shulvass, *From East to West* (Detroit: Wayne State University Press, 1971), pp. 19–37. On the extent of the decline in the total Polish population as a result of the devastation, see Jerzy Topolski, "Wpływ wojen połowy XVII wieku na sytuacje ekonomiczna Podlasia," in *Studia historica w 35-lecie pracy naukowej Henryka Łowmianskiego*, Aleksander Gieysztor, ed., (Warsaw: Państwowe Wydawnictwo Naukowe, 1958), pp. 324–28, who estimates that the population of Mazovia shrunk from approximately 990,000 people before the war to 360,000 in 1662–1663, a drop of about 65 percent. The population of Great Poland fell by 42 percent to 830,000 people in the same period, and that of Little Poland by 27 percent to 1.06 million people. Surprisingly, Topolski emphasizes the effects of increased child mortality and not emigration in the wake of the wars.

14. See Elizabeth Eisenstein, *The Printing Press as an Agent of Change*, vol. 1 (Cambridge: Cambridge University Press, 1979), pp. 71–73.

15. The development of printing did not totally absolve the need for manuscript copies. Books that were not available in the local marketplace and manuscripts from earlier ages that had yet to be printed still had to be copied by hand.

16. As Natalie Davis points out, the price of books was not the only impediment to purchasing printed works. Those living outside printing centers like Cracow and Lublin somehow had to connect with booksellers, who did not always have a book the buyer wanted. See Davis's article "Printing and the People," in a collection of her essays entitled *Society and Culture in Early Modern France* (Stanford: Stanford University Press, 1975), pp. 196–97.

Printing not only brought previously unavailable works to a relatively large audience but also increased the possibilities of preserving works for posterity. Two hundred copies of a book printed on high rag content paper dispersed among different owners in various places had a much better chance of surviving war, fire, theft, wear and tear, moisture, and the other vicissitudes that written records had to endure, than one manuscript.

Among the works of Polish rabbis that have survived to the present, two types are particularly useful in tracing those instances where rabbis shaped the law on the basis of economic and social factors in sixteenth- and seventeenth-century Poland. One is the glosses of Polish rabbis on earlier legal/talmudic texts; the other is the responsa literature, answers to specific questions asked of rabbis by colleagues or laymen unfamiliar with a point of law. The latter are particularly useful. Not only do they deal with concrete situations rather than theoretical textual interpretations, but they often reflect the values of both the rabbi answering the question and the community that asked it. No rabbi appointed himself an authority. If his views were not in harmony with those of his community, people would quickly stop referring their questions to him and consult someone else. That people continued to turn to a particular jurist time and time again can only mean that his approach to problems and his answers were in consonance with the values of his contemporaries.

There are obvious hazards in using such literature for historical purposes.[17] One problem is establishing the accuracy of texts. A sixteenth- or seventeenth-century responsum was usually written by its author and generally copied twice into a legible hand by a scribe before one copy was signed by the rabbi and sent to the questioner. The other copy was kept for the rabbi's files. In some cases the original letters that were signed and sent still exist; usually they do not.[18] Many sixteenth- and seventeenth-century Polish collections were set in type from the rabbi's files,[19] a process that pre-

17. No work takes a reader through the step by step textual difficulties and rewards of using responsa literature better than Haym Soloveitchik's *Shu"t ke-meqor histori* (Jerusalem: Zalman Shazar Center, 1990). While Soloveitchik's work focuses on responsa from eleventh-century Franco-Germany, the tools employed can be used with responsa written in a later age.18. A number of such responsa can be found in J.T.S. Rabbinics MS. 1542 that contains three signed responsa of Joel Sirkes (fols. 30b-31a, 73a-75a) that appear in Sirkes's *Responsa* (old), as numbers 85, 86, and 87.

19. See, for example, Sirkes, *Responsa* (new), no. 43 (end), that states that it has been copied from a holograph of Sirkes. The printed text is therefore likely but one step away from what Sirkes actually wrote.

sented opportunities for mistakes in transcription.[20] The resetting of type in subsequent editions increased the likelihood of errors.[21] In addition, responsa were subject to censorship by both Jewish communities anxious about the repercussions of a particular halakhic position and Christian authorities on the lookout for what they perceived as offensive passages.[22] In short, fidelity to the original text was generally inversely proportional to the number of hands through which a text passed between its writing and its printing.[23]

Manuscripts, on the other hand, remain of great historical value, but relatively few have been preserved. Once a collection was printed there was little reason to keep a manuscript copy. It was much more convenient to carry a neatly bound book than a bulky file bulging with papers (the beautifully

20. See Eisenstein, *The Printing Press as an Agent of Change*, vol. 1, pp. 108– 9.

21. Later editors recognized the numerous mistakes in the text of *She'elot u-teshubot ha-ge'onim batra'ey*, Löb ben Samuel Zebi Hirsch, ed., (Turka, 1763), and the fourth (Prague, 1816), fifth (Russia[?], 1820), and sixth editions (Chernovtsy, 1860) of the work each had additional corrections(!). Isaac Horowitz, who made corrections in the sixth edition, seems to have based his corrections solely on what he believed to be "better" readings; he had no manuscripts. He acknowledged that there were printer's mistakes in his own edition but could not correct them because the printers would not give him extra time.

22. Responsum no. 124 was removed from the Amsterdam (1711) edition of Moses Isserles's responsa by Jewish authorities for fear that it might aggravate an already serious problem in the Jewish community (see below, p. 86 n. 97) while two of Benjamin Slonik's responsa (nos. 29 and 86) discussing Christians were deleted from the 1833 edition of his work published in Sudylków.

23. Sometimes even first editions were recalled or edited. Soon after the first edition of Me'ir ben Gedaliah's responsa appeared in Venice (1618), the community ordered copies of the work returned and substituted a new page 14 (responsum no. 13) without comments deemed damaging to a local rabbi. The substitute page had the same layout as the one that it replaced in the hope that the change would go unnoticed (see David Fränkel, "Diqduqey-soferim," *'Alim le-bibliyogerafyah ve-qorot Yisra'el* 1.3 [1935]: 112–14; Isaac Rivkind, "Diqduqey-soferim," in *Sefer ha-yobel le-kebod Alekkesander Ma'rks*, Saul Lieberman, ed., [New York: Jewish Theological Seminary, 1950], pp. 427–28). The publisher of the first edition of *She'elot u-teshubot ha-ge'onim batra'ey*, Me'ir ben Solomon, asked (in a request that appeared only on the penultimate page of the first edition) that readers not judge him harshly for printing mistakes that occurred in the text. Such things were common, he said, because of the need to work quickly, errors in placing similar pieces of type, "wandering" letters, the inability of typesetters to read all portions of a manuscript, "and many similar" incidents. He also noted that he "corrected" the text to make it easier to read. One can only wonder whether his corrections changed the meaning of one or two poorly worded but important arguments.

bound collections of manuscripts often found in modern libraries are generally the work of modern binders). When they exist, manuscripts can provide historical information—such as the date and place of writing—that a printer anxious to save space often omitted from a legal discussion.[24] Nevertheless, a manuscript alone does not guarantee a faithfully transmitted text. Copyists, too, could be short of time, space, and/or concern and leave out data that printers using other copies included.[25] Uninterested in preserving material for later historians, scribes and printers were in business to make a profit and could hardly waste time trying to decipher a difficult script to insure a perfect transcription of words with little bearing on the halakhic argument.[26]

Yet even when a text has been reconstructed to represent what left the hand of an author, the historical use of responsa remains fraught with problems. The entire genre of responsa literature is dedicated to dealing with exceptions. There was little need to ask a prominent rabbi about well known customs that had been practiced for generations. Even if a rabbi were asked such a question, he had little reason to include it in a collection for posterity.[27] The unfamiliar was noteworthy. Yet what was novel may not have pervaded society. A question to a rabbi about a Jewish prostitute may include a novel legal argument; it does not mean that prostitution was a significant problem in Jewish society.

Responsa were not intended to be historical documents. Rabbis commonly left out the most important historical information in presenting what was asked of them, including only what they believed to be halakhicly

---

24. See, for example, Sirkes, *Responsa* (new), no. 94. J.T.S. Rabbinics MS. 1542 (fol. 85a) adds that the responsum was sent to Rabbi Zanvil.

25. The printed text of Joshua Höschel ben Joseph, *She'elot u-teshubot peney Yehoshu'a*, vol. 2 (Lvov, 1860), no. 97, for example, contains a number of lines of testimony given in Judeo-German that do not appear in Bodleian Neubauer MS. 842 (Opp. 76), fol. 207b. The printed text of Sirkes, *Responsa* (old), no. 104, adds that the responsum was written and signed at the fair in Lublin, a fact missing from J.T.S. Rabbinics MS. 1542 (fol. 84a).

26. Sirkes, *Responsa* (old), no. 97, *Responsa* (new), no. 79, and Isaac ben Samuel, *She'elot u-teshubot R. Yiẓḥaq ha-Levi* (Neuwied, 1736), no. 7, all describe the same event. The first text places the event in Izmir, the second in Sandomierz, and no place name is given in the third text. That the second text is the best working possibility is suggested not only from the provenance of the authors but from the mention of the *szóstak*, a Polish coin, in all three texts.

27. Rabbis may have had little say in which of their responsa were published. Most responsa collections from sixteenth- and seventeenth-century Poland were published posthumously.

germane. This habit is not only disconcerting in any attempt to reconstruct the realities of the past, but it is problematic for the student of halakhic history itself. One must also consider whether in the course of their presentations legists only raised questions to their approaches that they knew they could answer and ultimately use to strengthen their own arguments. The issues that a jurist chose not to pursue may be just as important as those he chose to develop. Textual criticisms may have been ignored in an attempt to achieve a predetermined goal.

Wherever possible, collateral information should be sought elsewhere: in parallel responsa in different collections; in responses of contemporaries to a *poseq's* decisions; in statutes or other works emanating from the Jewish community; even in the works of preachers.[28] Materials from non-Jewish sources can also shed light on what is being discussed in a responsum and what was taking place in Jewish society at large. The records of secular courts, where Jews often appeared as litigants and testified, can be of great help in expanding our knowledge of the Jewish community in Poland. Consideration must also be given to Jewish lay courts where Jewish litigants received arbitration from their peers instead of halakhic justice from scholars. Such courts imposed important restraints on the applicability and development of halakhic thought as did various ordinances enacted by lay leaders.

In analyzing and using the creative works of numerous authors for historical purposes, at some point one must ask who these men were. The question goes beyond amassing biographical data and is aimed at understanding something of their characters. Their decisions, whether consciously or unconsciously, were influenced by their personalities. A thorough investigation of this topic may best be left to psycho-historians, but at least some rudimentary information is germane to the topic at hand.

It is known that Solomon Luria, for example, was a fiercely independent legist and social critic. In part, our sense of the scope of his criticism is a function of the volume of his work; he wrote more than most and much of it has survived. But there is more. Luria rejected contemporary talmudic and legal methodology and dismissed the then current belief that legal opinions of earlier generations were almost sacrosanct. Maintaining that his

28. As in dealing with the responsa literature, the ordinances of the Jewish communities are generally assumed to be discussing actual problems faced or anticipated by Jewish leaders. The problems associated with the use of ethical writings and the works of preachers have already been noted by Baruch Mevorakh, review of '*Im ḥilufey tequfot*, by Ezriel Shochat, in *Kirjath Sepher* 37.2 (March 1962): 154.

generation had as much access to knowledge as did those that preceded it, Luria believed it incumbent upon scholars in each generation to comb the sources from their talmudic beginnings through the tosafists to their own day, analyzing and weighing each matter and all opinions before coming to a well considered opinion. To draw legal conclusions on the basis of a simple majority among three leading medieval authorities, as Rabbi Joseph Karo had done in his sixteenth-century code of Jewish law, the *Shulḥan 'aruk*, was, in Luria's opinion, simply wrong.[29]

Possessed by a mission to seek out the heart of talmudic matters, Luria had the independence and boldness of character to overturn almost any opinion in his passionate search for truth. By his own admission, a heavenly voice was urging him to write the *Yam shel Shelomoh*, an attempt to analyze each legal passage of the Talmud and all the relevant commentaries to arrive at a practical legal conclusion—an ambitious work by any account.[30] Not surprisingly, Luria derided rabbis who, in his view, did not delve into the depths of the halakhah at all and did not understand even one portion of tradition "properly." Old men ("*zeqenim*"; literally a term of respect in addition to a physical description) only in years, they followed a methodology that Luria condemned; yet they ruled the community.[31] Such a view of the world around him must have left Luria an embittered critic of both his colleagues and the society that empowered them.

Psychological and textual considerations notwithstanding, one must bear in mind that rabbis were communal functionaries burdened with many tasks and could not devote all their time to the consideration of profound issues. They sat on rabbinic courts, gave sermons in the synagogue, lectured in the yeshiva, and dealt with the most pressing religious issues presented to them from across Poland and beyond.[32] Rabbis were not just educators but

---

29. Luria also rejected Karo's attempt to reduce the halakhah to one book. According to Luria, the process of examining the law is ongoing and cannot be conclusively summarized in one book for all generations. A definitive handbook of Jewish law also ignored Luria's reading of Ecclesiastes 12.12, ". . . make many books without end . . ." (*YSS, Ḥullin*, introduction).

30. Luria, *YSS, Gittin* introduction; cf. Haim Hillel Ben Sasson, *Hagut ve-hanhagah* (Jerusalem: Mossad Bialik, 1959), pp. 21–22, regarding the scope of Luria's heavenly charge.

31. Luria, *YSS, Baba' Qamma'* 8.58. This information has been culled from Luria's introductions to each tractate.

32. Polish rabbis commonly dealt with problems from Lithuania, the Ottoman Empire, Austria, Germany, Bohemia, and Moravia. They also responded to questions from Italy (especially Isserles who had familial ties to Italy) and Amsterdam. The Jewish political leadership of Poland also concerned itself with happenings in western Europe. See Israel Halpern.

had to raise funds for and administer their schools. They had pastoral responsibilities: comforting mourners and rejoicing with congregants, often on the same day; listening to the most trivial of problems from people who had little knowledge of the law; and dealing with laymen, many of whom could undoubtedly be abusive to a man they employed. Not least of all, they had to spend some time with their own families, teaching their children and showing tenderness to their wives. Somehow they had to extract time from their days for study and thought. Not surprisingly, many wrote in their responsa that they were replying briefly and in a hurry because they had little time. This was no ivory tower. Perhaps that was best for men whose task it was to achieve a balance between the demands of religion and daily life.

Yehudim ve-yahadut be-mizraḥ Eyropah (Jerusaelm: Magnes, 1969), pp. 67–77, and Moshe Rosman, "Samkuto shel va'ad arba araẓot mi-ḥuẓ le-Polin," *Annual of Bar Ilan University* 24–25 (1989): 11–30, both of which deal mainly with the post-1656 period but contain some discussion of the earlier period.

Part One

Jewish Life in Early Modern Poland

1

Jews Among Poles

The beginnings of east European Jewry in general, and Polish Jewry in particular, are mired in obscurity. The first Jewish settlers, like other immigrants, must have seen in eastern Europe the prospects of a brighter future, but who they were, where they came from, and what exactly attracted them to these territories remains a matter of speculation.

Lack of information notwithstanding, the mysteries of early Jewish history in this region have been the source of much historical conjecture since the nineteenth century for both scholarly and political reasons. The numerous views can be compressed into two basic hypotheses.[1]

The first—and decidedly weaker—theory often involves the conversion of the Khazars to Judaism and suggests that the original east European Jewish communities had eastern, that is Palestinian, Byzantine, or Persian, antecedents and existed no later than the end of the first millennium of the common era. A second—and more likely—theory claims that the Jews of eastern Europe were predominantly of west European ancestry, hailing from the Germanic lands no later than the eleventh century. What is certain is that in the second half of the twelfth century a Rabbanite Jewish community existed in Poland. Likely of limited size, it appears to have been without local religious leadership,[2] but by the thirteenth century there were def-

1. Many of the sources dealing with this issue have been collected and evaluated by Bernard Weinryb in his "The Beginnings of East European Jewry in Legend and Historiography" in *Studies and Essays in Honor of Abraham A. Neuman,* Meir Ben-Horin, et al., eds., (Leiden: Brill, 1962), pp. 445–502. The categorization of the theories is Weinryb's (pp. 458–59). See too Weinryb's *The Jews of Poland* (Philadelphia: Jewish Publication Society, 1976), pp. 19–22. Weinryb's rejection of Old Russian sources must be tempered with the remarks of Henrik Birnbaum, "On Jewish Life and Anti-Jewish Sentiments in Medieval Russia," *Viator* 4 (1973): 225–55.

2. See Me'ir ben Baruch, *Teshubot R. Me'ir me-Roṭenburg* (Prague), M. Bloch, ed., (1895; reprint, Tel Aviv: n.p., 1969), no. 588; Isaac ben Moses, *Sefer or zaru'a* (1862; reprint, n.p., n.d.) vol. 1, no. 113. Regarding the approximate date and provenance of the responsum see E. E. Urbach, *Ba'aley ha-tosafot,* 4th ed. (Jerusalem: Mossad Bialik, 1980), pp. 213–14.

initely Jews of German descent in Poland, some of whom were connected to circles of Ḥasidey Ashkenaz.[3]

Jewish immigration to Poland continued in the fourteenth and fifteenth centuries as German Jews sought refuge in a land relatively free from religious persecutions. Although by the end of the fifteenth century there are estimated to have been between ten and fifteen thousand Jews in Poland,[4] it was not until the mid-sixteenth century that Polish Jewry began to blossom as an independent Jewish cultural center.

One of Europe's largest states, mid-sixteenth-century Poland stretched southward from Pomerania (Pomorze) along the Baltic Sea, across the agricultural lands, lakes, and forests of Great Poland (Wielkopolska) and over the fertile lowlands and mineral deposits of Little Poland (Malopolska) to the Carpathian Mountains. In the west the country extended from just east of the Oder River, past Warsaw—from 1611 the seat of the Polish capital—in impoverished Mazovia (Mazowsze), to the woodlands of Podlasie in the northeast and, further south, Red Ruthenia bordering on the lands of the Turks and Tartars. The Union of Lublin (1569) united the Kingdom of Poland and the Grand Duchy of Lithuania and brought the Lithuanian heartland, Byelorussia, and the underdeveloped but exceptionally rich Ukraine into Poland.[5]

Casimir?

The expanses of the Polish state encompassed not only numerous topographic areas but also a broad spectrum of peoples. Poland began to develop as a multi-ethnic state in the fourteenth century when Kazimierz the Great (r. 1333–1370) took control of Red Ruthenia and its non-Polish population. By the mid-seventeenth century ethnic Poles represented only forty percent of Poland's approximately ten million inhabitants.[6] Ukrainians, Byelorussians (White Russians), Russians, Lithuanians, Latvians, Estonians,

3. Israel Ta-Shma, "Le-toledot ha-Yehudim be-Polin be-me'ot ha-12—ha-13," *Zion* 53 (1988): 352.

4. Weinryb, *The Jews of Poland*, p. 32.

5. For an economic survey of Poland in the sixteenth and seventeenth centuries, see Andrzej Wyrobisz, "Economic Landscapes: Poland from the Fourteenth to the Seventeenth Century," in *East-Central Europe in Transition*, Antoni Mączak, et al., eds., (Cambridge: Cambridge University Press, 1985), pp. 36–46.

6. Irena Gieysztorowa, "Research into Demographic History of Poland. A Provisional Summing-up," *Acta Poloniae Historica* 18 (1968): 11.

as well as Germans, Italians, Jews, and Scots combined to make the ethnic minorities the demographic majority.[7]

The country was also religiously heterogeneous. The Reformation made major inroads especially among the German burghers, who were attracted to Lutheranism, and the nobility, who saw in Calvinism a means of circumventing the social and political hierarchy and the control of the Catholic and Orthodox clergy.[8] Even after a successful Counter Reformation, Roman Catholics constituted less than 50 percent of the population. Uniates, Greek Orthodox, Protestants (including Calvinists, Lutherans, Arians, and Czech Brethren), Armenians, Jews, Karaites, and Muslims together represented the demographic majority.

With such a diverse population, religious tolerance was a political, social, and economic necessity if Poland was to avert the strife that had rocked Germany in the wake of the Reformation.[9] However, only Christians—with the exception of Anti-trinitarians, who rejected the fundamental Christian beliefs, and Anabaptists, who were perceived to be dangerous to the established social order—were granted full religious freedom.[10] Yet even legal guarantees did not insure social and religious tolerance, and any harmony that had existed in Poland was disrupted by the Counter Reformation in the late sixteenth century. As for the Jews, their toleration by the

---

7. Scots, who appear to have begun coming to Poland in the fifteenth century for economic reasons, were an important segment of the merchant class in Poland. King Stephan Bathroy (r. 1576–1585) said regarding Scottish merchants, "Our court cannot be without them that supply us with all that is necessary," although by the seventeenth century most Scots in Poland were peddlers. In 1621 the Polish ambassador to England reported to the English monarch that there were approximately 30,000 Scots in Poland. See A. Francis Steuart, Introduction to *Papers Relating to the Scots in Poland* 1576–1793 (Edinburgh: T. and A. Constable, 1915), pp. ix-xxxvi, and W.B.[Wacław Borowy], *Scots in Old Poland* (Edinburgh: Oliver and Boyd, 1941), pp. 6–8.

8. Jarema Maciszewski, *Szlachta polska i jej państwo*, 2d ed., (Warsaw: Wiedza Powszechna, 1986), pp. 122–24.

9. The 1573 Confederation of Warsaw, agreed to by both the political and religious leadership, specifically stated that *dissidentes de religione* would tolerate one another in order to prevent unrest. See *Volumina Legum*, vol. 2 (1859; reprint, Warsaw: Wydawnictwa Artystyczne i Filmowe, 1980), 841–42.

10. Janusz Tazbir, "La tolérance religieuse en Pologne aux XVIe et XVIIe siècles," in *La Pologne au XIIe congres international des sciences historiques a Vienne* (Warsaw: Państwowe Wydawnicza Naukowe, 1965), p. 31. In Lithuania, one also had to be a member of the nobility to enjoy full religious toleration (Janusz Tazbir, *Reformacja w Polsce. Szkice o ludziach i doktrynie* [Warsaw: Książka i Wiedza, 1993], p. 106).

king and magnates not only raised the ire of Catholic clergymen but of those who competed with the Jews in the marketplace, particularly the lesser nobility and the burghers.[11] By the seventeenth century the emergence of a Polish national consciousness, defined in large part by religion, further eroded any ideal of religious tolerance.[12]

Prior to the Union of Lublin, approximately three million people lived in Poland. With the Union, the population swelled to about 7.5 million, of whom 40 percent were Eastern Orthodox.[13] The eastern borderlands were heavily rural, Great Poland and Little Poland less so, and Royal Prussia, where farming was most difficult, least so. While approximately 50 percent of the population in western countries such as Spain, Portugal, and the Low Countries lived in urban centers, in late sixteenth-century Poland, on average, less than one-third of the population did.[14] Of those who did live in towns, at least half were farmers who worked nearby fields.[15] Typically, residents without franchise comprised 50 to 80 percent of towns. Clergy members, whose numbers increased with the success of the Counter Reformation, represented up to 15 percent of certain centers (commonly, they were also part owners of the towns—as, for example, 35 percent of Cracow in 1580) while nobles and burghers made up the remainder of the townspeople.[16]

---

11. Frank Sysyn, "A Curse on both their Houses: Catholic Attitudes toward the Jews and Eastern Orthodox during the Khmel'nyts'kyi Uprising in Father Pawel Ruszel's *Fawor nibieski*," in *Israel and the Nations Essays Presented in Honor of Shmuel Ettinger*, Shmuel Almog, et al, eds., (Jerusalem: Historical Society of Israel, 1987), p. xix.

12. Zbigniew Wójcik, "Poland and Russia in the 17th Century: Problems of Internal Development," in *Poland at the 14th International Congress of Historical Sciences in San Francisco*, Bronisław Geremek and Antoni Mączak, eds., (Wrocław: Ossolineum, 1975), pp. 122–23.

13. *Historia chłopów polskich*, Stefan Inglot, ed., vol. 1 (Warsaw: Ludowa Spółdzelnia Wydawnicza, 1970), p. 41; Norman Davies, *God's Playground A History of Poland*, vol. 1 (New York: Columbia University Press, 1984), p. 215.

14. Some Polish historians have limited the urban population at the end of the sixteenth century to just twenty percent of the entire population. See Maria Bogucka, "The Towns of East-Central Europe," in *East-Central Europe in Transition*, Antoni Mączak, et al., eds., (Cambridge: Cambridge University Press, 1985), pp. 98–99.

15. *Historia chłopów*, p. 52. Andrzej Wyrobisz, "Small Towns in 16th and 17th-Century Poland," *Acta Poloniae Historica* 34 (1976): 157–58, claims that in small towns more than two thirds of the population made their living farming.

16. Maria Bogucka, "Polish Towns Between the Sixteenth and Eighteenth Centuries," in *A Republic of Nobles*, J. K. Fedorowicz, ed. and trans., (Cambridge: Cambridge University Press, 1982), p. 143.

The Jewish population in Poland in 1569 has been estimated at anywhere from 20,000(!) to 300,000 souls, generally on the basis of the same sources.[17] With such a wide divergence, these estimates can be both inaccurate and misleading. Jews were not evenly spread out across Poland, since not every geographic area offered the same opportunities to Jews. It may therefore be most useful to look both at general trends of Polish Jewish settlement and at local demographic patterns and statistics. Only about 15 percent of the Jewish population lived in western Poland. About 80 percent lived in towns, but not all Polish towns permitted Jewish residence.[18] Cracow, Gdansk, Lublin, and Warsaw, as well as many lesser commercial centers like Jarosław, did not officially tolerate Jewish settlement within town walls.[19] Some centers, mainly royal towns, took the extreme act of obtaining the right *de non tolerandis Judaeis* from the monarch, a privilege principally granted during the Counter Reformation.[20]

Like the urban non-Jewish Polish population, most Jews lived in small

---

17. The various views are cited by Zenon Guldon, *Żydzi i Szkoci w Polsce w XVI–XVII wieku* (Kielce: Wyzsza Szkoła Pedagogiczna im. Jana Kochanowskiego, 1990), pp. 127, 129. Guldon raises methodological problems in using taxes collected as a source for the demographic history of Polish Jewry during this period in his "Źródła i metody szacunków liczebności ludności żydowskiej w Polsce w XVI- XVIII wieku," *Kwartalnik Historii Kultury Materialnej* 34.2 (1986): 252–54.

18. Jerzy Topolski, "On the Role of the Jews in the Urbanization of Poland in the Early Modern Period," in *The Jews in Poland*, vol. 1, Andrzej Paluch, ed., (Cracow: Research Center on Jewish History and Culture in Poland, 1992), pp. 47, 48, regarding the percentage of Jews in western Poland and the towns.

19. There were exceptions to laws excluding Jews. In 1560 a Jew named Josko Piessak owned a house in Lublin next door to the town consul (Lublin Public Archive, *Księga miasta Lublina, Inscriptiones perpetuitatum civitatis Lublines* 129 [1541–1561], p. 455). In Cracow royal dispensations were granted to individual Jews to live in Cracow during the course of the sixteenth century (Bożena Wyrozumska, "Did King Jan Olbracht banish the Jews from Cracow?," in *The Jews in Poland*, vol. 1, Andrzej Paluch, ed., [Cracow: Research Center on Jewish History and Culture in Poland, 1992], pp. 30–31).

20. Only a small number of towns actually had the privilege of *de non tolerandis Judaeis*. See Ignacy Schiper, *Dzieje handlu żydowskiego na ziemiach polskich* (1937; reprint, Cracow: Krajowa Agencja Wydanicza, 1990), pp. 26–27, and Jacob Goldberg, "De non tolerandis Iudaeis," in *Studies in Jewish History Presented to Professor Raphael Mahler on His Seventy-fifth Birthday*, Samuel Yeivin, ed., (Merhavia, Israel: Poalim, 1974), pp. 41–42 and nn. 7 and 8. See, however, Gershon Hundert, "The Role of the Jews in Commerce in Early Modern Poland-Lithuania," *The Journal of European Economic History* 16.2 (Fall 1987): 253–54 and n. 18.

towns—both royal and private—where conditions were generally more favorable for them than in large centers.[21] The number of Jews in such towns could range from a few dozen families to just one or two.[22] For example, in 1591, of the forty-four homes in Zamość, a private town in southeastern Poland, nineteen were inhabited by Armenians, twelve by Greek Orthodox, five by Germans, three by Hungarians, two by Italians, two by Jews, and one by Scots. By 1657 there were a total of 222 homes in Zamość, nineteen of which belonged to Jews.[23] While such isolated settlement may have been historically unusual for Jews in Poland,[24] this pattern of settlement in small centers continued well into the seventeenth century during the expansion of the Ukraine.[25]

Although banned from establishing themselves within the limits of certain towns, Jews were typically allowed into the towns to trade and participate in fairs. To avail themselves of this opportunity, Jewish communities developed on the periphery of most of Poland's major economic hubs. The size of such settlements varied. There were sixty-nine Jewish homes in the

---

21. Gershon Hundert, "Security and Dependence: Perspectives on Seventeenth- Century Polish-Jewish Society Gained through a Study of Jewish Merchants in Little Poland," [Ph.D. diss., Columbia University, 1978], p. xv).

22. Maurycy Horn, "Działalność gospodarcza i pozycja materialna Żydów czerworuskich w świetle lustracji i inwentarzy z lat 1564–1570." *BZIH* 2/82 (April–June 1972): 18–19.

23. Janina Morgensztern, "Żydzi w Zamośćiu na przełomie XVI i XVII w.," *BZIH* 43–44 (July–December 1962): 3, 16.

24. Rabbi Ḥayyim ben Bezalel of Friedberg, who spent more than the first third of his life in Poland before settling in Worms in 1549, reported in the mid- 1570s that in Poland "everyone" lived in towns where there was a rabbi, unlike Germany where, he says, most Jews lived in small villages far away from Jewish communities (*Vikkuaḥ mayyim ḥayyim* [Amsterdam, 1712], p. 5b).

25. The constant opposition of the burghers in the royal towns, the pressures of the church particularly in the wake of the Counter Reformation, and the economic competition of the lower *szlachta* (nobility) made the numerous burgeoning private towns of the Ukraine quite appealing to Jews in western Poland. Samuel Ettinger estimates that across the Ukraine, in 1569, Jews lived in twenty-four settlements with a total Jewish population of 4,000 ("Ḥelqam shel ha-Yehudim be-qolonizazyah shel Uqr'enah [1569–1648]," *Zion* 21.3–4 [1956]: 124). By the 1648 uprising Jews lived in 115 Ukrainian settlements and numbered about 51,525 (Ettinger, "Ḥelqam shel ha-Yehudim," pp. 110–11, 119–24). Jews were not the only ones attracted to the Ukraine. The rich soil, abundant land, high wages, and significant tax abatements of the Ukraine lured colonizers from western Poland, Muscovite Russia, Red Ruthenia, northern Lithuania, and even from central Europe and Italy.

Jewish suburb of Lublin in 1570, about 1,035 Jews.[26] In 1583 the Christian population of Lublin is thought to have reached 5,175 people. Majer Bałaban, citing the treasury book of Kazimierz, where Jews had begun to move in the late fifteenth century after their rights had been severely limited in Cracow and their property had been looted or destroyed after a blaze in 1494, stated that there were 2,060 Jews in Kazimierz in 1578.[27] The estimate for the first half of the seventeenth century hovered around 4,500.[28] Nearby Cracow had approximately 28,000 residents.[29] In 1578 approximately 1,500 Jews lived in Lvov, where there were two Jewish communities, one inside the town walls and one outside. By 1648 both natural population growth and immigration from western Europe had helped swell Lvov's Jewish population to about 4,800 of the approximately total 30,000 residents.[30] The entire Lvov region, comprising 17 smaller towns such as Bruchnal, Olesko, and Kulików, plus Lvov itself, was home to about 27,410 people in 1578, about 10.2 percent of whom were Jews.[31] In Poznań Jews

---

26. Bella Mandelsberg-Schildkraut, *Meḥqarim le-toledot Yehudey Lublin* (Tel Aviv: Circle of Friends of the Late Bella Mandelsberg-Schildkraut, 1965), p. 66. Although Maurycy Horn argues for twelve people per house ("Działalność Gospodarcza, p. 17), Roman Szewczyk in his *Ludność lublina w latach* 1583–1650 (Lublin: KUL, 1947), p. 17, maintains that in Lublin the average family size was six people and that the "average" house housed fifteen people. Since Jews tended to marry younger than Poles and generally did not serve in the army, they probably had larger "average" families.

27. The view of M. Bałaban, *Dzieje Żydów w Krakowie i na Kazimierzu* (1304–1868), vol. 1 (1912; reprint, Cracow: Krajowa Agencja Wydawnicza, 1985), pp. 50–52, that the Jews were expelled from Cracow in 1495 has recently been challenged by Wyrozumska, "Did King Jan Olbracht banish the Jews from Cracow?," pp. 27–32, 36–37.

28. Bałaban, *Dzieje Żydów w Krakowie*, vol. 1, p. 102.

29. Unless noted otherwise, the total population figures for the Polish centers, all for the beginning of the seventeenth century, are taken from Bogucka's "Polish Towns," p. 138.

30. Maurycy Horn, *Żydzi na Rusi Czerwonej w XVI i pierwszej połowie XVII* w. (Warsaw: Państwowe Wydawnicza Naukowe, 1975), pp. 60–62; Maurycyz Horn, "Spoleczność żydowska w wielonarodowościowym Lwowie 1356–1696," BZIH 1/157 (January–March 1991): 4. Eleonora Nadel-Golobic, "Armenians and Jews in Medieval Lvov Their Role in Oriental Trade 1400–1600," *Cahiers du Monde Russe et Soviétique* 20.3–4 (July–December 1979): 352, cites research estimating the total population of Lvov between 1574 and 1591 at 12,344.

31. Horn, *Żydzi na Rusi Czerwonej*, pp. 63, 64. Horn suggests that in 1648 about 9,450 Jews lived in the region although he does not offer an estimate of the total population. With the exception of Żółkiew (over 20 Jewish homes) and Olesko (12 Jewish homes), the smaller towns in the Lvov region had but a handful of Jews (Majer Bałaban, *Żydzi lwowscy na przelomie XVIgo i XVIIgo wieku* [1906; reprint, Cracow: Orbita, n.d.], pp. 249–50).

lived in approximately 50 of the over 400 houses in the town in 1567. By 1619 there were some 762 Jewish families living in 141 homes.[32] Both Moses Isserles, rabbi of Cracow (Kazimierz), and Solomon Luria, who served as rabbi of Ostrog, Brest Litovsk, and later Lublin, related that in most Polish cities Jews were in the minority.[33]

As they had in medieval Germany, Jews in Poland generally lived in homes huddled together around one courtyard or along an alleyway—a pattern of settlement not always mandated by law but rather by self-interest and convenience.[34] These Jewish enclaves were often enclosed by a wall whose gates were locked at night for security reasons.[35] Jews had mixed feelings about having non-Jews in their midst. As early as 1558 the community in Lubmol (about twenty-five miles east of Chełm) believed that so long as Christians lived among them, they would not set fire to the Jewish quarter for fear of killing a fellow Christian.[36] In the mid-seventeenth century, however, Jews in Sandomierz feared the repossession of a bankrupt Jewish debtor's home "in the middle of the street of the Jews" by a non-Jewish creditor. Not only did the possible presence of a non-Jew in the Jewish sector cause the Jews to fret lest they have "no rest" but they also feared that the non-Jew might allow priests and (seminary) students

---

32. Zenon Guldon and Jacek Wijaczka, "Osadnictwo żydowskie w województwach Poznańskim i Kaliskim w XVI-XVII wieku," *BZIH* 162–163/2–3 (1992): 66, 73. Daniel Tollet, "Marchands et hommes d'affaires juifs dans la Pologne des Wasa (1588–1668)," (Ph.D. diss., Université de Paris, 1985), pp. 31–32, arrives at somewhat higher Jewish population figures for this period.

33. Moses Isserles, *She'elot u-teshubot ha-Rama'*, Asher Siev, ed., (Jerusalem: Feldheim, 1971), no. 61, p. 241; Solomon Luria, *She'elot u-teshubot ha- Maharshal* (Lublin, 1574), no. 17.

Kazimierz and Cracow were separate towns until 1800. Sixteenth- and seventeenth-century Jews, however, generally referred to themselves as residents of Cracow, a usage that has principally been followed here.

34. See, for example, Isserles, *Responsa*, no. 29, p. 169; no. 132, p. 512. Joshua Höschel, *Responsa*, pt. 2, no. 94, however, described a community connected by a gate to the courtyards of non-Jews. The gate was destroyed by a fire and the community did not bother to rebuild it for about fifteen years.

35. Jacob Katz has argued in his *Masoret u-mashber*, pp. 45–46, that, for essentially religious reasons, it was the Jewish community's ideal to live separately from the non-Jewish community.

36. Sirkes, *Responsa*, (old), no. 4. The community forbade any Jew, under the threat of excommunication, from purchasing either a house or land from Gentiles who lived within the Jewish town walls. The *qahal's* ordinance was renewed and strengthened in 1577, forcing anyone who had disobeyed the rule to sell the property in question back to non-Jews.

into the house from where, the Jews worried, they would harass the community.[37] Elsewhere, there was a popular notion that keeping a non-Jew out of the Jewish community was like keeping a lion at bay.[38] Isserles wrote that there were no non-Jews in the Jewish section of Kazimierz although they did pass through the streets.[39] In 1582 Rabbi Solomon ben Judah Leybush (d. 1591) noted that Jews in Chełm lived among "non-Jews, our wicked neighbors and our enemies" while "in the other holy communities 'it [Israel] is a nation that dwells alone' (Num. 23.9) and no foreigner mixes among them (cf. Job 15.19)."[40]

The central Polish government, with which Jews had to negotiate various matters, was made up of three legislative branches: a nominally hereditary monarchy, a royally appointed Senate, and a diet, the Sejm, whose members were drawn almost exclusively from the 7 to 10 percent of the population who were members of the nobility. The vast majority of the Polish population, the peasants, had no parliamentary voice.[41] With the exception of residents of Cracow, nor did town burghers, who made up about 10 to 15 percent of the total Polish population, many of whom were of German descent. The clergy too was without seats in the Sejm although Christian bishops were appointed to the Senate.

Royal legal jurisdiction was eroded in the course of the sixteenth century by a number of successive measures. With the adoption of the 1505 consti-

---

37. Joshua Höschel, *Responsa*, vol. 2, no. 97. As Dieter Fettke, *Juden und Nichtjuden im 16. und 17. Jahrhundert in Polen* (Frankfurt: P. Lang, 1986), p. 79, n. 284, suggests, the spelling "Ẓuyzmer" that appears in the text is likely a mistake for Sandomierz, usually written "Ẓuzmir" in Hebrew (at issue is the positioning of the "yud"). The word does not appear in Bodleian MS. 842 (Opp. 76), fol. 207b, a copy of this responsum.

38. Sirkes, *Responsa* (old), no. 18. Sirkes disagreed with the questioner's assumption. The non-Jew was only a "questionable lion," not a certain one. The use of the metaphor "lion" for a non-Jewish neighbor is talmudic in origin. See B.T., *Baba' Meẓi'a'* 108b.

39. Isserles, *Responsa*, no. 132, p. 512. Isserles noted that non-Jews controlled the gates of the town.

40. Solomon ben Judah Leybush, *Sefer pisqey u-she'elot u-teshubot Maharash me- Lublin*, I. Herskovitz, ed., (Brooklyn, N.Y.: n.p., 1988), no. 58, p. 16. See, however, Gershon Hundert, "An Advantage to Peculiarity? The Case of the Polish Commonwealth," *AJS Review* 6 (1981): 34–35, as well as his "Jewish Urban Residence in the Polish Commonwealth in the Early Modern Period," *The Jewish Journal of Sociology* 26.1 (June 1984): 27, who notes that in small towns such as Lubartów and Opole in the Lublin district, it was not unusual for Jews and Catholics to live interspersed, especially in the first half of the seventeenth century.

41. See Juliusz Bardach, "Le pouvoir monarchique en Pologne au Moyen Age," *Recueils de la société Jean Bodin pour l'histoire comparative des institutions* 21.2 (1969): 612.

tution, the Polish king was stripped of the right to legislate without the consent of the Sejm.[42] Legislation, which any member of the government could introduce, required the unanimous consent of all branches of government before becoming law. By the end of the sixteenth century, with the development of the manorial system, small towns under private jurisdiction accounted for more than 60 percent of all the towns in Great and Little Poland.[43] The legal independence of the estates, acquired at the expense of the crown and Sejm, added a significant degree of flexibility to the legal status of Jews and other minorities—notably Armenians—who could, and did, negotiate their legal status on these lands. By the seventeenth century the central government had withered; Poland became more a federation of territories and private estates than one large country.[44]

Not *servi camerae*, Polish Jews lived in one country but under many different authorities, none of whom could be ignored[45]—a situation not unknown in the annals of medieval Jewish life. Until the consolidation of the Spanish Empire under Ferdinand and Isabella, for example, nobles living in the border areas where the king's authority was limited commonly usurped

---

42. In 1518 the royal court's authority over appeals in cases between nobles and peasants was withdrawn (Davies, *God's Playground*, vol. 1, p. 212). In 1539 the king withdrew his judicial authority over the Jews living in towns owned by nobles (*Volumina Legum*, vol. 1, 550–51; the king, however, still collected taxes from the Jews on private estates and offered Jews some measure of legal protection—see Halpern, *Yehudim ve-yahadut be-mizraḥ Eyropah*, pp. 25–26). From 1563 the king had no mastery over lands owned by members of the nobility. Nobles were able to make their own laws, set up their own courts, and dictate the conditions of settlement for anyone who lived on their lands.

43. The reasons for the development of the manorial system have been the topic of much historical debate. See Jerzy Topolski, "Sixteenth-Century Poland and the Turning Point in European Economic Development," in *A Republic of Nobles*, J. K. Fedorowicz, ed. and trans., (Cambridge, 1982), pp. 74–90. For a more complete breakdown of the percentage of royal and private towns across Poland, see Andrzej Wyrobisz, "Rola miast prywatnych w Polsce w XVI i XVII wieku," *Przegląd Historyczny* 65 (1974): 19–24.

44. Juliusz Bardach, "Gouvernants et gouvernés en Pologne au Moyen-Age et aux temps modernes," *Standen en Landen* 36 (1965): 270, 276–79. Private towns were treated as commodities by their owners who sold them or collateralized them to other nobles who would have usufruct of the town until outstanding debts were repaid (Benjamin Slonik, *She'elot u-teshubot masa'at Benyamin* [Cracow, 1632], no. 27).

45. Philipp Bloch, *Die General-Privilegien der polnischen Judenschaft* (Posen, 1892), pp.107, 115. See too Salo Baron, *A Social and Religious History of the Jews*, vol. 16, 2d ed. (New York: Columbia University Press, 1976), vol. 16, p. 25; Katz, *Masoret u-mashber*, p. 23. See, however, M. Bałaban in *Beyt Yisra'el be-Polin*, I. Halperin, ed., vol. 1 (Jerusalem: Youth Department of the Zionist Organization, 1948), pp. 44–45.

authority over their lands and the Jews who lived in them while Jews living in lands adjacent to episcopal sees often fell under the control of the ruling bishops. By the thirteenth century Spanish aristocrats were receiving seignorial rights over Jews in their territories, a trend that accelerated in the fourteenth century.[46] Jews living under such conditions could not always rely on royal protection and thus could not afford to create alliances only with the royal court.

Since Jews had no uniform legal status in western Europe throughout the Middle Ages, the idea of negotiating legal rights when settling in a new area was also not new to them. Beginning in eleventh-century Germany, Jews sought written commitments from national, regional, and local powers that defined their rights and obligations with respect to the authorities. The first so- called "charter" given to Jews in eastern Europe was issued by Bolesław the Pious, duke of Kalisz, in 1264 to the Jews of Great Poland.[47] Early Polish charters allowed Jews to travel in the country, authorized them to have their own internal court system, clearly stated who had authority over them, and enumerated various laws regarding pawns. Later charters removed Jews from municipal jurisdiction, permitted them to build synagogues, maintain cemeteries, slaughter cattle and sell meat, and, in certain towns, authorized Jews to bear arms and dress like burghers. Taxes were also a common subject of discussion.[48]

In royal towns with large Jewish populations, the *qahal*, the local semi-autonomous Jewish communal government, received special privileges specifying its powers as well as outlining election procedures.[49] Since privileges not explicitly renewed by a sovereign's successor could be declared void, Jewish communities strove to have privileges reconfirmed by each successive monarch.[50] Because no privilege succeeded in dealing with every aspect of

46. Abraham Neuman, *The Jews in Spain*, vol. 1 (Philadelphia: Jewish Publication Society, 1942), pp. 15–18.

47. See *Volumina Legum*, vol. 1, 309–16.

48. See Jacob Goldberg, *Jewish Privileges in the Polish Commonwealth* (Jerusalem: Israel Academy of Sciences and Humanities, 1985), where over sixty charters are printed. Many of the later charters include citations from sixteenth- and seventeenth-century documents.

49. Stanisław Kutrzeba, *Historja źródeł dawnego prawa polskiego*, vol. 2 (1926?; reprint, Cracow: Krajowa Agencja Wydawnicza, 1987), p. 307; P.H. Wettstein, "Qadmoniyyot mepinqesa'ot yeshanim," *Ozar ha-sifrut* 4 (1892): 585.

50. John Felix Herboth of Dobromil, writing in 1606 to the bishop of Cracow concerning the Jews, argued that the charters given to the Jews should be canceled because, among other reasons, they were not renewed by Polish kings over the centuries (Czartoryski,

relationships between Jews and the local authorities, the parties had to grapple with new problems on an ongoing basis.[51] Individual Jews, usually those distinguished by their wealth or service to the royal court, also received privileges freeing them from certain tax obligations and removing them from the authority of courts that other Jews were subject to.[52]

In the mid-sixteenth century Solomon Luria wrote that the majority of Polish Jews made their livings through debt-for-merchandise agreements. According to Luria, merchants took goods from non-Jews with the understanding that they would return a stipulated sum at an upcoming fair. The merchant's profit depended on his selling the merchandise at a price greater than his expenses and his outstanding debt with his supplier.[53] In Cracow, at least during the 1620s and 1630s, money lending was considered the basis of Jewish subsistence, although Jews were also involved in crafts as well as local, regional, and international trade.[54] In Podolia, where there were many estates, Rabbi Benjamin Slonik (ca. 1550–ca. 1619) noted that *arendy* ("leases")[55] for selling liquor and malt were dominant Jewish occu-

---

Korzeniowski MS. 101 [1606], fols. 11, 13–14). Concerning Herboth (Herburt) see *Słownik geograficzny królestwa polskiego i innych krajów słowianskich*, F. Sulimierski, et al., eds., vol. 2 (Warsaw, 1882), s.v. "Dobromil." Despite Herboth's efforts, Jews received privileges in Dobromil in 1612 (Goldberg, *Jewish Privileges*, pp. 83–88). Goldberg notes that the privilege was granted "in order to counteract prevailing anti-Jewish prejudices, which are inconsistent with the spirit of Christian tolerance."

51. See Gershon Hundert, *The Jews in a Polish Private Town* (Baltimore: Johns Hopkins University Press, 1992), p. 21.

52. Goldberg, *Jewish Privileges*, pp. 8–9.

53. Luria, *YSS, Baba' Qamma'* 1.20. Also see Luria, in Isserles, *Responsa*, no. 4, p. 17, where he observed that all contemporary business was conducted on credit.

54. Sirkes, *Responsa* (new), no. 146. It is clear that Jews not only lent money but borrowed it as well (see Sirkes, *Responsa* [new], no. 29). See too Joseph ben Elijah of Zasław, *Sefer rekeb Eliyyahu* (Cracow, 1638), p. 12a, who decried the practice of some Jews who borrowed from non-Jews and used their wives and children as collateral! The same complaint appeared in the record book of the Lithuanian community (PH, nos. 44–45 [1623]). On Jews working in crafts and trade see Jan Małecki, "Żydzi w życiu gospodarczym Krakowa w XVI i pierwszej połowie XVII wieku," *Krzysztofory* 15 (1988): 14, 15–16, as well as Małecki, *Studia nad rynkiem regionalnym Krakowa w XVI wieku* (Warsaw: Państwowe Wydawnictwo Naukowe, 1963), p. 25, and, Wyrozumska, "Did King Olbracht banish the Jews from Cracow?," pp. 32–33.

55. The *arenda* was a lease offered by owners of estates who were anxious to guarantee their incomes and offered to sell the rights to income from the manor's operations, or a part thereof, for a specified period of time (often three years) in exchange for a fixed sum. For a

pations,[56] a description echoed by Rabbi Berechiah Berak ben Isaac Eiziq in the mid-seventeenth century.[57] The sale of alcoholic beverages was a particularly lucrative endeavor since water was generally not potable and peasants could not afford wine.[58] In the 1620s or 1630s, most Jews in Włodzimierz (Vladimir-Volynski) were said to make their livings selling meat to non-Jews.[59]

Jewish agricultural activity appears to have been restricted to animal husbandry and cultivating local yards.[60] In part, this was the result of Jews'

---

discussion of the *arenda* as well as its advantages and disadvantages for the estate owner, see Ettinger, "Ḥelqam shel ha-Yehudim," pp. 128–40, and M. J. Rosman, *The Lord's Jews* (Cambridge, Mass.: Harvard University Press, 1990), pp. 106–42, the later part of which deals mainly with the eighteenth century.

56. Similar leasing existed within towns where there were numerous municipal enterprises (see Jan Rutkowski, *Histoire économique de la Pologne avant les partages* [Paris: Champion, 1927], p. 157). However, Joshua Falk, writing around 1607, noted that in the areas adjacent to Poznań and Cracow as well as in other regions in Great Poland, Little Poland, and Red Ruthenia, Jews did not hold *arendy*, lease mills and beer houses, or farm tolls (*PVAA*, no. 72; Joshua Falk, *Qunṭeres me-ha-Semaʿ* [Żółkiew, 1833], p. 5a). The apparent reference to Jews in Cracow holding a monopoly on the sale of liquor and selling the beverage from their homes in the late sixteenth century (H. H. Ben Sasson, "Taqqanot issurey Shabbat shel Polin u-mashmaʿutan ha-ḥebratit ve-ha-kalkalit," *Zion* 21 [1956]: 188–90) must be reconsidered in light of E. Feldman's suggestion that the 1590 ordinances regarding Sabbath observance eminated from Lithuania (perhaps Brest Litovsk) and not Cracow (see E. Feldman, "Heykan u-bishbil mi nitaqqnu ha-taqqanot le-issur ha-melaʾkah be-Shabbat shel R. Meshulam Feybush me-Qeraʾqaʾ," *Zion* 34 [1969]: 93–94).

57. Slonik, *Responsa*, no. 43, an undated responsum that makes no mention of place (for a listing of the communities in which Slonik served see Nisson Shulman, *Authority and Community* [Hoboken, N.J.: Ktav, 1986], pp. 179–81); Berechiah Berak ben Isaac Eiziq, *Zeraʿ berak*, vol. 2 (Amsterdam, 1662), introduction.

58. Wine was generally imported from France, Spain, Italy, and, most often, from Hungary and thus was expensive compared to the cost of locally produced beer, apparently the most popular drink among Jews (Joshua Höschel, *Responsa*, vol. 2, no. 35), and liquor. Mead was very rarely found and, when it was, it too was prohibitively expensive, although it was commonly served at Jewish wedding feasts or the festive meal after a circumcision (Joel Sirkes, *Bayit ḥadash* [Cracow, 1631–1640], Oraḥ ḥayyim 182). See also Andrzej Wyczanski, *La consommation alimentaire en Pologne aux XVIe et XVIIe siècles* (Paris: Institut d'études slaves, 1985), pp. 33, 37. Tea and coffee, possible alternative beverages, were not readily available while cow's milk was always a possible source of infection before the introduction of pasteurization.

59. Judah Leb ben Enoch, *She'elot u-teshubot ḥinuk beyt Yehuda'* (Frankfurt, 1708), no. 20.

60. Jews did not generally own fields in the countryside (*She'elot u-teshubot ha-ge'onim batra'ey*, no. 24). Some houses had yards that were large enough for families to keep their

a n i -

urban and commercial tradition; they were also effectively barred from larger scale agriculture by Polish laws prohibiting their ownership of farm land.[61] The commercial orientation of Jews contrasted sharply with the agrarian activities of the non-Jewish majority with whom they interacted.

Historically, Ashkenazic Jewry's categorization of Christians as idol worshipers had created numerous legal barriers to Christian-Jewish interaction, at least from the Jewish perspective.[62] However, while not all jurists agreed, in the sixteenth century Luria removed Christians from the class of idol worshipers because they "believe in Divine providence."[63] A similar conclusion was reached by two of Luria's contemporaries who had been educated, at least in part, in Mediterranean societies that were perhaps more tolerant towards non- Jews.[64] Whether such rationales affected popular attitudes toward Christians is unclear.

---

mals in or to plant gardens (Sirkes, *Responsa* [old], no. 4). In at least one mid-seventeenth century Polish town, Jews had garden plots next to the town wall (Isaac ben Abraham of Poznan, *Responsa*, no. 44, p. 85). Halakhic questions regarding domestic animals were common. The problem of the *bekhor* (the first born of a cow belonging to a Jew which is forbidden to be used in the post-talmudic era, see Deuteronomy 15.19–23) is a reoccurring one in contemporary responsa literature. See, for example, Isserles, *Responsa*, no. 87; Joseph Katz, *She'elot u-teshubot she'erit Yosef*, Asher Siev, ed., (New York: Yeshiva University Press, 1984), no. 24; Luria, *Responsa*, no. 91; Sirkes, *Responsa* (old), no. 27. Luria, *YSS*, Beyẓah 5.6, raises a problem associated with sheep farming.

61. Przemysław Dąbkowski, *Prawo prywatne polskie*, vol. 1 (Lvov: Nakładem Towarzystwa dla Popierania Nauki Polskiej, 1910), p. 152, noted that Jews were barred from owning immovable property yet some Jews clearly owned their own homes (see above, p. 10).

62. On the nature of the prohibitions that limited the contact of Jews and "idol worshipers"—which medieval Ashkenaz believed Christians to be—see Jacob Katz, *Beyn Yehudim le-goyim* (Jerusalem: Mossad Bialik, 1960), pp. 35–45. Medieval Ashkenazic authorities, for the most part, tried to solve specific legal problems through talmudic interpretation rather than through the reclassification of Christianity. See Jacob Katz, "Soblanut datit be-shitato shel Rabbi Menaḥem ha-Me'iri be-halakhah u-be-filosofyah," *Zion* 18 (1953): 15– 16, and nn. 4 and 5.

63. Luria, *YSS, Baba' Qamma'* introduction.

64. See David ben Menasseh ha-Darshan, *Shir ha-ma'alot le-David* (Cracow, 1571), p. 10a, and Eliezer Ashkenazi, *Ma'asey Miẓrayim* (Venice, 1583), pp. 134b-135a, a passage already noticed by David Hoffmann in his *Der Schulchan-Aruch und die Rabbinen über das Verhältniss der Juden zu Andersgläubigen*, 2d ed. (Berlin, 1894), p. 18. Slonik, however, appears to have disagreed with those who recategorized Christianity. In his responsum no. 86, Slonik allowed Jews to lend their clothing to Christians who then wore them to church because he believed that the clothing was not part of the worship. This assumes that the actual church service was a form of idol worship.

The physical and spiritual distance between Jews and Christians did not preclude Jewish-Christian contacts,[65] and there seem to have been few impediments to Christian-Jewish communication.[66] Although among themselves Jews in central and western Poland were generally comfortable speaking a Judeo-German tongue—an early form of Yiddish—many Jews spoke the local language as well: various forms of Ruthenian in the east, and Polish in much of the rest of the country. The responsa literature from eastern communities, however, indicate that Jews expressed some of life's most emotional moments among themselves in the Slavic vernacular.[67] Rabbi Me'ir ha-Kohen Ashkenazi (fl. 1630–1645), for example, wrote that " . . . most sons of our covenant [i.e., fellow Jews] who live among us speak in the 'Russian' language (Ruthenian) . . . " He was quick to add, however, that " . . . God willing, the land will be filled with knowledge and everyone will speak one language, the German language [i.e., Judeo-German] . . . "[68]

There is much evidence of Jewish-Christian interaction. During the thrice yearly fairs in Lublin, Jews stayed in rooms rented in the homes of

65. See Baron, *A Social and Economic History*, vol. 16, pp. 52–61, as well as Katz, *Masoret u-mashber*, pp. 41–48.

66. The issue of Jews and the Slavic vernacular, particularly in eastern Poland, has occupied scholars since the late nineteenth century for both political and scholarly reasons. A brief but helpful evaluation of previous scholarly material appears in Moshé Altbauer, *Achievements and Tasks in the Field of Jewish-Slavic Language Contact Studies* (Los Angeles: n.p., 1972), pp. 1–2 with notes.

67. For examples see Avigdor Berger, "Teshubot Rabbi Manoaḥ Ha'ndel ba'al Ḥokmat Manoaḥ," *Sefer ha-zikkaron le-maran Rabbi Ya'aqob Beẓal'el Zolṭey*, Joseph Buksbaum, ed., (Jerusalem: Moriah, 1987), pp. 338–39; Sirkes, *Responsa* (old), no. 82; also Shabbetay ben Me'ir ha-Kohen, *Sefer geburat anashim* (Dessau, 1697), no. 9, authored by Me'ir Ashkenazi, from approximately 1641, in which the original Ruthenian(?) appears in Hebrew transliteration.

68. Shabbetay ben Me'ir ha-Kohen, *Responsa*, no. 1, authored by Me'ir Ashkenazi. The undated text was already noticed by Dubnow and is quoted in Chone Shmeruk, "Qavvim le-demutah shel sifrut Yiddish be-Polin u-be-Liṭa' 'ad gezerot Ta"Ḥ ve-Ta"Ṭ," *Tarbiz* 46 (1977): 261–62. Moshe Altbauer, *The Five Biblical Scrolls in a Sixteenth-Century Jewish Translation into Belorussian* (*Vilnius Codex 262*) (Jerusalem: Israel Academy of Sciences and Humanities, 1992), p. 23, has suggested that the Jews referred to in the responsum migrated to eastern Europe from the "Byzantine periphery" before the arrival of Jews from German lands and spoke the local Slavic tongue as "the process of their 'Ashkenazization' took many generations." There is little, if anything to substantiate such a claim. There are certainly no echoes of eastern religious practices in contemporary rabbinic literature.

non-Jews and cooked and attended to their "small needs" there.[69] Despite legislation in 1538 demanding that they wear a yellow hat to distinguish them from Christians,[70] Jews often dressed like Poles. Many worked among Poles and, some moralists of the day claimed, even wanted to be like Poles.[71] Some had very good Polish friends (in one instance termed "*ahubim*," lit., "beloved," but here a term for particularly good friends).[72] There were Jews who drank together with non-Jews,[73] ate in non-Jewish homes

---

69. Isserles, *Responsa*, no. 120, p. 479. The questioner said that Jews rented the rooms for the entire year even though they only stayed there during the fairs.

70. *Volumina Legum*, vol. 1, 525. The Church was not alone in demanding that Jews wear distinguishing clothing; Polish rabbis, like both their German predecessors and contemporaries, enjoined Jews to dress in a distinct fashion. Falk (*Qunṭeres*, p. 2b) complained against the common practice of wearing "clothes of the non-Jews" (on the situation among German Jews see Louis Finkelstein, *Jewish Self-Government in the Middle Ages*, 2d ed. [New York: Feldheim, 1964], pp. 225, 262–63). Despite the ordinance against their dressing like non-Jews, at least Jewish women in Poland continued to dress like the general population. If they did not, non-Jewish women would not have been anxious to borrow their dresses (see below, p. 19). See too Berechiah Berak ben Isaac Eiziq, *Zera' berak*, vol. 2, introduction, who complained that Polish Jews did not heed the repeated injunctions against wearing the clothing of non-Jews. Some men, however, may have dressed in a uniquely Jewish fashion. Sirkes wrote that since it was more dangerous for Jews to travel the highways than for non-Jews, Jewish merchants and travelers wore "non-Jewish" clothing when travelling to disguise their identity implying that they wore "Jewish" clothing at other times (*Bayit ḥadash*, Yoreh de'ah 156; the Constitution of Piotrkow [1538] specifically allowed Jews to remove the yellow hat when travelling because of the danger, an allowance also found in Christian Spain [Haim Beinart, "'Ha-siman ha-yehudi' be-Sefarad ve-qiyyum 'ẓav ha-siman' be-yemey ha-melakim ha-qatoliyyim," in *Israel and the Nations Essays Presented in Honor of Shmuel Ettinger*, Shmuel Almog, et al., eds., (Jerusalem: Historical Society of Israel, 1987), pp. 31, 32, 34, 35, 38]). A later observer, Jacob Gombiner (d. 1673), who served as rabbi of Leszno in Great Poland among other Polish towns, noted that " . . . the clothing of Jews is recognizable and all that see them recognize that they belong to a Jew . . . " (Jacob Gombiner, *Sefer shalom bayit*, I. Herskovitz, ed., [Brooklyn, N.Y.: n.p., 1988], no. 157). Cf., however, Katz, *Masoret u-mashber*, p. 22.

71. Hayyim ben Bezalel, *Sefer ha-ḥayyim* (Cracow, 1593), p. 39, quoted in Halperin, *PVAA*, p. 16, n. 4.

72. Joshua Höschel, *Responsa*, pt. 1, Oraḥ ḥayyim no. 14.

73. Luria, *Responsa*, no. 72; Falk, *Qunṭeres*, p. 2b; *PVAA*, p. 16, n. 4; Abraham Horowitz, *Yesh noḥalim* (Amsterdam, 1701), p. 35b. Despite Polish legal codes prohibiting Christians from eating and drinking with Jews (Bartłomiej Groicki, *Porządek sądów y spraw prawa mieyskich prawa maydeburskiego w Koronie Polskiey* [Warsaw: Wydawnicza Prawnicze, 1953], p. 59; see too *Volumina Legum*, vol. 2, 624), Polish sources confirm that it indeed took place. See Daniel Tollet, "La place faite aux juifs dans la société Polonaise (fin du XVIe s., XVIIe s.): Representation social et aspects juridiques," *Revue des études juives* 138 (July–December 1979): 538.

and establishments,[74] had business partnerships with non-Jews,[75] traveled together with them,[76] and even defended their towns together with non-Jews.[77] While educated Jews and Christians may have engaged in formal religious debates, there seemed to have been little hesitancy by more common Jews to lend their jewelry and clothing to Christians to wear to church on their holidays.[78] Melodies from the theater and tunes that were sung in churches found their way into the synagogue (i.e., the Jewish liturgy was

---

74. Isserles, *Shulḥan 'aruk,* Oraḥ ḥayyim 193.3; Luria, *Responsa,* no. 72; Moses Meth, *Sefer maṭeh Mosheh* (Jerusalem: Ozar ha-poseqim, 1978), no. 150, who stated that (a) Luria himself ate in a non-Jew's home and even had a quorum for Grace After Meals there (cf. Isserles's opinion in *Shulḥan 'aruk*) and (b) there was once a meal for the Redemption of the First Born in the house of a non-Jew with non-Jews present.

As early as May 1539 Catholic leaders in Płock complained that Catholics met and spoke with Jews in homes, baths, and eating establishments (. . . *in domibus, balneis, collationibus* . . .). A similar complaint against "many citizens [i.e., burghers] and nobles of Płock" who had recently eaten and drunk at a banquet together with Jews was leveled by the clergy in the midst of a campaign against reformers in September 1551 (see Boleslaus Ulanowski, "Acta Capituli Plocensis ab anno 1514 ad anno 1577," *Archiwum Komisyi Historycznej* 10 [1916], nos. 149 [p. 188] and 207 [p. 213]).

75. See, for example, the case of Prosper Provana and the Jew Joachin then living in Cracow who in 1577 formed a partnership to produce and sell salt. A copy of the agreement has been translated into Hebrew by S. A. Cygielman, "Shutfut polanit-yehudit be-yiẓur melaḥ mezuqaq be-shanim 1577–1580," *Zion* 51.2 (1986): 221–22. Also see Gershon Hundert, "The Implications of Jewish Economic Activities for Christian-Jewish Relations in the Polish Commonwealth" in *The Jews in Poland,* Chimen Abramsky, et al., eds. (Oxford: Blackwell, 1986), p. 61, as well as Slonik, *Responsa,* no. 27.

76. Luria, *Responsa,* no. 94; *YSS, Ḥullin* 8.22, 8.44; *Qiddushin* 4.21.

77. Maurycy Horn, *Powinności wojenne Żydów w Rzeczypospolitej w XVI i XVII wieku* (Warsaw: Państwowe Wydawnicza Naukowe, 1978), p. 81. In 1625, however, the Wiszenski pre-Diet complained that in Przemyśl " . . . in times of danger you cannot find [the] Jews to mount a defence with proper help, neither with their powder, nor with shotguns, nor with their persons do they wish to participate in such action" (cited in Andrzej Link-Lenczowski, "Ludność Zydowska w świetle uchwał sejmikowych XVI-XVIII w.," in *Żydzi w dawnej Rzeczypolitej,* Andrzej Link- Lenczowski, ed., [Wrocław: Ossolineum, 1991], p. 156).

78. On Jewish-Christian debates see Judah M. Rosenthal, "Marcin Czechowic and Jacob of Bełżyce Arian-Jewish Encounters in 16th Century Poland," PAAJR 34 (1966): 81–86. As Rosenthal acknowledged, there has been some question whether Jacob of Bełżyce ever existed. The issue of lending clothing to Christians to wear to church prompted a question to Slonik who allowed the custom (Slonik, *Responsa,* no. 86). Borrowing fancy clothing for special occasions such as weddings was common. See Luria, *YSS, Baba' Qamma'* 8.31, who mentions the custom among Jews.

sung to contemporary music).[79] Although Jewish documents were usually dated according to the Hebrew date and month in the years from creation, in some cases, Jews—probably unconsciously—became caught up in the Christian mode of marking time. Jewish documents referred to the fair to be held at Lublin on "Gra'mniẓ," a Hebraized abbreviation of *Matki Boskiej Gromnicznej* (Feast of the Purification of Our Lady), instead of the corresponding Hebrew date or the more neutral February 2.[80] Yet no matter how much Jews interacted with Christians and assimilated their ideas, Jews—at least the rabbinic elite whose writings are our source of information about this period— did not consider themselves totally implanted in Polish society.

Despite this lack of rootedness, there was stability and a general sense of security in the lives of most Polish Jews, at least until the late 1640s and 1650s when the Cossack uprising and the Swedish invasions wreaked havoc on Jewish life. Before then Judah Löw (known by the acronym *MaHaRaL*; ca. 1525–1609), who served as rabbi of Poznań from 1592 until 1597 when he returned to Prague, wrote that unlike earlier generations who had to observe the law under very difficult conditions, "now we sit in our homes, each person in tranquility and quiet."[81] Similarly, in the early seventeenth century, Me'ir Ashkenazi commented that many Jews live under "their vine and under their fig tree" in Poland and have children and grandchildren, a play on two biblical verses discussing idyllic times.[82] Jews' economic success and the level of political autonomy that they had attained must have imbued them with a feeling of confidence and optimism about life in Poland.[83]

To be sure, Jews endured antisemitic attacks prior to 1648. Peasants,

---

79. Slonik, *Responsa*, no. 6; Sirkes, *Responsa* (old), no. 127.

80. See *PVAA*: 542–544, s.v. "*yeridim*," for other such examples.

81. Judah Löw ben Bezalel, *Derek ḥayyim*, chap. 6, quoted in Simhah Assaf, *Meqorot le-toledot ha-ḥinuk be-Yisra'el*, vol. 1 (Tel Aviv: Dvir, 1924), p. 50. Löw, who is thought to have been born in Poznań, may have served as rabbi of the community from 1584–1588 as well. See Yizhaq Yudolov, "Teshubot Maharal me-Per'ag," in *Sefer ha-zikkaron le-maran Rabbi Ya'aqob Beẓal'el Zolṭey*, Joseph Buksbaum, ed., (Jerusalem: Moriah, 1987), pp. 264–65.

82. In Shabbetay ben Me'ir ha-Kohen, *Responsa*, no. 1. The reference to "their vine and under their fig tree" is a play on 1 Kings 5.5, which speaks of times of peace and security, and Micah 4.4, a description of Messianic times.

83. Jacob Katz, "Beyn TaTN"U le-Ta"Ḥ ve-Ta"Ṭ," in *Sefer ha-yobel le- Yiẓḥaq Baer*, Salo Baron, et al., ed., (Jerusalem: Historical Society of Israel, 1961), pp. 328–29.

plebs, burghers, and nobles could, and did, turn violent in their dealings with Jews.[84] Jewish communities in Lublin, Lvov, Cracow, Płock, and Poznań suffered harrassment by Jesuit students and/or local residents over the years, while Jews in Gombin, Kalisz, Łęczyca, Lublin, Przemyśl, Sandomierz, and elsewhere endured charges of host desecration that undoubtedly undermined their collective sense of security.[85] On an individual level, attacks on Jews were commonplace despite the occasional efforts of non-Jews to protect them.[86] Luria believed that it was physically safer for Jews to remain in their own communities beset with the plague than to try to flee the dreaded disease by moving to a non-Jewish town.[87] Nevertheless, on the whole, Jews felt a certain degree of physical security in Poland. Some, however, were quite aware that the situation could easily change.

As they had in the Middle Ages, the Jewish intellectual leadership believed that the Jewish community was tolerated by the host community essentially for economic reasons.[88] Isserles's oft-quoted remark that " . . . in these states where their [the non-Jews'] anger has not risen up against us like in the German states" and his prayer, "May it be so until the coming of

84. Daniel Tollet, "Les manifestations anti-Juives dans la Pologne des Wasa (1588–1668)," *Revue d'histoire moderne et contemporaine* 33 (July–September 1986): 427–39, analyzes such attacks in Poznań and Cracow suggesting that such incidents were economically motivated. Also see Hundert, "The Implications of Jewish Economic Activities," p. 56, n. 4, regarding Cracow and Lublin.

85. See the list of incidents of blood libel and host desecration accusations leveled against Polish Jews during the sixteenth and seventeenth centuries compiled by Hannah Węgrzynek, *"Czarna legenda" Żydów* (Warsaw: Wydawnictwo Bellona, 1995), pp. 182–94. Also see Shmuel Arthur Cygielman, *Yehudey Polin ve-Lita' 'ad shenat Ta"Ḥ (1648)* (Jerusalem: Zalman Shazar Center, 1991), pp. 238–40. Although the papacy had banned charging Jews with ritual murder and host desecration such claims persisted in Poland. Cygielman suggests that the Polish church supported such accusations to strengthen itself both politically and ideologically in the wake of the Counter Reformation (pp. 234–35). On the ongoing efforts of Polish Jewry to protect itself from such slander see Węgrzynek, op.cit., pp. 150–56, also to be found in her "Ludność Żydowka wobec oskarżeń o popełnianie przestępstw o charakterze rytualnym," *Kwartalnik Historyczny* 101.4 (1994), pp. 18–24.

86. See Cygielman, *Yehudey Polin ve-Liṭa'*, p. 233.

87. Luria, *YSS, Baba' Qamma'* 6.26.

88. Slonik, *Responsa*, no. 3, quotes a statement of Rabbi Asher ben Yehi'el to this effect. Not only did Slonik not question the assumption but he used it as the basis of his decision. Also see Katz, *Masoret u-mashber*, pp. 23–26, and Daniel Tollet, "Merchants and Businessmen in Poznań and Cracow, 1588–1668," in *The Jews in Poland*, Chimen Abramsky, et al., eds., (Oxford: Blackwell, 1986), p. 23.

our Messiah," were tacit admissions that the secure existence Jews enjoyed in Poland was subject to change.[89] Elsewhere Isserles clearly expressed his awareness of the possibilities for unfavorable developments.

> . . . Because unless God [had] left a remainder [of the Jewish people] in this land [i.e., Poland], God forbid Israel would become one who is cursed and damned like a faithless wife [see Num. 5.11–31]. But with the help of Him who is wrapped in light, the heart of the king and his ministers is turned towards us that he wants us, thank God, as long as the announcers of darkness do not speak like the piercing of a sword [see Prov. 12.18, B.T., *Nedarim* 22a].[90]

Isserles was not alone in his point of view. During the conclaves of Polish nobles, Jews said special penitential prayers beseeching God for mercy and that nothing harmful to the wellbeing of the Jewish people would result from the meeting.[91] Like Jews living in Arab lands throughout much of the Middle Ages, Polish Jews realized that their safety and prosperity always depended on the goodwill of others whose motives were rarely altruistic.[92]

Jewish religious practices of the period reflected this sense of vulnerability. Fearing that the parchment would be stolen and defiled, some Jews claimed that they were afraid to fulfill the biblical precept (Deut. 6.9) to put a mezuzah on their front door post.[93] Solomon Luria suggested that Jews abandoned saying "birkat ha-reḥabah" (a blessing said in the street as mourners return from burying their dead) because they feared the "wicked-

---

89. Isserles, *Responsa*, no. 95, p. 417. Isserles's prayer, "may it be so until the coming of our Messiah," belies some level of insecurity. See too Joseph ben Elijah, *Sefer rekeb Eliyyahu*, p. 2a.

90. Isserles, *Responsa*, no. 63, p. 289. These remarks are made after a reference to the expulsion of the Jews from Bohemia. The responsum is not dated so it is difficult to determine whether Isserles is referring to the expulsion of 1542 or 1559–1561 or both. The "announcers of darkness" is likely an allusion to informers (see, however, B.T., *'Erubin* 53b).

91. Eliezer Ashkenazi, *Seliḥot u-pizmonim* (Lublin, 1614); reprinted in *PVAA*, no. 89.

92. See Leon Nemoy, review of *Jews of Arab Lands*, by Norman Stillman, in *Jewish Quarterly Review* 71 (October 1980): 124.

93. David ben Samuel ha-Levi, *Ṭurey zahab* (Lublin, 1646), Yoreh de'ah 265.5. I assume that the Jews feared that non-Jews would steal the mezuzah, not other Jews. Even if this fear was only a justification for the non-observance of a precept—they also claimed that the outside was dirty and unsuitable for a holy parchment—David ben Samuel's inclusion of the reason indicates that he must have thought it plausible.

ness" of the non- Jews who would see this public religious act.[94] Solomon ben Judah Leybush feared that if he gave too strict a penance to an adulterous woman in 1582, not only would Christian neighbors mock the Jews but there would be "misfortunes" for the community as well.[95]

Jewish communal leaders were assiduous in their efforts to protect the community's physical well being. Joel Sirkes, rabbi of numerous centers in Lithuania and Poland and of Cracow from 1620 until his death in 1640, for example, was unequivocal in seeking revenge for the murder of a Jew by a non-Jew. Failure to press the Polish authorities for punishment of the perpetrator consistent with the letter of the law (in this case capital punishment) could leave the impression that Jews were easy prey.[96]

As in so many places before, Jews perceived their existence in Poland as tenuous and vulnerable.[97] Perhaps Luria was somewhat extreme when he declared, ". . . but now that we are in a land that does not belong to us and [we] are like slaves under the hand of their masters . . ."[98] Nevertheless, the

94. Luria, *YSS, Ketubbot* 1.22. Like in the case of David ben Samuel ha-Levi cited above, even if this was simply a justification for what was already the practice, the environment allowed it to ring true.

95. Solomon ben Judah Leybush, *Responsa*, no. 58, p. 16.

96. Sirkes, *Responsa* (new), no. 52. Sirkes wrote, " . . . for who knows for how many days and years [we] must wait to bury her in order to try and get revenge so that Israel will not be a waif [*hefqer*] among them [the non-Jews], God forbid . . . " Similar concerns underlay Me'ir ben Gedaliah's opinion in his responsum from 1615 regarding punishing a Jewish murderer (Me'ir ben Gedaliah of Lublin, *She'elot u-teshubot Me'ir me-Lublin* [Venice, 1618], no. 138; a copy of the responsum from Neubauer MS. 846 [Oppenheimer MS. 327] has been published by Isaac Lewin, *Me-boqer le-'ereb*, [Jerusalem, 1981], pp. 107–14) as well as the decision of Menahem Mendel Krochmal, *She'elot u-teshubot ẓemaḥ ẓedeq* (Amsterdam, 1675), no. 111, to obligate the community to pay for information and bribes that would help bring a perpetrator to justice. The community must have felt that pressuring the Polish authorities would not jeopardize their status or, if it would, in such instances the potential benefits outweighed the liabilities. Solomon ben Judah Leybush, *Responsa*, no. 88, pp. 24–25, however, believed that communities, as extended family members, sought revenge in fulfillment of the biblical precept in Numbers 35.16–21.

97. Some of these issues are discussed in Murray Rosman's "Reflections on the State of Polish-Jewish Historical Study," *Jewish History* 3.2 (Fall 1988): 115– 30. Rosman rejected the trend among Polish historians for many years to view the Jews as resident aliens (p. 117). Yet, at least in rabbinic literature, this is how the Jews portrayed themselves. Rosman is well aware that Polish Jews knew that their security was fragile. See his "Jewish Perceptions of Insecurity and Powerlessness in Sixteenth-Eighteenth Century Poland," *Polin* 1 (1986): 19–27.

98. Luria, *YSS, Yebamot* 4.49. The statement, made in the context of discussing the mortal danger to Jews of accepting converts in Poland and praying that there will always be a safe haven for Jews among the nations as long as the exile continues, can hardly be considered typological. On Luria and converts see too Katz, *Beyn Yehudim le-goyim*, pp. 146–48.

reality of sixteenth- and seventeenth-century laws excluding Jews from full participation in the Polish economy and others that banned Jews from certain cities would not let Jews forget that they were not equals with the Christian population. In addition, their own laws and customs aimed at separating them from other cultures. Yet for the most part, life remained relatively peaceful for Jews in Poland until 1648.

The quality of Jewish life and the direction of its intellectual achievement in the period under consideration were certainly influenced by the Polish environment, which dictated much of the rabbinic agenda. The matters of *arenda* and inn-keeping that almost all rabbinic authorities in Poland dealt with were local developments that raised halakhic problems. The scarcity of fresh produce in Polish markets during the long winters made *ḥadash* ("new"), the biblical prohibition against eating grains that had sprouted since the previous Passover (see Lev. 23.9–14), a precept that Polish Jews could not observe.[99]

Even issues that had little apparent bearing on time and place were affected by the realities of the day. The drop of non-kosher fat falling on a kosher pot was a perennial problem wherever Jews lived.[100] Polish Jews had trouble eking out a living; they could not afford to throw out a pot of only questionable *kashrut*.[101] Thus rabbis had to concern themselves with the economics of observance. After all, according to the Talmud, the Torah itself "had mercy on the money of Israel."[102] It was a religious obligation to help Jews support themselves and legal leniency could broaden the possibility of economic self-sufficiency.[103] Failure to do so was religiously irresponsible.

---

99. See, among other sources, Sirkes, *Bayit ḥadash*, Yoreh de'ah 293.3.

100. There were, on average, four utility bowls and about six pots in an eighteenth-century "middle class" (non-kosher) home in Poznań and Warsaw (Miroslawa Gajewska, "Wyposażenie w sprzęty mieszczanskich gospodarstw domowych," in *Dom i mieszkanie w Polsce [druga połowa XVII-XIX w.*], Zofia Kamienska, ed., [Wrocław: Zakład Narodowy im. Ossolinskich, 1975], pp. 167–68).

101. See Luria, *YSS*, *Ketubbot* 1.8, 1.12; *Yebamot* 6.40. Luria believed that the difficulties of life in the Diaspora sapped all the happiness out of life.

102. For example, B.T., *Menaḥot* 76b; *Ḥullin* 49b. For a discussion of the talmudic rule, which has limited parameters, see Meyer Berlin (Bar-Ilan) and Shlomo Zevin, eds., *Enẓiqloppedyah talmudit* vol. 11, pp. 240–45 (esp. p. 245), and vol. 10, pp. 32–41.

103. See Joshua Falk, *Qunṭeres*, p. 10b; Joshua Höschel, *Responsa*, vol. 2, no. 25. See also Haym Soloveitchik, "Religious Law and Change: The Medieval Ashkenazic Example," *AJS Review* 12.2 (Fall 1987): 219, where Rabbi Jacob (Rabbenu Tam), confronted with a group that refused to avail themselves of legal allowances in interest taking, declared "I deem it per-

In dealing with halakhic problems, Polish Jewish jurists were not only sensitive to *realia*, such as the cost of pots. Social concerns also informed their legal thought, just as they had in every time and place, whether openly expressed or not. No responsible rabbi considering the case of young orphans or facing a woman who could not remarry because her husband was lost or believed dead could be devoid of compassion. Yet rabbis were not the only Jewish authorities in contemporary Poland. Their power was both complemented and circumscribed by the organs of Jewish self-government whose jurisdiction was recognized both by the halakhah and the Polish authorities.

Rabbis are political leaders as well... was this always so like when the church had all the real power or is it a phenomena distinct to Poland?

---

fectly permissible, indeed a divine mandate, so as to provide sustenance for my co-religionists." The historical environment is what necessitated Rabbi Jacob's "radical judicial construction" that eased religious restrictions on intra-Jewish credit. Had Jews had other economic options there would have been little reason for Rabbi Jacob's actions.

2

The Jewish Community

Beyond the many obligations placed on individuals by the halakhah, Polish Jews were also obliged to obey the laws of Poland, including those of the local municipalities within which they lived. As non-citizens, however, they had few civil obligations to the state beyond the compulsory payment of taxes to the Crown.[1] On the other hand, another authority imposed a broad range of duties on them: the highly developed Jewish community.[2]

Long before the sixteenth century, Jewish law had accepted the notion that organizations could obligate members to observe extra-halakhic rules and regulations.[3] It was assumed that each member accepted the obligations of membership by formally joining the group,[4] and those who failed to obey its bylaws were often punished. Guilds, for example, fined members who violated pricing and trade agreements. Similarly, Cracow business groups appointed tribunals and invested them with the authority to enforce their decisions.[5]

All organizations in the Jewish community functioned under the auspices of the semi-autonomous Jewish community council, or *qahal.* The *qahal* collected and paid taxes to the government and the municipality, secured political support for the community among Polish officials, set up schools for those who could not afford private tutors, maintained Jewish

1. A brief survey of the various taxes paid by the Jews during the sixteenth and seventeenth centuries can be found in Daniel Tollet, "Les Juifs et le trésor royal polonais sous les règnes des Wasa, de 1588 à 1668," in *The Jews in Poland,* vol. 1, Andrzej Paluch, ed., (Cracow: Research Center on Jewish History and Culture in Poland, 1992), pp. 53–54.

2. Even Jews who lived in isolated settlements generally had connections with a nearby Jewish community where they would pray a number of times a year and in whose cemetery they may have expected to be buried.

3. See, for example, the records copied in Wettstein, "Qadmoniyyot," pp. 603, 604–5. On guilds see Mark Wischnitzer, *A History of Jewish Crafts,* with a Foreword by Salo W. Baron (New York: Jonathan David, 1965), p. 214.

4. See B.T., *Baba' Batra'* 9a; *Ṭur,* Ḥoshen mishpaṭ 231 (end).

5. Signing the agreement obligated adherence to the bylaws of 1613 of a Cracow business group of 1613 (Wettstein, "Qadmoniyyot," p. 602).

hospitals, fixed local streets, and so on. It had the power to assess and tax, judge damages, enjoin people from settling in the community, and fine members. It also had the authority to make and enforce ordinances.

These communal rules and ordinances were not enacted by halakhic authorities but rather by the lay leadership that controlled the community. The leadership was elected annually by tax-paying members who gathered each spring to determine who would serve in the local electoral college.[6] The nine people chosen by lot, none of whom could be related to any of the other eight, then appointed the town's leaders, including its *ro'shim* (among whom the titular leadership of the community rotated each month), and the "good men" (*tobim*; alternates for the *ro'shim*).[7] Despite the elaborate arrangements, the wealthy tended to have a disproportionate say in the council, just as they did in the Polish municipalities.[8] Unlike in the Jewish community of mid-sixteenth-century Salonika (Thessaloniki) where

---

6. Such was the custom in Cracow which was in no way unique (see Bałaban, Dzieje Żydów, vol. 1, p. 240). Tollet, "Merchands," pp. 522–30, maintains that almost 35 percent of the votes in the Poznań and Cracow communities were controlled by small and middle merchants. Bałaban, p. xxi, asserts that leaders of the *qahal* zealously guarded their positions and power and that despite the use of a lottery the same people tended to occupy the positions of leadership year after year. See too Dov Avron's comments in his edition of *Pinqas ha-kesherim shel qehillat Pozna'* (1621–1835) (Jerusalem: Mekize Nirdamim, 1967), pp. xi-xii.

7. A similar custom existed in Żółkiew where a number of the "electors" (*borerim*) chose the senior leaders of the community (Salomon Buber, *Qiryah nisgabah* [Cracow: Ha-eshkol, 1903], p. 82, an ordinance dating from 1620).

8. On the inordinate role of the wealthy see Krochmal, *Responsa*, no. 2. A native of Poland who moved to Bohemia, Krochmal, writing in the mid-seventeenth century, quoted his questioners who stated that "in all large and important communities" the custom was to give the wealthy a greater say in running the community than the poor—a custom that Krochmal rejected as improper. Also see Katz, *Responsa*, no. 18, p. 59, where the wealthiest family in town, a family that contributed 80 percent of the total tax revenues, was anxious to have a disproportionate say in running the town. See also Samuel Edels, *Ḥiddushey aggadot* (Lublin-Cracow, 1627–1632), *Soṭah* 40a; Weinryb, *The Jews of Poland*, pp. 73–74; Gershon D. Hundert, "On the Jewish Community in Poland during the Seventeenth Century: Some Comparative Perspectives," *Revue des études juives* 142 (July–December 1983): 351; Bałaban, *Dzieje Żydów*, p. xxi. Israel Halperin, "Mibneh ha-va'adim be-Eyropah ha-mizraḥit ve-ha-merkazit be-me'ah ha-17 ve-ha-18," in *World Congress of Jewish Studies*, vol. 1 (Jerusalem: Magnes, 1952), p. 444, has noted that community leaders did not see themselves as democratically elected representatives of the people but, at least those who were sincere about holding office, as communal guardians. Their role was to act in the best interests of the community and no one was better suited for that task, it was thought, than the wealthy who were knowledgeable about the ways of the world, an assumption that not even critics of communal leadership disputed.

rich, "middle class," and poor formally shared communal power, only those who paid taxes participated in the communal self-government of the Polish Jewish community.[9]

Rabbis were excluded from the leadership of Jewish communal self-government—a phenomenon that had already begun in many of the large communities in fifteenth-century Germany.[10] In Poland as elsewhere, rabbis maintained their role as religious authorities; they were rarely political leaders.[11]

The *qahal* was imbued with power by the Polish government that, like the medieval hosts of the Jewish community, was interested in dealing with the Jews as a single corporate body, particularly for taxation purposes. But the *qahal's* authority also emanated from tradition. With the dawn of the Ashkenazic community in the eleventh century, rabbis such as Rabbenu Gershom, Joseph Tub Elem, and Meshulam ben Qaloniymus moored the community's right to judge damages and tax its members in the talmudic concept of *hefqer beyt din hefqer* (confiscation by the court).[12] In the twelfth and thirteenth centuries, the community's powers, including its prerogative to make ordinances and fine its members, were anchored more deeply through a legal comparison between the local *qahal* and the Sanhedrin, or

9. On the contemporary division of power in the "Shalom" community in Salonika see Samuel de Medina, *She'elot u-teshubot Maharshdam* (1862; reprint, n.p., n.d.), Yoreh de'ah no. 152 (question), and, more generally in Salonika, Isaac Adarbi (ca. 1510–ca. 1584), *She'elot u-teshubot dibrey ribot* (Sudilakov, 1833), no. 124. Also see Leah Bornstein, "Ha-hanhagah shel ha-qehillah ha-Yehudit be-mizraḥ ha-qarob me-shilhey ha-me'ah ha-16 ve-'ad sof ha-me'ah ha-18" (Ph.D. diss., Bar Ilan University, 1978), p. 96. Although Adarbi's questioner described this division of power as "the custom of all communities," De Medina for one, who served as a rabbi in his native Salonika until his death in 1589, believed that the wealthy were entitled to control the community (Oraḥ ḥayyim no. 37). The notion that only taxpaying residents should have a voice in running the community was an old one in the Ashkenazic world, stretching back at least to the thirteenth century (Mosheh Frank, *Qehillot Ashkenaz u-batey dineyhen* [Tel Aviv: Dvir, 1937], p. vi).

10. See Mordecai Breuer, "Ma'amad ha-rabbanut be-hanhagatan shel qehillot Ashkenaz be-me'ah ha-16," *Zion* 41 (1976): 47–54, 61, 62, 65–66, who argues that the prestige of the Ashkenazic rabbinate declined greatly in the fifteenth century and that laymen, not rabbis, ruled most urban communities. Nevertheless, talmudic scholarship appears to have entitled one to a voice in communal government even if the scholar was poor (see Krochmal, Responsa, no. 2).

11. The situation was similar in contemporary Venice. See David Malkiel, *A Separate Republic* (Jerusalem: Magnes, 1991), pp. 17, 175–76.

12. Yitzhak Baer, "Ha-yesodot ve-ha-hatḥalot shel irgun ha-qehillah ha-Yehudit be-yemey ha-beynayyim," *Zion* 15 (1950): 29–30.

High Court of talmudic times, that had the power to punish as well as to make ordinances.[13] By the 1550s these matters had become so accepted that Isserles, like others before him, could say that the *qahal's* authority to enact laws was based on custom and accepted by every resident simply by his or her continuing to live in the town.[14]

While each community administered matters within its own boundaries, there were issues that crossed jurisdictions. In part to deal with such matters in a relatively non-partisan manner, regional councils evolved across Poland, first in Mazovia and Great Poland, and by the mid-seventeenth century, in the eastern portion of the country.[15] Like the local *qahal*, regional administrations were governed by lay councils that usually convened in the largest Jewish community in the area and recorded their decisions in a record book or *pinqas*. The council also appointed a "chief rabbi," generally the rabbi of the main center in the region, who presided over a regional court.[16]

---

13. See Samuel Morell, "The Constitutional Limits of Communal Government in Rabbinic Law," *Jewish Social Studies* 33.2–3 (April–July 1971): 89–90; Menachem Elon, "Power and Authority: Halachic Stance of the Traditional Community and its Contemporary Implications," in *Kinship and Consent*, Daniel J. Elazar, ed., (Ramat Gan: Turtledove, 1981), p. 191, and Gerald J. Blidstein, "Individual and Community in the Middle Ages: Halakhic Theory," in the same volume, pp. 218–223. The legal basis for deciding cases and punishing those who disobeyed communal decisions remains unclear. See Finkelstein, *Jewish Self-Government*, pp. 7–10.

14. Isserles, *Responsa*, no. 73, p. 309; *Shulḥan ʿaruk*, Ḥoshen mishpaṭ 2.1. There were limitations on the *qahal's* power. It could not make ordinances that were against communal interests (Isserles, p. 309; Sirkes, *Responsa* [old], no. 60) or impose new forms of taxation without unanimous consent (Isserles, p. 310).

15. Bałaban has argued that regional Jewish councils were an outgrowth of the development of satellite communities in the fourteenth century. Before these communities were able to establish their own synagogues, cemeteries, and hire their own rabbis, they relied on the established town for religious services and paid their taxes to the Polish authorities in conjunction with the large town. As a result, members of the large town assumed a degree of hegemony over smaller centers near their borders. As the small communities developed, they were anxious to exert their independence (Bałaban in *Beyt Yisra'el be-Polin*, vol. 1, pp. 59–62). See, for example, Isserles, *Responsa*, no. 73, p. 308; *PVAA*, no. 104.

Regional authorities also sought and obtained letters from the king confirming their rights. See, for example, Mathias Bersohn, *Dyplomataryusz dotyczący Żydów w dawney Polsce na źródłach archiwalnych osnuty (1388–1782)* (Warsaw: Edward Nicz, 1910), no. 57, pp. 50–52, a letter from the king granting the Jews of Great Poland and Mazovia the right to appoint a chief rabbi. On the history of the regional synod in Great Poland see Louis Lewin, *Die Landessynode der grosspolnischen Judenschaft* (Frankfurt: J. Kauffmann, 1926), pp. 18–29, much of which goes beyond the seventeenth century.

16. See Me'ir ben Gedaliah, *Responsa*, no. 88.

Regional synods dealt not only with matters such as taxation but with religious problems.[17] Representatives from Volhynia, for example, gathered in Włodzimierz in 1602 together with the head of the rabbinic court to enact ordinances dealing with the desecration of the Sabbath and the non-observance of other precepts which were, in part, a result of Jewish involvement in estate management. Participants carried the results of the discussions back to their communities, where local councils instituted and enforced them.[18]

At some point in the mid-sixteenth century, the collective needs of Polish Jewry brought about the organization of formal meetings of Jewish leaders from across Poland. Precisely when these meetings began to take place remains unclear, but the forum for the meetings was the commercial fair held at Lublin, where already in the 1530s, if not earlier, rabbis and laymen had gathered up to three times a year to conduct their personal business as well as to exchange news and ideas.[19] By the 1550s regional leaders attending the fair had assumed the role, if not of judges, then of mediators in disputes between communities.[20] During the following decade the Lithuanian Jewish Community Council appointed laymen and rabbis to supervise the

17. Although Majer Bałaban has argued that the establishment of the Council of Four Lands, the national political body of Polish Jewry, and internal regional bickering caused the regional councils to degenerate into simply tax collection vehicles, evidence from the records of the synods of Great Poland demonstrates that the regional councils were involved with much more than tax collection well into the eighteenth century. See Majer Bałaban, *Historia i literatura żydowska*, vol. 3, (1925; reprint, Warsaw: Wydawnictwa Artystyczne i Filmowe, 1982), pp. 219–220; *Beyt Yisra'el be-Polin*, vol. 1, p. 60. Partial records of the synods of Great Poland were published by Lewin in his *Die Landessynode*. See too Bałaban, *Historia*, vol. 3, p. 333.

18. The enactments of the 1602 meeting in Włodzimierz were published by H. H. Ben Sasson, "Taqqanot issurey Shabbat," pp. 195–206.

19. *PVAA*, p. i. In 1533 Zygmunt I issued an order that mentioned that a matter between two Jews was brought before the rabbis when they were in Lublin. As Halperin pointed out, this does not mean that there was an established national court in Lublin but it does illustrate that Jews gathered in Lublin and could convene a court if necessary. That Jews came to Lublin specifically at the time of the fairs is supported by a 1540 document from Zygmunt I concerning Shalom Shakna and the Jews who gathered in Lublin for the fairs (*PVAA*, p. xix).

20. See Isserles, *Responsa*, no. 73, p. 308. Isserles noted that "some time ago" the litigants from two towns involved in a tax jurisdiction dispute stood together with members of their local communities "before the *parnasim* (leaders) of the *medinah* (region)" at the Lublin fair. Given the emergence of Jewish self government at Lublin in the course of the sixteenth century and the role of the leaders in this case as arbitrators of a regional dispute, viewing this as the precursor of the Council of Four Lands may not be imprudent. Concern-

Lublin fairs and, in addition, named three judges to handle any matters that arose during the fair.[21] By 1576 the court of the "three lands" (Great Poland, Little Poland, and Red Ruthenia) was firmly established and empowered to call litigants to appear before it in Lublin, even important rabbis like Joseph Katz (d. 1591), who served on the rabbinic court and as head of a yeshiva in Cracow.[22]

The Council of Four Lands (*va'ad arba' arazot*), whose constituent regions fluctuated from three to five—Great Poland, Little Poland, Volhynia, Red Ruthenia, and Lithuania—until the mid-seventeenth century, did not just sponsor a court. Composed of elders of each of the regions across the country as well as representatives of some large centers such as Cracow, the Council acted as the representative of the Jewish community to the Polish government. It also concerned itself with the internal workings of local Jewish communities, particularly with matters that transcended local borders and threatened to have an adverse effect on the image of Jews in Polish eyes. It also oversaw the division of the tax burden due the monarch into portions from each of the various regions.

Rabbis do not appear to have participated in the meetings of the Council but rather gathered separately to exchange ideas and deal collectively with difficult halakhic problems that confronted them in their communities or in the yeshiva.[23] Problems that evaded easy solution at the conclave were assigned to one of the attendees for further work. Sirkes, for example, wrote that when scholars met in Lublin in the spring of 1632 and remained in doubt regarding a particular bill of divorce, they asked him to look into the matter further when he returned home. All agreed to be bound by his final decision.[24]

---

ing the dating of this responsum: Isserles sent the responsum to Rabbi Me'ir Katzenellenbogen in Padua for comment and Katzenellenbogen replied at some length (Isserles, *Responsa*, no. 75). Although Katzenellenbogen died in 1565 at the age of ninety-two, already in 1559 his son, Samuel, wrote to Isserles that his father was in poor health and almost unable to write (Isserles, *Responsa*, no. 69). This, combined with Isserles's statement that the case took place "sometime ago" easily places the court in the 1550s if not earlier.

21. Israel Halperin, "Re'shito shel va'ad medinat Liṭa' ve-yaḥaso el va'ad arba' araẓot," *Zion* 3 (1938): 53–54.

22. Katz, *Responsa*, no. 42, p. 123.

23. Luria, *Responsa*, no. 65; Me'ir ben Gedaliah, *Responsa*, no. 79. It is unclear whether the rabbis met formally or informally.

24. Sirkes, *Responsa* (old), no. 91. A similar example appears in Isaac ben Abraham of Poznań, *Responsa*, no. 119, p. 272, who was assigned the case because the questioner lived in his area.

The signatures of rabbis and laymen rarely appeared on the same document from Council meetings unless there was specific mention of one group joining the other to issue a decree or grant an approbation. If both were represented on a document there was a clear demarcation between them and each group was referred to by a different name: the rabbis were called the *ra'shey yeshibot* ("heads of the rabbinic academies") and the laymen the *ra'shey medinot* ("heads of the regions").[25]

There were exceptions to this division of political and religious leadership. A notable one involved Abraham Rapoport (1584–1651), rabbi of Lvov, whose name appeared among those of laymen on a 1642 proclamation of the Council. Yet even with Rapoport's signature on the proclamation, lay leaders turned to the rabbinic leaders as a group to support the decision to grant a Cracow printer a monopoly to sell a certain work for a specified time. The rabbis did so with a separate proclamation of their own.[26]

As in the Jewish community in contemporary Venice, Polish rabbis and lay leaders depended upon each other to strengthen one another's authority and implement decisions.[27] For example, in 1612, to the great consternation of Rabbi Mordecai Jaffe (ca. 1535–1612) of Poznań, who was ill and not in Lublin, rabbis at the fair tried to persuade the leaders of the Council to announce that a contested bill of divorce given to a woman in Vienna was valid.[28] Their efforts failed, but such an announcement by the Council would not only have lent the prestige of Polish Jewry to those arguing that the divorce was valid but would have been repeated across the land by fairgoers returning home—making opposition to the woman's remarriage

25. *PVAA,* no. 89, 96–97, 178. From time to time each group was called a different name. The *ra'shey medinot* were sometimes referred to as the *manhigey ha-medinot* ("leaders of the regions") or *manhigey dalet arazot* ("leaders of [the] Four Lands"); the rabbis were called *ge'onim* ("brilliant ones"; see *PVAA,* index; see too no. 178, from which it is clear that the term signified the rabbis, and Halperin's notes on p. 492 [1637]). Nothing suggests a particular significance to the use of any one name over the other.

26. *PVAA,* pp. 181–82; see also p. 30 and n. 3; cf., however, Bałaban, *Dzieje Żydów,* vol. 1, p. 270.

27. On Venice see Malkiel, *A Separate Republic,* pp. 186–87.

28. Me'ir ben Gedaliah, *Responsa,* no. 125. Jaffe wrote to the leaders in an attempt both to refute the rumor that he now approved of the divorce and to convince the leaders not to announce that the woman could remarry. On the Vienna case in general see Isaac Lewin, "Le-she'elat ha-'get me-Vina'," in his *Me-boqer le-'ereb* (Jerusalem: Mossad ha-Rav Kook, 1981), pp. 115–16.

much more difficult to sustain. Other examples: Rabbi Joshua Falk (d. 1614) relied on the communal leadership to disseminate his 1607 rulings regarding usury.[29] Falk was also concerned about one family owning an *arenda* for a tavern and living alone in an isolated village lest the husband travel and leave his wife alone among the drinking clientele. The lay leadership responded by prohibiting a single family from owning an *arenda* under such circumstances. Two Jewish families would have to live together.[30]

The Council invested the rabbinate with authority. For example, it threatened to close any printing press and excommunicate any printer and his associates who dared print Judaica in Poland without a rabbinic approbation.[31] As for the rabbis, they recognized the Council and its authority to fine and punish people, to hand Jews over to the Polish authorities, and even to expel them from Poland.[32] They also acknowledged the Council's right to regulate the marketplace with ordinances that supplemented the halakhah. Although the rabbinic stance on such ordinances was not always clearly defined, they never questioned the notion of communal sovereignty.[33]

In the last quarter of the sixteenth century, for example, Joseph Katz was asked whether a Jew who purchased the debt of a fellow Jew from a Gentile creditor was entitled to seek repayment from the Jewish debtor. Katz considered the matter in a typical responsum, citing numerous authorities to build his case. Arriving at a negative conclusion, Katz tried to discourage the practice by using a two-pronged approach. First, he recalled that the rabbis of the Talmud had frowned on anyone who used an authorization to collect a debt.[34] If the rabbis opposed the use of an authorization issued by a Jew, Katz reasoned, then certainly they opposed its use if received from a non-Jew. Second, Katz noted that he had heard that "a number of years

---

29. Falk, *Qunṭeres*, p. 3a.

30. Falk, *Quntres*, pp. 2b-3a (also quoted in *PVAA*, no. 52). See too Morgensztern, "Żydzi w Zamośćiu," p. 4.

31. *PVAA*, no. 16. Only original works required an approbation. Reprints did not.

32. Sirkes, *Responsa* (new), no. 43. Halperin dates the letter to 1623 (see *PVAA*, no. 110). See too Slonik, *Responsa*, no. 33, regarding the local communities.

33. See, for example, Isserles, *Responsa*, no. 73; Sirkes, *Responsa* (old), no. 60. An ordinance of Moravian Jewry accepted at Gaya in 1650 empowered the rabbi of the region to rule on the meaning of any ordianance that proved to be ambiguous (*TMM*, no. 292).

34. B.T., *Shabu'ot* 31a, the opinion of the third-century scholar Rab. Later authorities encouraged the use of a power of attorney to collect a debt under certain circumstances. See *Ṭur*, Ḥoshen mishpaṭ 123 (end) with the comments of Joseph Karo.

ago" an ordinance had been made in the regions (*medinot)* that no Jew should buy the debt of another Jew held by a non-Jew.[35] The ordinance was a not a legal determinate, yet it was a useful support in a call for change.

While Polish rabbis accepted the ordinances (*taqqanot*) of the lay councils and quoted them in their responsa as part of the realities of contemporary life, the *taqqanot* did not represent legal precedents for Polish rabbis and did not enter the realm of contemporary Jewish jurisprudence. Never used as legal proof texts with which to make an argument, the ordinances stood in sharp contrast to the decisions of the medieval synods of German and French Jewry, in particular the ordinances of Speyer, Worms, and Mainz, whose proclamations entered the Ashkenazic legal tradition and which Polish halakists quoted with almost the same degree of authority as they did the works of the tosafists.

The difference between the medieval ordinances and those of the Council of Four Lands lay in the makeup of the legislators. The communal councils of medieval German Jewry, like those of Andalusian Jewry during its Golden Age and Egyptian Jewry during much of the Fatimid period, were comprised of rabbinic scholars;[36] those of Polish Jewry were made up of laymen. It was the tosafists themselves, their teachers, and students who authored the *taqqanot* of the German and French synods. Their ordinances entered the pantheon of Ashkenazic legal thought as the creative works of great legists.[37] The *taqqanot* of the Council of Four Lands and most local councils remained the creation of laymen.[38]

Like all contemporary institutions, the Council was dedicated to supporting religious observance both financially and with the weight of its authority. Religion was the matrix of the community's value system. Thus merchants found using inaccurate weights and measurements in the mar-

---

35. Katz, *Responsa,* no. 58, pp. 143–44. The *medinot* may well refer to the Council of Four Lands as the heads of the Council came to be known as the *ra'shey medinot.*

36. On Andalusian Jewry see Ross Brann, *The Compunctious Poet: Cultural Ambiguity and Hebrew Poetry in Muslim Spain* (Baltimore: Johns Hopkins University Press, 1991), p. 13; on the Jews in Fatimid Egypt see S. D. Goitein, *A Mediterranean Society,* vol. 1 (Berkeley: University of California Press, 1971), pp. 30–31.

37. The texts and translations of many of these ordinances are collected in Finkelstein's *Jewish Self-Government*, pp. 111–256.

38. Ordinances dealing with religious observance that were drawn up by the heads of rabbinic courts and heads of the rabbinic academies, either alone or in conjunction with the laity, were viewed as halakhic precedents by latter legalists. See H.H. Ben Sasson, "Taqqanot issurey Shabbat," pp. 183–85, or Falk's *Qunteres* that was ensconced in the legal tradition. See too David ben Samuel ha-Levi's gloss on *Shulḥan 'aruk,* Oraḥ ḥayyim 566.2.

kets of Cracow were not accused of cheating per se, but rather of transgressing positive and negative biblical commandments.[39] Calling into question their status as observant Jews and responsible members of society was the greatest societal embarrassment.

While the community and its resources supported the institutions central to a life of piety, public institutions were much less susceptible to the pressures of daily life on religious observance than individuals. People had to eke out a living—for many, an almost all-consuming task.[40] They had emotions and desires that often conflicted with the prescriptions of religious life. Because of this reality, perhaps the truest measure of the level of a society's religiosity was not the laws generated by its public institutions but rather the level of personal piety among its members.

39. Majer Bałaban, "Die Krakauer Judengemeinde-Ordnung von 1595 und ihre Nachtrage," *Jahrbuch der Jüdish-Literarischen Gesellschaft* 10 (1912): 356.

40. Joseph Solomon Delmedigo, *Sefer ma'yan gannim* (Odessa, 1865), pp. 128–29; *Sefer eylam* (Odessa, 1864–1867), pp. 92–93. Delmedigo claimed that many Polish and Lithuanian Jews were ignorant and spent their time trying to make a living which was difficult. See too Shmeruk, "Qavvim le-demutah," pp. 279–80, who cites Isaac Sulkes, author of a Judeo-German translation of Song of Songs published in 1579, who wrote a number of times that people were forced to abandon study when they were young due to the burden of making a living and paying taxes.

3

Personal Piety

Jewish society in sixteenth- and seventeenth-century Poland assumed that its members would adhere to a religious lifestyle—one based upon familiarity with the halakhah and Jewish customs (*minhagim*) as well as fundamental Jewish beliefs. Formal education, however, did not focus on teaching youngsters this knowledge. The education of young boys concentrated on the reading and writing of Hebrew and familiarization with the Pentateuch. It took for granted that they, like girls, would absorb the system of Jewish laws, customs, and beliefs somewhere other than in school: the home, the synagogue, and, to a great extent, "the street."[1]

The transmission of Jewish values in this manner seems to have been effective. Although the average sixteenth- and seventeenth-century Polish Jew—both male and female—may not have completely understood the philosophic and/or theosophic underpinnings of Judaism, few failed to learn how to behave in a fashion that society, including Christian society, deemed "Jewish."[2] Nevertheless, rabbis and preachers were not without numerous critiques of their lay contemporaries.[3] Such criticisms were not wholly unexpected; no preacher has ever been completely satisfied with those he seeks to lead. Moreover, many rabbis felt themselves to be have been held in low public esteem and/or to have lacked real influence in their communities. For example, Samuel Edels (1555–1631), rabbi of Lublin and later Ostróg, observed that scholars were regularly embarrassed and

1.On the role of the family and synagogue in educating youngsters see Katz, *Masoret u-mashber*, pp. 214–16.

2. Rabbi Ephraim of Łęczyca (Luntshits; 1550–1619) offered a biting critique of the educational system of his day in which he complained that even advanced students learned Mishnah and Talmud without knowing about the unity of God and accepting the "yoke of fearing Him" (*'Ammudey shesh*, quoted in Assaf, *Meqorot le-toledot ha-ḥinuk*, vol. 1, p. 61).

3. For example, writing in 1636 Menahem Man Ashkenazi, rabbi of Rymanów, accused the masses of being the "spreading gall and wormwood" that Moses warned of in Deuteronomy 29.17 (Sirkes, *Responsa* [new], no. 29).

their admonishments ignored;[4] Solomon Luria believed that the "hand of the masses" had grown more powerful than the voice of the rabbis even in halakhic matters;[5] and Sirkes argued that the heads of rabbinic academies should be allowed to accept remuneration until they became wealthy because wealth was the only way to imbue scholars with practical authority.[6] Society, he believed, respected only wealth, not scholarship.[7]

Another gap in values between rabbis—particularly the elite who were well versed and engaged in ongoing research in Jewish sources—and the generally uneducated laity, involved in worldly pursuits, was their divergent understandings of what a religious life meant. Professional rabbis who dedicated their lives to studying, understanding, and fulfilling the minutiae of the law assumed that laymen, most of whom had neither the skills nor the

---

4. Edels, *Ḥiddushey aggadot, Shabbat* 119b. Polish rabbis were not the only contemporary religious leaders whose public protests fell upon deaf ears. Priests in sixteenth-century Spain had similar, if not worse, problems. During high mass, lay people talked back to the priests who reproved them for their religious lapses (William A. Christian, Jr., *Local Religion in Sixteenth-Century Spain* [Princeton: Princeton University Press, 1981], pp. 166–67). Polish preachers may have suffered similarly in their parishes (see Ben Sasson, *Hagut*, pp. 52–54).

5. Luria, *YSS, Ketubbot* 2.42. Like other Polish rabbis, Luria often lamented that members of the community did not listen to him. He wistfully declared that he would try to change things in the community if only he had the power.

6. Sirkes, *Bayit ḥadash*, Yoreh de'ah 246. A similar text appears in his *Responsa* (old), no. 52. Sirkes, who was careful to limit his allowance to the head of the yeshiva—he himself was head of the school in Cracow for a number of years, idealized the past and suggested that people listened to scholars of old even though they were not rich. The generation of halakists that followed Sirkes expanded his position to apply to the heads of rabbinic courts as well. See David ben Samuel ha-Levi, *Ṭurey zahab*, Yoreh de'ah 246, n. 7, and Shabbetay ben Me'ir ha-Kohen, *Siftey kohen* (Cracow, 1646–1647), Yoreh de'ah 246, n. 20. Sirkes's view was, however, not without a detractor. See the critique of Eliezer Ashkenazi, *Damaseq Eli'ezer*, vol. 1 (Lublin, 1646), pp. 88b-89a. The Ashkenazic rabbinate had already been professionalized in the fifteenth century. See Israel Yuval, *Ḥakamim be-doram* (Jerusalem: Magnes, 1988), pp. 398–404, and Mordechai Breuer, *Rabbanut Ashkenaz be-yemey ha-beynayyim* (Jerusalem: Zalman Shazar Center, 1976), pp. 18–19.

7. Rabbis were not the only authorities ignored. Communal ordinances were repeated time and time again, presumably because people did not obey them the first time. Joshua Falk, quoting earlier sources, wrote that if the letter of the law that disqualified anyone who disobeyed the ordinances of the communities from acting as a witness was enforced, not even one in a thousand could ever testify (*Sefer me'irat 'eynayim* [Prague, 1606], 34, n. 10). While Falk cites a source from medieval Germany, his quotation suggests that the issue was germane in his day as well. See too Sirkes, *Bayit ḥadash*, Ḥoshen mishpaṭ 34.7.

time for such study, would simply follow rabbinic counsel.[8] In contrast, not only were the laity's perceptions of religiosity not always informed by the letter of the law; they were often impervious to such information.[9]

Solomon Luria, for example, was asked whether someone "whose head is heavy" may sit and eat without a head covering. To Luria the answer was obvious: there is no prohibition against sitting in one place bare-headed although it is considered an act of piety to cover one's head when mentioning God's name. "Nevertheless," he advised his questioner,

> it appears to me that even though there is no prohibition in [doing] this and not even an aspect of piety when one does not mention the Name, at any rate a scholar should be careful since people take this to be irreverence and lawlessness as if one transgresses Jewish custom (*dat Yehudit*). And even one who studies in his room should not rely on this in case an ignoramus sees him and belittles him. It was not for naught that the rabbis said "Everything that is prohibited because of appearance is prohibited even in inside rooms." And now I will reveal the embarrassment of Ashkenazic Jewry: certainly they do not have misgivings about one who drinks *yayin nesek* [non-kosher wine] in a hotel of non-Jews and eats fish cooked in their [non-kosher] pots (and the stringent one is one who believes the innkeeper that they did not cook in this pot [i.e., it was a new pot]) and they do not check after him and they honor him if he is rich and powerful. But whoever eats and drinks [only] kosher [food] but without a head covering, they consider him as if he left the fold. Therefore a scholar's eyes [must] be in his head that he should know to be careful that they should not catch him . . .[10]

---

8. Joseph ben Elijah, head of the rabbinic court of Zasław in the 1630s, complained that most people did not understand the very Hebrew prayers that they said every single day (Joseph ben Elijah, *Sefer rekeb Eliyyahu*, p. 18b). Without a knowledge of Hebrew, most Polish Jews who wanted to learn about their religion had to turn to "women's books," simplified works written in Judeo-German. On this genre of literature see Agnes Romer Segal, "Yiddish Works on Women's Commandments in the Sixteenth Century," in *Studies in Yiddish Literature and Folklore* (Jerusalem: Hebrew University, 1986), pp. 39–40, 45–51, and Chava Weissler, "The Religion of Traditional Ashkenazic Women: Some Methodological Issues," *AJS Review* 12.1 (Spring 1987): 77–86.

9. Simone Luzzatto's (ca. 1582–1663) portrayal of the yeshivas and study halls of Poland in the 1630s as full of thousands of youngsters diligently pouring over Jewish law would seem to be an exaggeration (quoted in Chone Shmeruk, "Baḥurim me-Ashkenaz be-yeshibot Polin," in *Sefer ha-yobel le-Yiẓḥaq Baer*, Salo Baron, et al., eds., [Jerusalem: Historical Society of Israel, 1960], pp. 304–5). Perhaps thousands of Jewish children received elementary education; few received advanced training.

10. Luria, *Responsa*, no. 72.

Evidently popular conceptions of "proper Jewish behavior" created a sociological gauge of piety more influential than the laws of the Talmud and one that scholars dared not disregard if they wished to safeguard their reputations.

In other words, in searching out some of the issues that laymen believed defined the religious life, much more telling than anomalous acts or rabbinic reactions to those acts were the reactions of contemporary lay observers to deviant behavior. How did they respond to sin? Simply put, "What did the neighbors think?"[11]

Occasionally, the neighbors' perceptions were incorporated into responsa. For example, the following report from the early seventeenth century reflects their views in a matter of sexual promiscuity, a social taboo in both the Jewish and Christian communities.

> . . . A married woman came home with a particular male guest who was passing by the town in which the woman lived. The woman's husband was not in town. There was also no one else in the house except for an important woman who saw the two of them coming and then they vanished from her sight and she did not know where they went. Then a great fear fell upon her and she thought that maybe they went to the cellar. As quick as the blink of an eye, she heard the sound of the hinges of the cellar door and her fear increased. She went from the "winter house" to near the cellar and she heard the cellar doors close. While she was standing there, several other women came and asked whether she had seen the aforementioned woman with X, the guest, and where did they go since the cart driver will [soon] be on his way. The woman replied that she saw both of them coming to the house and then she lost sight of them. The women [who had come] said that maybe they went into the cellar and they [all] waited for them to come out. Then one woman said, "Let us light a candle and look for them in the cellar," but in the middle of her saying this the aforementioned woman came from the cellar and said that X was sitting in the cellar in the cold and would like to drink some mead there. While she was talking X came behind her from the cellar in front of all the people standing there and they saw that the back of the woman's scarf was dirty with mud and the earth of the cellar [presumably

---

11. Behavior that simply contradicts the law cannot automatically be declared deviant. Certain practices, such as jay-walking in most modern cities, gain communal acceptance despite their technical illegality and do not illicit communal sanctions. Deviance therefore depends more on society's response to behavior than the legal character of a particular action. See Kai Erikson, *Wayward Puritans* (New York: Wiley, 1966), pp. 6–24.

> she was surprised and turned around at his approach]. Based on these things the whole city was talking about the woman who adulterated with X.[12]

Not only was the woman the talk of her town, but travelers returning from the Lublin fair who passed through the unnamed city on their way back to Cracow brought the gossip home with them until all Cracow too was buzzing with the news.

Extramarital affairs were not unknown in contemporary society. Rabbi Me'ir ben Gedaliah of Lublin (1558–1616) wrote that "in our great sins many people" stumble and have sex with non-Jewish women,[13] which infringed upon a rabbinic prohibition. Those who engaged in it, as well as Jewish society at large, may have seen it as less offensive than sexual intercourse between a Jewish man and a married Jewish woman, which, as in the above quoted case, was unmistakably a violation of the seventh commandment forbidding adultery and by no means condoned by Jewish society.

A related case from Sirkes's responsa involved a particular widow in the 1620s who remarried and gave birth to a fully developed girl seven months after her second marriage. Word quickly spread that the woman had become pregnant from a man other than her present husband and that in order "to hide her disgusting acts," she hastily found and married her current mate.[14] Socially embarrassed to have become pregnant out of wedlock, the woman, if the rumors were well founded, was anxious to protect her name as soon as she was aware that there would be incontrovertible evidence of her misdeeds.[15]

---

12. Sirkes, *Responsa* (old), no. 98. I have translated some of the Hebrew phrases with English equivalents. The statement has been reformulated by Sirkes, who says that he was confronted with this problem just after his arrival in Cracow in 1619.

13. Me'ir ben Gedaliah, *Responsa*, no. 16. Also see Shmeruk, "Qavvim le-demutah," p. 292, who cites Benjamin Wolf, author of an ethical treatise published between 1548–1572, who warned Jewish men about being enticed by harlots (in addition to drinking with non-Jews and getting drunk). It is not clear whether such harlots were Jewish or not.

14. Sirkes, *Responsa* (old), no. 100. The responsum is dated 1629. See too Sirkes, *Responsa* (new), nos. 56, 57.

15. Two similar cases appear. In the responsa of Me'ir ben Gedaliah there is a case of a woman who became pregnant and then married and was suspected of having killed the child on the day it was born. In the hierarchy of Jewish law, murder, including the murder of a newborn, is a much graver offense than premarital sex, but the social stigma attached to premarital pregnancy may have been more than the woman was forever willing to be reminded of (*Responsa*, no. 80). A comparable theme appears in an undated case of a husband who was

In part the erotic nature of such events must have caught the imagination of the community. One wonders if religious zealousness alone would have pushed people to go peeping through holes in the door to spy on a man and woman in bed.[16] But there was also communal disgust at such behavior. The neighbors who caught the man and woman in the cellar were aghast. The "important woman" in the house was overcome with fear, presumably the fear of confronting imminent sexual impropriety, and the pregnant woman dreaded the social consequences of being an unwed mother. There was undoubtedly sexual laxity in the Jewish community, particularly among those who had had sexual experiences but who were now forced into abstinence (e.g., widows/widowers, travelling salesmen as well as their wives waiting for them at home),[17] but those bold enough to have illicit liaisons were not commonly so brazen as to do so openly. Generally, only those who were careless were publicly exposed. Even loose women tried to make themselves look respectable by claiming that their paramours were their husbands.[18]

Menahem Mendel Krochmal (d. 1661), a native of Cracow who studied and taught in Polish yeshivas before becoming rabbi of Mikulov (Nikolsburg) and other towns in Moravia, wrote, "Praise to God that the licentious of the generation are not common." Krochmal believed the deterrent to such aberrant behavior was fear of punishment, especially punishment by the non-Jewish courts.[19] He wistfully added, ". . . if only the fear of the judgment of Heaven would weigh upon them as the[ir] fear of the judg-

---

away from home and returned to rumors and eye witness reports that his wife had been having an affair with a young man. The woman had tried to abort the illegitimate child of the liaison by taking a liquid concoction (Sirkes, *Responsa* [old], no. 99). The psychological variables in these two cases, however, make them problematic historical sources.

16. See Isaac ben Samuel ha-Levi, *Responsa*, no. 40.

17. See Jacob Katz, "Nisu'im ve-ḥayyey ishut be-moẓa'ey yemey ha-beynayyim," *Zion* 10.1–2 (1945): 44–45, who expands on the types of people who were susceptible to falling prey to desire. Katz's conclusion—that sinners viewed their acts as sins since they came to rabbis to find some means of penitence—is more suspect. Certainly, those who repented viewed their actions as sins; but what did those who did not seek penance think?

18. See Joshua Höschel, *Responsa*, pt. 1, Eben ha-'ezer, no. 1.

19. In the wake of the Counter Reformation, Catholic reformers sought to suppress illicit sexual relations more systematically than had been done in earlier generations. Protestants too treated such cases harshly. See James Brundage, *Law, Sex, and Christian Society in Medieval Europe* (Chicago: University of Chicago Press, 1987), pp. 557, 569.

ment of man."[20] At least in the eyes of one of the most important contemporary rabbinic figures, the sexual mores of Judaism held firm, even if not entirely for the proper religious reasons.

Such was not the case in other matters of observance, particularly when money and/or power was involved. The religious prohibition against stealing from non-Jews was unequivocal by the sixteenth century, although talmudic rabbis had argued over the source of the measure.[21] By mid-seventeenth century, however, the problem of Polish Jews stealing from non-Jews had become so acute that Rabbi Me'ir ben Abraham Zak quipped, "In our great sins the thieves and robbers have multiplied [so much] that we can no longer count [them]."[22] With a play on a talmudic phrase, he claimed that most thieves of the day were Jews.[23]

---

20. Krochmal, *Responsa*, no. 55. The comment is made about Moravia; however, Krochmal applies his opinion to Isserles's comments on *Shulḥan 'aruk*, implying that he never knew a different reality, including during the period when he studied in Poland. The examples of sexual misconduct reflected in the responsa literature are almost all from the seventeenth century. However, even late sixteenth-century ordinances attempted to prevent any possible sexual enticement. See Bałaban, "Die Krakauer Judengemeinde-Ordnung," p. 89.

21. See B.T., *Baba' Qamma'* 113a-b; J.T., *Baba' Qamma'* 4.3, 4b. Cf., however, B.T., *Baba' Meẓi'a'* 111b. Luria expresses no hesitation in ruling that stealing from a non-Jew is a biblical prohibition (*YSS, Baba' Qamma'* 10.20). See too *Shulḥan 'aruk*, Ḥoshen mishpaṭ 348.2, 359.1, together with the glosses of both Joshua Falk and Shabbetay ben Me'ir ha-Kohen.

22. Thievery and dealing in fenced goods posed a serious security risk for both the individuals involved and the Jewish community. The *qahal* in Cracow was so concerned about the ramifications of Jews dealing in stolen goods that in 1595 it explicity forbade any of its members from buying suspect goods from non-Jews. When the *qahal* caught thieves, as it did in 1649 and 1650, they were expelled from the community (Wettstein, "Qadmoniyyot," pp. 594, 614—a case of theft from a fellow Jew, 617). Individuals caught stealing by the Polish authorities were jailed and could be executed for their crimes (Luria, *YSS, Qiddushin* 1.28; Me'ir ben Gedaliah, *Responsa*, no. 24). A noble who found that a Jew had either stolen from him or possessed property stolen from him could press the community to surrender the accused.

Zak deplored the quickness with which the Jewish community tried to buy the freedom of Jewish thieves and other "sinners" incarcerated by the Polish authorities. This removed any deterrent that the threat of punishment might have held. Zak says that he would not have given a penny to save them from death (Abraham Rapoport, *She'elot u-teshubot eytan ha-ezraḥi* [Ostrog, 1796], no. 45; cf. *Shulḥan 'aruk*, Yoreh de'ah 252.6).

23. Rapoport, *Responsa*, no. 45. Zak was not the first to complain about Jewish thievery. Earlier in the century Edels too bemoaned that many Jews had attained their wealth through stealing from non-Jews (Edels, *Ḥiddushey aggadot, Ketubbot* 67b). Solomon Luria also remarked that these types of sins were common (*Responsa*, no. 33).

To be sure, Jewish society perceived gradations among thieves. When a rumor spread that a particular witness was a known thief, Me'ir ben Gedaliah of Lublin, who served as head of the rabbinic court in Cracow (1587), Lvov (1599), and Lublin (1613), asked people in his community what they knew about the man. Reliable people who knew him replied that yes, he was a thief, but he only stole from non-Jews.[24] The statement betrays an attitude among some thieves (and observers) that stealing from non-Jews was somehow acceptable or at least a lesser evil than stealing from Jews. It did not seem to matter that the Talmud and later jurists had categorically banned stealing from anyone.

Evidence, however, points to the fact that Jews stole from Jews as well, even if indirectly. The 1595 ordinances of the Cracow Jewish community indicate that many people granted themselves legal dispensation to steal, withhold payments of debts, and not pay taxes to the community.[25] Rabbi Manoah ben Shemariyah Handel (d. 1612) complained that many of the Jewish poor of his day were charlatans who used deceit to collect from the community chest.[26] In Cracow, even a trusted communal functionary who had long served in the rabbinic court and signed bills of divorce was later exposed as, and admitted to having been, a thief. Like many others, he also bought stolen goods from Christian thieves.[27]

It appears that life's hardships led some Jews to view theft and dealing in stolen goods to be permissible.[28] Isaac Sulkes contended that, particularly

---

24. Me'ir ben Gedaliah, *Responsa*, no. 25.

25. Bałaban, "Die Krakauer Judengemeinde-Ordnung," p. 335. The ordinance refers to those who borrowed money and then claimed that they could not pay it back. The record book labels this as stealing. See too Edels, *Ḥiddushey aggadot, Shabbat* 119b. Concerning non-payment of taxes to the community, see Bałaban, p. 356.

26. Berger, "Teshubot Rabbi Manoaḥ Ha'ndel," p. 345.

27. Slonik, *Responsa*, no. 51; Me'ir ben Gedaliah, *Responsa*, no. 81; Handel in Isaac Lewin, *Demuyyot ve-eyru'im hisṭoriyim* (Jerusalem: Mossad ha-Rav Kook, 1988), p. 23, dated 1608. Both the latter two sources contain only partial information about this case faced by Rabbi Feybish of Cracow. At least in late medieval Germany, such communal functionaries had often attained a higher level of education then most other members of the community (see Yuval, *Ḥakamim be-doram*, p. 280) and if this was so in Poland as well then their deviant behavior is all the more noteworthy. Further references to Jews dealing in stolen goods are found in Sirkes, *Responsa* (old), no. 12. Also Katz, *Responsa*, no. 78; Luria, *Responsa*, no. 33, regarding a case in Neustadt.

28. There are specific instances in tort law where the Talmud distinguishes between the property of Jews and that of non-Jews and declares the money of non-Jews to be without ownership (see B.T., *Baba' Qamma'* 37b-38a). The attitude of Polish Jews may be an out-

in big cities, making a living was so difficult that businessmen could not be honest.[29] His claim was not new. Even the thirteenth-century German Jewish pietists (*Ḥasidey Ashkenaz*) tacitly acknowledged that at times the poor had to steal to make ends meet.[30]

Yet a sinner in one area of Jewish law could demonstrate profound religious commitment in other facets of Jewish life. For example, one responsum sheds light on a Moravian Jew who had marauded and stolen, together with two non-Jews, until he was caught and imprisoned in 1641. The day before his trial, sitting fettered and jailed in a fortress, the accused was planning his escape and wrote to fellow Jews in the nearby town. He asked that they prepare matzot for him as well as fringes for his torn *ẓiẓit* (four-cornered garment; see Numbers 15.37–40). In deference to the dietary laws, during his captivity he had refused to eat the bread given to him and only ate peas and beans cooked in water and salt. He had spent the entire period of his incarceration in "fasting [sic] and prayer." Ultimately, his escape attempt failed. When his body was dragged from the moat, phylacteries and a small prayer book were found among his belongings.[31]

There is abundant evidence that even the rabbinate was not free from graft.[32] Recently ordained rabbis who came from wealthy families but who had not yet come close to mastering the corpus of rabbinic law were able to "buy" themselves yeshivas—setting up schools and attracting students by promising them generous financial support.[33] A small number of communal rabbis obtained their positions through bribery, giving money or loans to unscrupulous local Jewish leaders with the expectation of an office in return.[34]

---

growth of this legal double standard that also occurs in other areas of jurisprudence. It is permitted, for example, for a Jew to take interest from non-Jews but not from fellow Jews. A lost object need not be returned to a non-Jew. Given such a frame of reference, in a society where making a living was difficult and there was an antagonism between religions, the rationalization that one may steal from a non-Jew is not difficult to understand.

29. Quoted in Shmeruk, "Qavvim le-demutah," p. 282.

30. Judah ben Samuel he-ḥasid, *Sefer ḥasidim*, Jehuda Wistinetzki, ed., with Introduction by J. Freimann (Frankfurt: Wahrmann, 1924), no. 1126.

31. Joshua Höschel, *Responsa*, pt. 2 no. 62. The responsum was written early in 1643 in Cracow.

32. Siev demonstrates that this was an old problem in both the Ashkenazic and Spanish Jewish communities (Isserles, *Responsa*, no. 123, n. 1).

33. Katz, *Responsa*, no. 19, p. 63; Luria, *YSS, Baba' Qamma'* 8.58.

34. See Isserles, *Responsa*, no. 123, pp. 483–84. Isserles voided the appointment of any rabbi who gained his position with the help of the secular authorities. See too Katz, *Responsa*, no. 19, p. 63.

Records from as early as 1587 indicate that the Polish Jewish community banned such dishonest appointments. The ban, apparently, was not totally effective and had to be repeated in 1597, again in 1628 in Lithuania, and again in 1640 and 1641 in Poland at the urging of Yom Tob Lipman Heller.[35] Samuel Edels, writing in the early seventeenth century, complained that no one seemed to pay attention to the rules or punishments associated with such behavior. People were either unaware or indifferent to the Talmud's comparison of one who appoints an unworthy judge or hires a judge on the basis of graft to someone who plants idol worship in Israel[36] (Polish rabbis served as local judges). Rabbis and their agents continued to seek honor by buying the rabbinate, the power of which, Edels adds, they were quick to abuse.[37]

Deceit also manifested itself in other activities of the religious elite. Luria complained that a few rabbis had recently been stringent in matters of engagement gifts and considered the gifts to be a form of marriage. If the engagement broke off, these rabbis required a bill of divorce from the couple that had exchanged gifts. Luria believed that the frequent application of this legal opinion was motivated not by concern for Jewish law but by greed: each bill of divorce meant more money for the rabbi and his scribe.[38] Luria, who resented the positions of power that many contemporary rabbis held, had doubts about the moral integrity of some of his colleagues, men whom he claimed accepted presents and payments while publicly condemning

---

35. Heller himself became involved in trying to oust Josel of Łokacze, who Heller claimed had bought the rabbinate, from his post. See the sources quoted by Halperin in *PVAA*, nos. 176, 178–79. Somewhat surprisingly, local rabbinic leaders were lenient with Josel, whose community let him remain as rabbi for six months beyond the expiration of his contract so that he could collect the "huge" debts that were owed him by its members. See M. Brann, "Additions a l'autobiographie de Lipman Heller," *Revue des études juives* 21 (1890): 273. Brann suggests that the first signatory on the letter from Włodzimierz supporting Josel may have been Rabbi David ben Samuel ha-Levi (n. 4).

36. B.T., *Sanhedrin* 7b.

37. Edels writes that contemporary rabbis made a number of enactments and declarations in an attempt to stop this practice but to no avail. Edels calls on the laity not to stand up for such imposters or call them "rabbi" (*Ḥiddushey aggadot, Sanhedrin* 7b). See too Berechiah Berak, *Zera' berak*, vol. 2, introduction. Also see Edels's *Ḥiddushey aggadot, Baba' Batra'* 73b and *Soṭah* 40a. Edels longed for the talmudic example in which rabbis and scholars chose the rabbinic leadership, not members of the laity who made their choice based on the rabbi's wealth. Rabbis may, however, have had a say in the nomination of the heads of academies. See Bersohn, *Dyplomataryusz*, pp. 77–78, no. 106.

38. Luria, *YSS, Qiddushin* 2.19.

such behavior.[39] Similarly, in the mid-seventeenth century, Joshua Höschel found unprincipled judges in his midst whom he accused of being quick to render decisions in order to increase their case loads and their incomes (judges were generally paid by the litigants).[40]

Perhaps more important than these accusations of dishonesty was the negative image of the rabbi and the communal leadership that such practices fostered in the eyes of laymen. For example, Abraham Ashkenazi, a pharmacist from Włodzimierz who claimed that he tried to follow in the ways of the Torah, considered the communal leadership, including the rabbis, to be corrupt. They engaged in flattery, exploited their power,[41] and sought bribes.[42] In some instances rabbis overly concerned about the respect due them fined anyone who publicly embarrassed them. This angered communities and led people to believe that the rabbis studied a lot only to be able to impose and collect such fines.[43] Preachers too cried out against lay leaders who assumed positions of power through nepotism rather than on the basis of ability.[44] Others complained that in making monetary com-

39. Luria, *YSS, Baba' Qamma'* 8.58.

40. Sirkes, *Responsa* (old), no. 51. The responsum is unsigned but is the same as that found in *She'elot u- teshubot ha-ge'onim batra'ey*, no. 48, which is signed "Joshua," presumably Joshua Höschel. In part, the responsum deals with the propriety of judges accepting payment for their work.

41. See Luria, *YSS, Ḥullin* 8.42, who complains that unworthy rabbis actively sought honor by doing things that made them look much more important than they were.

42. Abraham Ashkenazi, *Sam ḥayyim* (Prague, 1590), quoted in Israel Zinberg, *A History of Jewish Literature*, vol. 7, Bernard Martin, trans. and ed., (Cleveland: Press of Case Western Reserve University, 1975), pp. 155–56. Ashkenzai was a self-proclaimed "uneducated" pharmacist in Włodzimierz. He warned that if the heads of the talmudic academies did not use corporal punishment their young students would "carnival" the entire term (p. 3b [the microfiche copy available to me has no pagination; I have numbered the title page 1a]; perhaps typically, parents too complained that their sons were not studying hard enough [Shmeruk, "Baḥurim me-Ashkenaz be-yeshibot Polin," pp. 309–10]). Ashkenazi also reprimanded students for chasing the girls.

43. Luria, *YSS, Baba' Qamma'* 8.58. The Talmud allows scholars to collect a fine from constituents who embarrass them publicly. However, halakhkic authorities prior to Luria had already argued that the law was not applicable in contemporary times and therefore rabbis were not entitled to collect a fine. Still, some Polish rabbis were insistent about the matter. Luria writes that an insulted rabbi does deserve an apology. In order to avoid negative public opinion, however, if a rabbinical scholar does collect a fine, he should be careful to give the money to charity and not use it for his personal needs.

44. Joseph ben Elijah, *Sefer yesod Yosef* (Cracow, 1638), 2.2, p. 17a.

promises to avoid perceived physical threats to the community, the leadership was stealing from the people on a daily basis.[45] People also objected to the leadership's laxity in enforcing ordinances against the wealthier classes such as businessmen and tax collectors.[46] In large towns the wealthy and the learned had joined forces to disenfranchise the poorer members of society, an arrangement that must have increased intracommunal tensions.[47]

As in every generation and locale, the Jewish community had its share of individuals who succumbed to desire and/or lethargy, sexual deviance, and fraud. There was the butcher who sold non-kosher meat to unsuspecting consumers instead of absorbing the loss himself.[48] There were recalcitrant husbands who spitefully refused to give their wives bills of divorce[49] and there were menstruating women who deceived their husbands and had intercourse with them while ritually unclean.[50] Domestic violence was condemned but not unheard of.[51] Murder too,

45. Katz, *Responsa*, no. 78. The statement comes from two Jews obligated to repay the community for its payment to a noble who had threatened to retaliate against the community for the thievery of the two Jews. The two were not consulted during the negotiations. Nevertheless, the statement that the community steals from its members daily reflects a deep-seated hostility towards communal management.

46. Louis Lewin, *Neue Materialien zur Geschichte der Vierländersynode* (Frankfurt: Kauffmann, 1905), vol. 1, p. 10, no. 28, dated 1645.

47. Krochmal, *Responsa*, no. 2. Wealthy members of the community asked how the uneducated could be equated to scholars and be granted a say in running the community. Krochmal opposed this position and ruled that votes should be based on numbers, not wealth. Also see Katz, *Responsa*, no. 18, p. 59, where Katz agreed to the request of a wealthy family that contributed 80 percent of the town's tax revenue to have a disproportionate voice in making community decisions.

48. *She'elot u-teshubot ha-ge'onim batra'ey*, no. 19.

49. There are numerous examples of this problem in rabbinic legal literature. One even occurs in homiletic literature. See David ha-Darshan, *Shir ha-ma'alot*, p. 15a, regarding a teacher of the young from Cracow who left his wife for more than twelve years and continually ignored the coaxing of the community to give her a bill of divorce.

50. Sirkes, *Responsa* (new), no. 84; *She'elot u-teshubot ha-ge'onim batra'ey*, no. 26.

51. Although there are only three explicit cases of wife-beating mentioned in the responsa literature of this period (Katz, *Responsa*, no. 66; Luria, *Responsa*, no. 69 [only a threat to beat the wife]; Rapoport, *Responsa*, no. 43), such behavior had already been labeled improper for a "son of the covenant" by Me'ir of Rothenburg (quoted in the following citation). See too Luria, *YSS*, *Baba' Qamma'* 3.21, where Luria states that wife-beating is improper even if the husband claims that he married his wife with the understanding that he would beat her if she did not obey him. Nevertheless, Luria writes, many have been mis-

even Jew killing Jew, was uncommon but not unknown among Polish Jewry.[52]

Others transgressed the law inadvertently, thinking that they knew the halakhah when they did not. The woman who heard testimony that her husband had been killed while traveling and then proceeded to remarry without rabbinic permission probably did not think that she needed to ask a rabbi whether she could remarry.[53] Others were not well versed in the laws concerning Sabbath observance and profaned the holy day through the use of a non-Jewish agent to do prohibited work for them on the Sabbath. Since the Jew himself did no work and there were indeed situations in which a Jew could tell a non-Jew to perform a task for him or her on the Sabbath, people came to see the use of a non-Jewish agent as something permitted for all activities.[54] The problem of profanation of the Sabbath became so severe that communities appointed individuals to educate society about the Sabbath laws and enforce them.[55]

But these examples were exceptions to the generally high level of Jewish observance in sixteenth- and seventeenth-century Poland. Certainly, Polish Jews did not want others to generalize about their community on the basis of those who violated Jewish law. Writing after the massacres of 1648, Nathan Hanover described the Polish community idyllically.

---

taken in this matter. See too Isaac ben Eliakum of Poznań's ethical treatise *Leb ṭob* (Prague, 1620), quoted in Zinberg, *A History of Jewish Literature*, vol. 7, p. 163, who writes, "It is the most assured principle that no son of Israel may strike his wife . . . it is not Jewish, but a great and grievous sin . . ."

52. Me'ir ben Gedaliah, *Responsa*, no. 138, where the man was accused of two murders. Mordechai Nadav, "Ma'aseh allimut hadadiyyim beyn Yehudim le-lo' Yehudim be-Lita' lifney 1648," *Gal-Ed* 7–8 (1985): 44–52, demonstrates that in Lithuania Jews were not only victims in violent confrontations with non-Jews but also perpetrators. Nadav points out that such disputes usually arose over business dealings, particularly estate leasing, although Jews also made preemptive attacks against Jesuit students.

53. Slonik, *Responsa*, no. 105. The case took place no later than 1616. The man, together with a non-Jew, was sent with money and goods by his non-Jewish employer to trade in Volhynia.

54. See Katz, *Goy shel Shabbat*, pp. 73–83. As Katz points out, this was a perennial problem that was exacerbated in sixteenth- and seventeenth-century Poland (p. 82).

55. Joseph ben Elijah, *Sefer rekeb Eliyyahu*, p. 22a; Luria, *YSS*, *Beyẓah* 3.25, among others. Also see Ben Sasson, "Taqqanot issurey Shabbat," pp. 183–87, and the ordinances on pp. 195–203.

> And now I will begin to describe the practices of the Jews in the Kingdom of Poland, which were founded on principles of righteousness and steadfastness . . . for throughout the dispersions of Israel there was nowhere so much learning as in the Kingdom of Poland . . . There was scarcely a house in all the Kingdom of Poland where its members did not occupy themselves with the study of the Torah. Either the head of the family was himself a scholar, or else his son, or his son-in-law studied, or one of the young men eating at his table . . . In each community great honor was accorded to the head of the academy. His words were heard by rich and poor alike. None questioned his authority. Without him no one raised his hand or foot, and as he commanded so it came to be . . . There was in Poland so much interest in learning that no three people sat down to a meal without discussing the words of Torah, for throughout the repast everyone indulged in debating matters of the Law and puzzling passages in the Midrashim in order to observe: "Thy law is in my inmost parts" (Psalms 40.9).[56]

The discrepancy between Hanover's portrayal of Polish Jewry and that garnered from responsa is not surprising. The image of a pious, scholarly community made the tragedy of its violent destruction all the more poignant— the very impression that Hanover wished to convey to his readers.[57] In contrast, the examples from responsa literature drew from the atypical events of daily life. Exemplary behavior escaped the notice of a lit-

---

56. Nathan Hanover, *Abyss of Despair* (Yeven Metzulah), Abraham J. Mesch, trans., (New York: Bloch, 1950), pp. 110–21.

57. While almost all literary memorials to the Chmielnicki massacres portray a society in which scholars toiled and achieved great heights, it was axiomatic for all writers that the destruction was meted out by God as a punishment for the sins of Polish Jewry. As Hanover asks in concluding his description of the catastrophe, "What can we say, what can we speak, or how can we justify ourselves? Shall we say we have not sinned? Behold, our iniquities testify against us. For we have sinned, and the Lord found out the iniquity of his servants. Would the Holy One, blessed be He, dispense judgment without justice?" (Hanover, *Abyss of Despair*, p. 109). Seventeenth-century Polish Jews could not conceive of undeserved suffering, at least not openly. Some, like Berechiah Berak (*Zera' berak*, vol. 2, introduction) and Bezalel ben Solomon the Preacher (quoted in Katz, *Goy shel Shabbat*, p. 83), tried to itemize the sins that brought about the destruction, but most were content to make a vague reference to "great sins" or the forsaking of Torah and the commandments without dwelling on the issue (see, for example, Shabbetay ben Me'ir ha-Kohen, *Megillat 'eyfah*, in Halperin, *Beyt Yisra'el ba-Polin*, vol. 2, pp. 252–55, and the sources quoted in Jonas Gurland, *Leqorot ha-gezerot 'al Yisra'el* [1887–1892; reprint, Jerusalem: Kedem, 1972], vol. 1, p. 28; vol. 2, p. 20; vol. 6, p. 11).

erary genre dedicated to solving legal problems, except in those occasional cases where "over-diligence" in observance raised questions about the law.[58]

The vast majority of urban Polish Jewry attended communal prayer services instead of praying at home[59] and few ignored an excommunication of the community.[60] Jews even endured financial loss maintaining their beliefs. Their businesses were closed on late Friday afternoons, Saturdays, and Jewish holidays, while the stores of non-Jews remained open. In addition, Jews sometimes found themselves at a legal disadvantage in Polish courts, as happened in 1604 when Moses, a Jew from Lublin, refused to take an oath and swear by the name of Jesus.[61]

It seems that at some point everyone, even if unwittingly, transgressed a biblical or rabbinic commandment. Sins were a spiritual blemish that nagged at the heart and mind. The Ashkenazic tradition recognized this and prescribed various penitences to atone for sins that some people anxiously sought out.[62] The depth of this religious consciousness and the desire to be free from sin that could be found among laymen in contemporary

---

58. See, for example, Shabbetay ben Me'ir ha-Kohen, *Responsa*, no. 10; Luria, *YSS, Ḥullin* 5.11; Joshua Höschel, *Responsa*, pt. 2 no. 39.

59. Joshua Höschel, *Responsa*, pt. 1, Oraḥ ḥayyim, no. 7.

60. Sirkes, *Responsa* (old), no. 4.

61. *Księgi miasta Lublina* 22 (1604), fols. 6v-7. An oath in Polish court invoked the name of Jesus. Polish courts, like many courts in western Europe in the Middle Ages that wanted to facilitate Jewish participation in commercial life (see Joseph Ziegler, "Reflections on the Jewry Oath in the Middle Ages," in *Christianity and Judaism*, Studies in Church History, no. 29, Diana Wood, ed., [Oxford: Blackwell, 1992] p. 210), often allowed Jews to go to the synagogue and take an oath that was religiously acceptable to them there. An example appears in the Cracow Public Archives (Wawel) *Varia* 12 (1642–1647), fol. 723, where the Jew said "I, Zacharais, swear to omnipotent God who created heaven and earth, who gave the Ten Commandments on Mount Zion [sic] by his faithful servant Moses . . ." It concludes reaffirming that the statement is true based on God as the giver of the Ten Commandments and if it is not true the swearer asks that his flesh and blood be punished. (Professor Juliusz Bardach of the University of Warsaw has told me that there were a number of different versions of the oath. See, for example, Groicki, *Porządek sądów*, pp. 60–61, 150–51.) Why this does not seem to have been an option in the case of Moses of Lublin remains unclear.

62. The Ashkenazic legacy with respect to penances appears to have begun with the thirteenth-century German pietists. See Ya'aqob Elbaum, *Teshubat ha-leb ve-qabbalat yessurim* (Jerusalem: Magnes, 1992), pp. 11–17, as well as 18–36, for some indication of their penetration into Ashkenazic legal thought in the fourteenth and fifteenth centuries. As in the Catholic Church, the need to confess the sin in order to receive a penance must certainly have deterred many from coming forward. See Jean Delumeau, *Sin and Fear: The Emergence of a Western Guilt Culture*, Eric Nicholson, trans., (New York: St. Martin's, 1990), pp. 463, 466, 469–70.

Poland was perhaps nowhere better displayed than in the following case of a Jew from "Russia" (likely the Ukraine) who migrated to Pinców, a town near Cracow.

Sometime between 1648 and 1651 this unnamed man came to a rabbinic court and admitted to having had "bad thoughts" that led to masturbation. He also confessed to having been naked with an unclothed, married woman. They did not have sexual intercourse. The two rabbis who heard his admission sometime before 1648 offered him an unspecified means of penitence which he appears to have accepted. The Chmielnicki massacres intervened between then and his second appearance before a rabbinic court. The massacres must have poignantly stirred the man's conscience because he returned to court in the belief that his penitence may have been too light and that not only did his sin remain but it had caused the massacre of tens of thousands of Jews in 1648. He stood before the court seeking a stricter punishment that would surely expiate his sin and neutralize its consequences for the Jewish people.[63]

Like other rabbis through the ages, Polish rabbis emerged from their talmudic studies steeped in a book culture with which the vast majority of Jewish society was only superficially acquainted. Like other rabbis, they defined religiosity in far more halakhicly correct terms than the laity, who more often calibrated what it meant to be a Jew in sixteenth- and seventeenth-century Poland in terms of Sabbath and festival rituals, circumcision, kashrut, head coverings for males, and communal prayer for those living in areas able to support it. To be sure, laymen did not perform all the details of these rituals scrupulously, yet most observed them in a way that society collectively found acceptable.

In the face of this well-established sense of what Jewish observance entailed to the laity of a given community, its rabbis could only struggle to impose their more stringent conceptions upon it. This endeavor almost inevitably led them to complain about laxity in certain areas. Needless to say, such complaints about public behavior are neither surprising nor unique. What was unusual about rabbis in medieval and late medieval Ashkenaz

63. Wettstein, "Qadmoniyyot," pp. 614–16. The information is recorded in the record book of the Jewish community of Cracow in 1651, together with a warning signed by Yom Tob Lipman Heller that no one should malign the man since he has repented. There is also a call for others in the community of Pinców who may have sinned in such a fashion to repent.

was that they did not look askance at public behavior but perceived of it as something that the law had to be reconciled with rather than something that had to be changed to conform with the law.[64] At the same time, Polish rabbis were rarely guided by common custom unless they knew it to be well informed. In seeking to reconcile stringency with public behavior, they had to show legal flexibility and creativity as teachers, jurists, and committed Jews. The considerations and inclinations diplayed in their deliberations reveal not only the development of Jewish law but also the nature of the relationship between the rabbinic leadership and the contemporary Jewish community.

64. On the relationship between common custom and religious law in Ashkenaz during the twelfth and thirteenth centuries, see Soloveitchik, "Religious Law and Change," pp. 211–12, 220–21. Yedidya Dinari, *Ḥakmey Ashkenaz be-shalhey yemey ha-beynayyim* (Jerusalem: Mossad Bialik, 1984), pp. 196–97, 203–4, maintains that fifteenth-century German rabbis saw it as one of their most important tasks to justify legally public practice, even those that prima facie appeared halakhicly improper. A custom that clearly violated a talmudic ruling, however, was rejected (pp. 216–17).

Part Two

Social and Economic Realities and the Law

4

Social Issues as Halakhic Determinants

In confronting legal and communal problems, Polish rabbis had to weigh not only the demands of the halakhah but also the emotional, physical, spiritual, and economic needs of their constituents. Human needs and the spirit of the law, however, were not always in harmony.

Needless to say, such tensions were not new to the halakhic process. Already in talmudic times rabbis had responded to such pressures by allowing seemingly non-halakhic criteria such as compassion and respect for others to shape halakhic decisions. In matters of *'agunot* (women whose husbands had disappeared without giving a bill of divorce or who refused to give one—in either case such women could not remarry), for example, the Talmud recognized the bleakness of the woman's plight and accepted forms of testimony with regard to the husband's status that the halakhah generally did not tolerate. One witness was sufficient to confirm the death of a missing husband, even though generally two witnesses were required to establish a married woman's right to remarry (e.g., to validate a bill of divorce).[1] Even the casual remark of a non-Jew was deemed sufficient to establish the death of a missing husband.[2]

There were other areas in which the Talmud recognized social values as mitigating factors in legal decision-making. "Respect for human beings" or human dignity (*kabod ha-beriyyot*) was declared to set aside a negative bibli-

---

1. *Yebamot* 16.7, *'Eduyyot* 8.5, from which it is clear that not all rabbis accepted this principle in mishnaic times (late first, second centuries). Although the Mishnah did not explicitly state that the motivation for this and similar forms of leniency with respect to *'agunot* was compassion, Maimonides later articulated such a rationale (*Code of Law*, Divorce 13.28). Not only was freeing the woman viewed as a religious duty, but needless stringency came to be viewed as a sin. See the sources cited by Yizhaq Kahana, *Sefer ha-'agunot* (Jerusalem: Mossad Harav Kook, 1954), pp. 17–25.

2. B.T., *Yebamot* 121b-122a. The remark had to be made without any pretext of legal testimony.

cal precept.[3] Elsewhere, the Talmud ruled that no rabbinic body could impose a restriction (*gezerah*) on the community, no matter how necessary it believed the restriction to be, unless the majority of the lay community could endure it.[4] The rabbis were also willing to compromise to insure public safety. Ideally, the lighting of Hanukkah candles, a rabbinic ordinance, was to be done in the doorway of the house so that passers-by would see the lights and remember the miracle of Hanukkah. However, in locales where the non-Jewish population took offense at this practice and threatened the Jews, the rabbis allowed the candles to be lit indoors.[5]

The talmudic sages were also concerned with the community's spiritual well-being. Their desire to keep people far from sin led them to impose extra regulations, particularly in the realm of the Sabbath and festival laws, when they were concerned that certain actions permitted by the letter of law might be misconstrued and lead people to believe prohibited acts to be permitted.[6] The desire to maintain public observance could also lead to extraordinary measures to ease the difficulty of observance. For example, according to the Mishnah,

> A woman who had five doubtful births or five doubtful issues (see Lev. 15.25–30) only brings one [sacrificial] offering and then she may eat sacrificial flesh [since she is then considered ritually clean]. She does not have to bring the other [four offerings]. If she had five certain issues or five certain births she must bring one offering and then she may eat sacrificial flesh; she is still obligated to bring the other [four] offerings. It once happened in Jerusalem that the price of a pair of doves [used by women for these sacrifices] rose to [two] golden dinars. Rabbi Simeon ben Gamli'el took an oath, "I will not sleep tonight until they cost [two silver] dinars!" He entered the rabbinic court and taught: "A woman who has five certain births or five certain issues need only bring one offering and then she may partake of sacrifi-

3. B.T., *Berakot* 19b. The concept was qualified by the *amora'im* to apply only to Deuteronomy 17.11, the prohibition that invested the rabbis with the authority to make edicts. In effect, the notion of human dignity overruled one negative biblical commandment, but all rabbinic statutes since their authority stemmed from Deuteronomy 17.11. Over the centuries the concept was rarely formally invoked. See Gerald Blidstein, "'Gadol kabod ha-beriyyot'— 'iyyunim be-gilguleyha shel halakhah," *Shenaton ha-mishpaṭ ha-'ibri* 9–10 (1982–1983): 128–29, 178–81, and Aharon Lichtenstein, "Kabod ha-beriyyot," *Maḥanayim* 5 (1993): 14–15.

4. B.T., *'Abodah zarah* 36a-b.

5. B.T., *Shabbat* 21b with the comments of Rashi. See too B.T., *Sukkah* 14b.

6. B.T., *Beyẓah* 9a and elsewhere; J.T., *Mo'ed Qaṭan* 1.2, 80b.

cial flesh and she is not obligated to bring the other [four offerings]." Thereupon the price of two birds stood at two quarters of a [silver] dinar.[7]

Rabbi Simeon ben Gamli'el feared that if the cost of birds rose too high, poor women would not be able to afford to bring the proper sacrifices and, out of sheer despair, would forsake the law and eat consecrated food in a state of ritual impurity. He therefore temporarily suspended the tradition in the hope of ultimately strengthening it.

Even in issues that were not strictly legal matters, talmudic rabbis exercised a social conscience. The Talmud related that "originally" burying the dead was so costly that the expense of burial was more difficult for the family than the pain of death itself. People began to abandon bodies rather than bear the expense of burial. In an attempt to ease the burden on the bereaved, Rabbi Gamli'el (late first century), a wealthy man, set an example for others by having himself buried in simple cotton shrouds.[8]

Experts in the fine points of Talmud, Polish rabbis were familiar with such concepts and included them as considerations in their legal discussions. They also inherited a method of grappling with extra-halakhic concerns from the tosafists, who had often reinterpreted talmudic texts and limited their applicability to contemporary situations, particularly when the community's livelihood was threatened or in cases of severe financial loss.[9] Thus the legal methodology and social concerns of both the past and present helped fashion the character of Polish jurisprudence.

Of course, each jurist had to decide when such methods of reinterpretation were applicable. Not all problems moved rabbis to seek an accommodation with the halakhah. Certain issues, however, particularly those of social justice, demanded this type of rabbinic response.

Concern for the Underprivileged

During his tenure as rabbi in Cracow, for example, Moses Isserles faced the following case that pitted halakhic demands against legitimate human concerns.

---

7. *Keritut* 1.7.

8. B.T., *Ketubbot* 8b. Only a man who could afford to have himself buried in grand fashion could effectively counter the trend.

9. See Shalom Albeck, "Yaḥaso shel Rabbenu Tam le-ba'ayot zemano," *Zion* 19 (1954): 104–41; Jacob Katz, "Ma'arib be-zemano ve-she-lo' be-zemano," *Zion* 35 (1970): 35–60, especially pp. 39–49; Soloveitchik, "Religious Law," pp. 205–21, and "Can Halakhic Texts Talk History?" *AJS Review* 3 (1978): 152–96.

There was a poor man in the land who betrothed his grown daughter [i.e., she was older than twelve] to her proper mate. And during the time of her engagement . . . the father died . . . and the daughter was left bereaved. She was without father or mother and only [had] relatives who forsook her and averted their eyes from her, except for one relative, her mother's brother, who brought her into his home, for she had no relative closer than he. And when the time for her wedding came, when it was proper to prepare the meal and the necessities for the wedding, there was no dowry or other needs. Yet everyone told her that she should ritually immerse herself and prepare for her wedding because she would have a dowry. And this virgin did as her female neighbors told her. She listened to their voice and they covered her with the veil on Friday as is done to virgins.

And when the shadows of evening became long and the day [the Sabbath] was almost sanctified, when her relatives were to give the dowry, they tightened their hands and did not give as they were supposed to, and there was about a third missing from the dowry. Also, the groom reneged and did not want to marry her and did not pay attention to all the words of the town leaders who spoke to him saying that he should not embarrass a daughter of Israel because of contemptible money. But he did not want to listen, and he closed his ear like a deaf asp and did not listen to the voice of those whispering to him, nor did the rebuke of the scholar move him. And because of these arguments and fights time passed, as they [the rabbis] said, "There is no marriage contract without a quarrel." And the work of Satan succeeded until it was about an hour and one-half into the Sabbath when they reconciled themselves and the groom agreed to enter under the marriage canopy and, in order not to embarrass a worthy daughter of Israel, I arose and performed the marriage at this time.[10]

Isserles's actions appear to have blatantly contradicted the halakhah prohibiting marriages on the Sabbath.[11] Yet what motivated him was, as he said, "clear to all that enter the gate of our town." He feared that if he did not perform the wedding then and there, not only would the bride have been embarrassed but the engagement would likely have been broken off. Isserles felt obliged to marry the couple. Not all of his colleagues, however, accepted his concerns as legitimate rationales for violating the law.

I hear after me a voice of great rushing that they have caused it to be proclaimed in the camp, "Look after Moses," regarding my recent performance

10. Isserles, *Responsa*, no. 125, pp. 488–89.

11. *Beyẓah* 5.2; Ṭur, Oraḥ ḥayyim 336.

> of a marriage . . . and since they are maligning me I have come to remove their complaints from me, to bring a proof and my reasons and [legal] justification with me and what I relied on to say in such a case, "Come and marry."

Pressured by other rabbis, Isserles felt compelled to articulate the halakhic basis of his actions. To support his decision, he turned not to the Talmud but to a debate between Rashi and Rabbenu ("our rabbi") Jacob ben Me'ir Tam (d. 1170) over the legal meaning of the Mishnah prohibiting Sabbath marriages.

> Every act for which one is liable because of a *shebut* [a rabbinic prohibition intended to insure Sabbath rest], be it an optional act or a religious precept, [if the rabbis prohibited it] on the Sabbath, one is liable for it also on a festival . . . and these are [prohibited] optional acts: they may not sit in judgment, they may not marry . . . (*Beyẓah* 5.2)

Rashi interpreted the Mishnah according to its plain sense: marriages were prohibited on the Sabbath and festivals under all circumstances. However, Jacob Tam argued that even though it did not say so explicitly, due to the importance of the commandment to "be fruitful and multiply" (Gen. 1.28), the Mishnah did not include a man without a wife and children in the prohibition of marrying on the Sabbath.[12] Faced with a dispute between these titans of Ashkenazic jurisprudence, Isserles could not simply side with Jacob Tam. He needed an ironclad argument to support his view, especially since major legal authorities like Rabbi Asher ben Yehi'el (ca. 1250– 1327) and his son Rabbi Jacob (d. 1340) had followed Rashi's interpretation.[13]

First Isserles attempted to transform Rashi's reading of the text from a conflicting opinion into a supporting source by questioning the textual implications and emerging with a new interpretation of Rashi: a man without wife and children may marry on the Sabbath. Yet as Isserles himself realized, Rashi had always been quoted as an opponent of Sabbath marriages under any circumstances. Isserles had to deal with Rashi based on the assumptions of history.

---

12. *Tosafot*, B.T., *Beyẓah* 36b. See too Jacob ben Me'ir Tam, *Sefer ha-yashar le-Rabbenu Tam, ḥeleq ha-she'elot ve-ha-teshubot*, E. Margoliot and S. Rosenthal, eds., (1898; reprint, Jerusalem: n.p., 1965), p. 101, which was unknown to Isserles.

13. Asher ben Yehi'el on B.T., *Beyẓah* 36b; *Ṭur*, Oraḥ ḥayyim 339.

With little latitude to maneuver, he therefore tried a different legal tack and spelled out for his readers the consequences of his not having performed the wedding. A grown orphan would have been humiliated, waiting in her bridal clothes the entire Sabbath for a Saturday night wedding that in of itself would have been a source of embarrassment since, in opposition to the custom of Poles, Jewish weddings were generally not held on Sundays (Saturday night is considered part of Sunday in Jewish chronology).[14] There was also the distinct possibility that the wedding would have been called off altogether, causing the jilted woman further embarrassment and perhaps permanently tainting her in the eyes of future suitors. Faced with such possibilities, Isserles declared that the case before him was an emergency (*sha'at ha-deḥaq*), and that in such an instance one may rely on Jacob Tam.

Still aware that his actions contradicted accepted custom, Isserles attempted to broaden his base of support for reliance on Jacob Tam. Since the prohibition of marrying on the Sabbath was rabbinic, Isserles invoked the talmudic principle that "respect for human beings"—in this case saving the orphan from humiliation—overrode the negative biblical precept that was the source of rabbinic authority. That principle, in his argument, rendered the ordinance against Sabbath marriages inoperable. Not satisfied, Isserles found a precedent for ignoring a rabbinic prohibition in the contemporary custom of marrying off daughters before they attained religious majority.[15] In the case of the orphan, too, Isserles argued, circumstances demanded that the applicable rabbinic prohibition should be ignored. "All this," he wrote, "I put before my eyes to rely on the words of Rabbenu Tam and other jurists who allow [a marriage on the Sabbath] in an emergency."[16]

---

14. While the Talmud prohibited Friday and Sunday weddings fearing that they would lead to desecration of the Sabbath (B.T., *Ketubbot* 4b–5a), Friday weddings were commonplace in medieval Ashkenaz. See Abraham Freimann, *Seder qiddushin ve-nisu'in aḥarey ḥatimat ha-talmud* (1945; reprint, Jerusalem: Mossad Harav Kook, 1964), pp. 29–30, Ze'ev Falk, *Jewish Matrimonial Law in the Middle Ages* (London: Oxford University Press, 1966), p. 44, n. 2, as well as Esther Cohen and Elliott Horowitz, "In Search of the Sacred: Jews, Christians, and Rituals of Marriage in the later Middle Ages," *Journal of Medieval and Renaissance Studies* 20.2 (Fall 1990): 227–28, nn. 10–12.

15. See B.T., *Qiddushin* 41a. Isserles argued that the custom of his day could be justified because "we are now few in number." The tosafists maintained that this was allowed because of the continually growing "difficulties of the Diaspora."

16. Isserles, apparently, did not know that Jacob Tam eventually reversed himself and ruled Sabbath weddings to be prohibited in all circumstances. See below, n. 25.

Having attempted to neutralize opposing opinions among previous Ashkenazic authorities and to find reasons and precedents to support his actions, Isserles continued. In an approach similar to that of the tosafists,[17] he tried to prove that the very basis of the prohibition, the talmudic concern that one might come to write the marriage contract on the Sabbath, did not apply in an age when the *ḥazzan* (cantor),[18] not the groom, wrote the contract.[19] The Talmud did not concern itself with the possibility that a professional scribe would desecrate the Sabbath to write a contract for someone else.[20] As for the Jerusalem Talmud's rationale that weddings were prohibited on the Sabbath because of "purchasing" —applicable in any age (the husband acquires the wife with respect to her labor and the objects she might find)[21]—Isserles fell back on the tradition that "it appears that our Talmud [i.e., the Babylonian] is primary against the Jerusalem [Talmud] and so rabbinic authorities have always ruled."[22]

Isserles had delegitimized what appeared to be a legitimate question. "However," he acknowledged, "many arise against me and dismiss my ideas [claiming that] perhaps [we] should differentiate between betrothal and entering the marriage canopy, which may be prohibited according to everyone . . . " because it is actually purchasing on the Sabbath. Isserles addressed and refuted such concerns with textual arguments and a charge that those who appeared to be stringent in the law were actually being lenient in another aspect of the law: they took no heed of the damage that their position would inflict upon the woman.

Aware that despite his textual arguments, tradition still placed him in a weak position, Isserles then invoked a proof sometimes used in the Talmud:

---

17. Isserles was well aware of the parallel and quoted a similar attempt by the tosafists (B.T., *Beyẓah* 30a) to strengthen his own approach.

18. Already in the Middle Ages, if not earlier, the term "*ḥazzan*" had taken on the meaning of "cantor" in addition to "sexton" (see Eliezer Ben Yehuda, *Millon ha-lashon ha-'ibrit*, N. Tur-Sinai, ed., [New York: Thomas Yoseloff, 1959], s.v. "*ḥazzan*"). At least in the first half of the seventeenth century, Polish Jews seem to use the term "*ḥazzan*" to refer exclusively to the cantor (see PVAA, index, s.v. "*ḥazzan*").

19. See B.T., *Beyẓah* 37a. Isserles's unarticulated assumption was that the subject of the talmudic phrase "lest one write" is none other than the groom.

20. Isserles added that since cantors always prepared such contracts well in advance of the ceremony, there was no reason to worry about the talmudic ordinance in his time. Later Isserles attempted to bolster his position, arguing that the Talmud did not prohibit divorce on the Sabbath for fear that the divorce would be written on the Sabbath. Bills of divorce were routinely written by professionals and professionals would not come to violate the Sabbath.

21. J.T., *Yoma'* 1.1, 38d; *Ketubbot* 1.1, 24d.

22. Isserles, *Responsa*, no. 125, p. 492.

"Go out and see how people conduct themselves."[23] In Cracow there were often five or six weddings on Fridays, some of whose ceremonies lasted into the Sabbath, with nobody complaining. What difference was there, Isserles asked, between the beginning of the Sabbath and an hour or two into the night? Here Isserles did not invoke public practice as a proof as much as the silence of his colleagues in the face of apparent public negligence. Surely, if there was something wrong with Friday weddings, local rabbis would have tried to quell the practice. Their ongoing acquiescence proved that there must have been some generally accepted, albeit unarticulated, allowance for the custom.

Finally, Isserles suggested that the rabbis of the Talmud had never made an ordinance prohiting Sabbath marriages when there was a time of need (*ẓorek ha-sha'ah*). While Isserles acknowledged that one should be careful to avoid such an exigency, the possibility that delaying the wedding might ruin the match, embarrass the woman, or cause similar grief constituted to Isserles's mind a bona fide and legal need.

All told, despite the fact that a rabbinic ordinance could not be ignored, social concerns propelled Isserles to make no fewer than seven attempts to show the inapplicability of the ordinance prohibiting Sabbath marriages in this case. Without doubt, he did not think of all these arguments on the spot but, in the quiet of his study, was able to construct a reinterpretation of a number of legal approaches that even included a barb for colleagues who looked the other way when Friday weddings lasted into the Sabbath but who may have been hesitant to accept any of his lines of reasoning. Agreeing that Sabbath marriages remained banned, he could not suffer to see the prohibition exact such a high human cost in this instance.

Isserles was not shy about publicizing his position. After Karo ruled in his *Shulḥan 'aruk* that "One does not judge or marry [on the Sabbath]," Isserles noted in his gloss,

> And there are those who permit one to marry when he does not have a wife and children. And it is possible that it is permitted to enter under the wedding canopy too. And even though the law is not so [but like Rashi] nevertheless we rely on this in an emergency also because human dignity is very important. It is not uncommon that they [i.e., the families] are not able to agree on the dowry on Friday until night-time. [Even so] we enter the canopy and make the wedding on the Sabbath night since they already pre-

23. B.T., *Berakot* 45a.

pared the meal and the wedding and it would be an embarrassment to the bride and the groom if they did not enter [the canopy] then and there. However, ideally one should be careful not to come to this.[24]

Some half a century after Isserles's death, on a Sabbath eve in Cracow, a groom balked at accepting the dowry that had been scrounged together for a poor orphan bride. To settle their differences, bride and groom appeared in front of a Polish court. Later, on that very Friday night, Joel Sirkes married the couple, basing his actions upon Isserles's opinion and precedent. Isserles's ruling, however, was insufficient to silence a local critic, and Sirkes was forced to defend the Sabbath wedding.

To do so, Sirkes tried to strengthen Isserles's ruling by widening the range of extra-halakhic concerns that may be invoked to set aside a rabbinic prohibition.[25] He found a paradigmatic case in the talmudic discussion of the parent of a bride or groom who died after the wedding meal had been prepared but before the wedding took place.[26] Conflicted by the biblical injunction to mourn the dead versus concern for extreme and imminent financial loss, the rabbis were lenient with regard to the biblical commandment and allowed both the ceremony and the consummation of the marriage to take place. Sirkes argued *a minori ad maius* that if with regard to a biblical prohibition the rabbis were lenient due to financial loss, then certainly when considering a rabbinic ordinance in an instance where a poor orphan who had nothing but what was raised for her, whose wedding banquet would go to waste, whose engagement might be canceled if the wedding was delayed, and who might remain a spinster "until her head turned white," the rabbis would have been lenient and allowed the orphan to marry on the Sabbath. Concern for impending financial loss as well as for the woman's welfare, Sirkes argued by analogy, should constitute grounds for suspending a rabbinic prohibition.

---

24. *Shulḥan 'arukh*, Oraḥ ḥayyim 339.4.

25. Sirkes, *Responsa* (new), no. 42. See also Sirkes, *Bayit ḥadash*, Oraḥ ḥayyim 339, where he reported that Jacob Tam eventually retreated from his position and prohibited all Sabbath marriages. Nevertheless, once the wedding process stretched into Friday night, Sirkes was willing to rely on Jacob Tam's original opinion in conjunction with the idea of *kabod ha-beriyyot* and concern for financial loss. Sirkes was publicly mocked for this decision by the local cantor, with whom he had a tempestuous relationship. The conflict ultimately erupted in a vitriolic quarrel one Sabbath morning during the reading of the Torah. The responsum is not dated.

26. B.T., *Ketubbot* 3b-4a.

Prodded by practical dilemmas, both Isserles and Sirkes expanded and applied talmudic principles and used tosafist methodology to resolve a conflict between the halakhah and social values. In the aforementioned cases, the values—avoidance of embarrassing someone and concern for financial loss—were in consonance with classical rabbinic thought. One must consider whether Polish rabbis exhibited the same enthusiasm about reconciling the halakhah with values that had no talmudic precedent or openly contradicted traditional Jewish morals.

Dealing with Women in the Marketplace

As part of an attempt to minimize sexual urges outside of marriage and prevent sexual promiscuity, the Talmud prohibited men from looking at women or their colored clothes (even when not being worn), from speaking to women, and even from sending them regards through their husbands.[27] Perhaps some Jewish men could avoid them. Like in the Middle Ages, however, more than a few women in sixteenth- and seventeenth-century Poland were engaged in commerce, working either from their homes or in the marketplace.[28] Others supplemented the family income by serving as cooks, wet nurses, and house servants to wealthy Jewish families; or like Jewish women in different countries, there were those who were involved in business, either with their husbands or independently.[29] In addition, even nonworking women were involved in commerce. When they went to the market to buy food and other daily necessities, businessmen had to look at women, talk to women, and deal with women; it was practically unavoidable.

---

27. B.T., *'Abodah zarah* 20a–b; B.T., *Qiddushin* 70a–b and *tosafot.* These laws were strengthened by their inclusion in Karo's *Shulḥan 'aruk,* Eben ha-'ezer 21.1,6 with some amendments.

28. Medieval Jewish women were very active in money lending (William Jordan, *Women and Credit in Pre-Industrial and Developing Societies* [Philadelphia: University of Pennsylvania Press, 1993], p. 21–22). Writing in the seventeenth century, Me'ir Ashkenazi noted that a particular woman "sat at home as is the way of all women" (*Sefer geburat anashim,* no. 6).

29. Bałaban, "Die Krakauer Judengemeinde-Ordnung," pp. 100–101; Wettstein, "Qadmoniyyot," p. 618; Sirkes, *Responsa* (old), nos. 50, 78; David ben Menasseh Darshan, *Shir ha-ma'alot,* p. 12a; Howard Adelman, "Rabbis and Reality: Public Activities of Jewish Women in Italy during the Renaissance and Catholic Restoration," *Jewish History* 5.1 (Spring 1991): 35–36.

Given the generally low level of rabbinic education among the populace, it is doubtful that the majority of people gave any thought to the question of the halakhic permissibility of talking to a prospective customer who happened to be female; few probably would have even recognized it as a problem. Yet for a leading talmudist and jurist such as Solomon Luria, talmudic passages that conflicted with public practice were provoking.

Forced to deal with the incongruity between contemporary practice and the halakhah, Luria looked to an earlier authority to transform what appeared to be a talmudic injunction into practical advice: "Everything according to what a man knows about himself," he cited in the name of Rabbi Yom Tob ben Abraham Ishbili (known by the acronym *RiYTB'a*; ca. 1250–1330, Spain). If a man is easily excited sexually, Luria wrote, he should not even look at the colored clothes of women; but if he is able to control his desires and no thoughts of lust arise in him, then he can not only look at their clothing but speak with women and look at them.[30] Thus an earlier authority who had transformed a group of laws into subjective rather than objective strictures provided the basis for a reconciliation of tradition and practice.

Significantly, this acceptance of a subjective reading of the law did not carry over into areas where public practice did not challenge the halakhah. Although men and women mingled at weddings,[31] Luria noted with approval that the custom at wedding feasts in most places in "my region" was to entertain the sexes in separate buildings; this was in accordance with the view of the thirteenth-century pietist Samuel he-Ḥasid in *Sefer ḥasidim* that it is inappropriate to recite the phrase, "Let us bless our God that joy is in His abode" (a special insertion in the Grace After Meals at weddings), when men and women sit together. There can be no joy, the pietist declared,

30. Luria, *YSS, Qiddushin* 4.25, cf. 4.4; Yom Tob ben Abraham Ishbili, *Ḥiddushey ha-Riyṭba', maseket Qiddushin*, Abraham Dinin, ed., (Jerusalem: Mossad Harav Kook, 1985), p. 819.

In the introductory heading to this section Luria noted,

> . . . and everything is according to what his eyes see and also [that] he controls his desire and can overcome it. [Therefore] it is permissible for him, to speak to [women], to look at a prohibited women ['*ervah*; i.e., a married woman], and to ask after her well being. And the whole world relies on this when they deal, talk, and look at women.

On the authorship of the headings to each section of *YSS*, see Meir Raffeld, "Ha-Maharshal ve-'Ha-yam shel Shelomoh,'" (Ph.D. diss., Bar Ilan University, 1990), pp. 151–52.

31. See Luria, *YSS, Giṭṭin* 1.18.

when there are thoughts of sin. With practice supporting that earlier dictum, Luria believed that the prohibition was to be supported, not weakened by reinterpretation.[32]

Where, however, this prohibition was not observed, Mordecai Jaffe, for one, felt obliged to reconcile public practice with tradition by reinterpretation, rather than trying to alter either of them. As Luria had done with respect to the marketplace, Jaffe speculated that social conditions had changed. Without quoting Ishbili, he suggested that because contemporary women commonly mingled with men in the course of daily activities, they did not normally elicit "thoughts of sin." The sexes could therefore sit together during Grace.[33] Yet there were limits to such interpretive reconciliations of practice and prohibition. Luria and, a number of years later, Sirkes specifically disapproved of the common practice of Jewish men being bathed by non-Jewish women—no matter how high the level of a man's perceived self-control.[34]

Whereas the problems relating to the physical presence of women in the marketplace were easily overcome by relying on the textual reinterpretation of an earlier jurist, the issue of a husband's liability for his wife's business dealings was somewhat more complex. According to the Talmud, "Whatever a woman acquires, her husband acquires."[35] A woman therefore has no ownership over anything that she buys, makes, or even finds during her marriage and, without joint tenancy, has no legal right to use "family" funds.[36] Technically, then, a married woman could not transact business or incur debt, let alone shop for household needs.[37] According to the Talmud,

---

32. Luria quotes Judah ben Samuel he-Ḥasid's *Sefer ḥasidim* (Reuben Margoliot, ed., [Jerusalem: Mossad Harav Kook, 1957], nos. 393, 1120) to support this custom (*YSS, Ketubbot* 1.20).

33. Mordecai Jaffe, *Sefer lebush ha-ḥur* (Lublin, 1590), *Minhagim*, no. 36. Sirkes, *Responsa* (new), no. 55, recorded in 1627 that the custom of *Sefer ḥasidim* was observed in Cracow (cf. Sirkes, *Bayit ḥadash,* Eben ha-ʿezer 62 [end]).

34. On the practice see Isserles, *Shulḥan ʿarukh,* Eben ha-ʿezer 21.5. On the reaction see Luria, *YSS, Qiddushin* 4.25; Sirkes, *Bayit ḥadash,* Eben ha-ʿezer 21. See, however, Joshua Falk, *Derishah,* Eben ha-ʿezer (Lublin, 1638), 21, n. 3, who accepted the custom.

35. B.T., *Giṭṭin* 77a.

36. *Babaʾ Meẓiʿaʾ* 1.5, regarding what a woman finds.

37. The Mishnah made exceptions and allowed women to sell woolen goods in Judah, cotton goods in the Galilee, and calves in Sharon (the plain along the Mediterranean coast between Jaffa and Carmel). See *Babaʾ Qammaʾ* 10.9 and the accompanying talmudic text (119a).

if a wife somehow assumes a debt, her husband does not have to repay it, and a creditor should know better than to extend credit to a woman without her husband's consent. In sixteenth-century Poland, where some women helped run family businesses, this dictum represented an intolerable legal predicament.[38]

This issue was not new. It had already been raised in the twelfth century by Rabbi Eliezer ben Nathan of Mainz (ca. 1090–1170), one of the early tosafists, during a period in which women of various social ranks also participated in running family businesses. Eliezer argued that women minded stores, traded, borrowed and lent money, repaid debts and accepted payments, took pledges and left pledges. It was therefore clear that even though they were never formally empowered, they were acting as agents of their husbands, who therefore bore responsibility for their actions.[39] Reality dictated that this was a husband's intention. Eliezer added that if a wife incurred a debt before witnesses, her husband would have to pay it; if there were no witnesses she would have to swear against the creditor's claim. Eliezer maintained that such an ordinance in the marketplace (*taqqanat ha-shuq*) was a necessity, one upon which everyone's livelihood depended.[40]

If no one had raised this issue again between the twelfth and sixteenth centuries, Solomon Luria might have had little trouble explaining legally what had become the norm in Polish society. However, in the late fifteenth century, Rabbi Joseph Colon (northern Italy), in a very influential set of responsa, wrote that Eliezer's ruling declared the wife to be an agent only in small dealings—otherwise, he said, no Jewish woman could have bought the groceries! In large sums, though—in which women did not customarily

38. Women who worked with their husbands in the house generally did so in their husbands' presence and were assumed to act with their husbands' consent. Therefore their actions were binding (Luria, *Responsa*, no. 99; *YSS, Baba' Qamma'* 8.28, 29). The Cracow ordinances of 1595 prohibited anyone from transacting business with a woman outside of her house without the express consent of her husband (Bałaban, "Die Krakauer Judengemeinde-Ordnung," p. 102). Yet some women supported their husbands and controlled the family finances (*YSS, Baba' Qamma'* 8.29).

39. Eliezer ben Nathan, *Sefer Ra'aban* (1926; reprint, Jerusalem: n.p., 1975), pt. 1, no. 115, p. 83b. Also see his comments on B.T., *Baba' Qamma'*, pp. 191a, 195b. See also B.T., *Ketubbot* 86b-87a and Rashi's comments, a source not cited by Eliezer.

40. Me'ir ben Baruch of Rothenburg rejected Eliezer's ordinance and maintained that whatever a wife takes possession of belongs to her husband (Mordecai ben Hillel ha-Kohen, *Sefer Morddekay 'al Baba' Qamma'*, no. 89). See, however, Luria, *YSS, Baba' Qamma'* 8.29.

deal—a wife was not to be considered an agent and her husband bore no responsibility for her actions.[41]

Colon's responsum imposed a serious restriction on the activities of those Jewish women in Poland who supported their families—and on their husbands. Essentially agreeing with Colon, Luria tried to stretch the limits of Eliezer ben Nathan's thought by allowing custom and judges to determine a husband's unarticulated intentions in each individual case.[42] Eliezer's opinion became a question to be determined by a judge: had the husband wanted his wife to act as an agent or not?—as opposed to an encompassing legal principle. In small sums one could assume, like Eliezer, that he had; with regard to larger sums, a judge had to make the determination. Luria had no doubts that "even large amounts the husband was obligated to pay, everything according to the matter and the custom of the place and the wisdom of the judge." A woman who controlled the family business "must have" been appointed as an agent by her husband; Luria just could not prove it with a legal rule.[43] Trying to rely on earlier practice, Luria quoted Eliezer's observations that "now [i.e., in the twelfth century] that women are guardians of their husbands, we accept anything [from them] . . . and the managers of charity take . . . even large [donations] . . . " from women, suggesting that the working assumption had always been that husbands wanted their wives to act as their agents. Nevertheless, local judges would have the last word if need be.[44]

Here, too, there is no evidence to suggest that the laity gave the matter a moment's thought. A husband who refused to pay his wife's debts would soon find himself ostracized by the marketplace and his business would quickly collapse. Women routinely dealt with men in the marketplace and ran businesses, apparently without any discernible concern about constantly

---

41. Joseph Colon, *She'elot u-teshubot ha-Mahariq* (Venice, 1519), no. 193 (no. 192 in the Cremona [1557] edition). While historically Colon's ruling must be considered in the context of his attempt to establish a husband's control over family finances and protect him from financial collusion between his wife and son, this was of little consequence to Luria. Colon was held in high esteem by Polish rabbis and cited often in Isserles's glosses to *Shulḥan 'arukh.* Also see Katz, *Responsa,* no. 16, no. 17, pp. 51, 55–56, and Luria, *YSS, Baba' Qamma'* 8.72.

42. Luria, *YSS, Baba' Qamma'* 8.29.

43. Luria, *YSS, Baba' Qamma'* 8.29. See, however, *YSS, Baba' Qamma'* 10.59, where Luria quoted Eliezer ben Nathan that women were agents for their husbands. Luria qualified this by adding that the wife's status depended on the arrangement between her and her husband.

44. Luria, *YSS, Baba' Qamma'* 8.29. See Eliezer ben Nathan, *Sefer Ra'aban,* p. 195b.

transgressing rabbinic law. Concern about the discrepancy between law and practice was only expressed by rabbinic scholars, who were the only ones knowledgeable enough to recognize the problem. However, there was no point in their raising the issue with a community that could not possibly adjust its behavior. Luria, at least, chose to follow the approach of earlier authorities—that is, to reconcile public practice with the halakhah, even if prima facie that practice was at odds with the values of the rabbis of the Talmud.

Expanding the Rights of Daughters to Familial Wealth

Since biblical times, not only had the position of Jewish women changed in the marketplace, but in the value system of Jewish society in general and the family in particular. The Torah had mandated that only males could inherit familial wealth.[45] This is not to say that in rabbinic Judaism daughters did not receive any share of the family's assets. All daughters, even orphans, were assured of a dowry, but unrestricted inheritances were a different matter.[46]

Already in the first centuries of the common era, if not earlier, this stricture conflicted with contemporary values and there were attempts to improve a daughter's lot by encouraging parents (perhaps more correctly, fathers) to increase the size of dowries. Rabbis of the period ordered that if a woman predeceased her husband, the husband would continue to have use of the dowry during his lifetime. Upon his death, however, the dowry would pass solely to the male children of this union rather than being distributed among all the husband's heirs. The assumption was that a bride's parents would dower her more generously if they were sure that the funds would remain in their family through their grandchildren.[47]

---

45. While alive, parents could give their daughters assets as they pleased, but they could not halakhicly bequeath them an inheritance unless there were no sons (see Numbers 27.1–11). The law was codified in *Baba' Batra'* 8.2, 4–5; B.T., 126b.

46. The Talmud insisted that orphaned daughters receive one tenth of their late father's wealth as a dowry when they were married (B.T., *Ketubbot* 68a-b). This arrangement continued to be observed at least into the eleventh century in Franco-Germany (see *Teshubot ḥakmey Ẓarfat ve-Lotir*, Joel Müller, ed., [1881; reprint, Jerusalem: n.p., 1967], no. 94). Later in the Middle Ages, not only orphans but all daughters received cash dowries. See E. Horowitz, "'Haknasat kallah' be-geṭṭo Veneẓiyah: beyn masoret le-ḥiddush u-beyn idey'al le-meẓi'ut," *Tarbiz* 56 (1987): 348–50.

47. B.T., *Ketubbot* 52b-53a with Rashi's comments.

This so called "male children marriage contract" engendered skepticism among some talmudic rabbis, who saw the passing of assets to daughters as a violation of the biblical demand that only males assume familial wealth.[48] It was quickly countered, however, that making a daughter more attractive with an unstinting dowry was a means of fulfilling a different biblical command: "Give your daughters to men [in marriage]" (Jeremiah 29.6).[49]

In the course of the first millennium of the common era, this form of marriage contract fell into disuse in Babylonia due to the legal difficulties involved in implementing it and, rather paradoxically, because daughters were routinely given very large sums—so large that one ninth-century rabbi wishfully mused, "Today, if only a man would give his son as much as he gives his daughter."[50] However, the contract continued to be used, albeit spottily, in Franco-Germany well into the Middle Ages.[51]

Disregarding the spirit of the Masoretic Text, which the rabbis of the Talmud themselves had slighted in this matter, some Jewish parents in medieval Germany sought an alternative to the "male children marriage contract" to insure that their daughters/sons-in-law would receive a portion of their legacy. In thirteenth-century Germany, Rabbi Me'ir ben Baruch of Rothenburg received an inquiry concerning an "inheritance contract" that effectively granted a son-in-law a portion in a man's estate, equal to that which he believed each of his sons would receive after his death, as a gift. The son-in-law took legal possession of the assets on the day of the gift but could not take physical possession until after the father died. Me'ir was

---

48. Numerous biblical verses emphasized the importance of preserving the proper rules of inheritance (see Adolf Büchler, "Seqirah talmudit hisṭorit 'al ha'abarat naḥalah min ha-ben 'al yedey ha-ab," *The Hebrew University, Jerusalem. Inauguration April 1, 1925* [Jerusalem: n.p., 1925], pp. 95–96). However, as Büchler pointed out, already in early rabbinic literature there were fathers who attempted to exclude children from inheriting their share (pp. 78–95).

49. B.T., *Ketubbot* 52b.

50. See the remarks of Rabbi Haninah ben Rabbi Judah quoted in Simhah Assaf, "Biṭtulah shel ketubbat benin dikrin," *Ha-ẓofeh le-ḥokmat Yisra'el* 10 (1926): 23.

51. Me'ir ben Baruch of Rothenburg was asked whether the "male children marriage contract" was still applicable, implying that the questioner did not see it widely used in his surroundings, if used at all. See *Teshubot Maymoniyyot, Nashim*, no. 26; Me'ir ben Baruch, *Responsa* (Prague), no. 248 (compare, however, the Cremona [1557] edition, no. 116). Also see Asher ben Yehi'el, *She'elot u-teshubot le-Rabbeynu Asher ben Yeḥi'el*, Yitzhaq Yudolov, ed., (Jerusalem: Machon Yerushalayim, 1994), no. 36, section 6, who reported that he had seen the contract used in Germany.

asked whether the son-in-law enjoyed the same rights to assets acquired by the father between the time of the gift and the father's death as he did to those given to him directly by the father. In his responsum, Me'ir said he did not, effectively discriminating against daughters/sons-in-law if family assets increased between the time of the giving of the gift and a father's demise.[52]

German Jewry's development of this "inheritance contract" reflected the values of medieval urban German society in general, whereby daughters enjoyed equality with sons in the realm of inheritance law.[53] In Jewish communities elsewhere—in Egypt, for example, Jews bequeathed little if anything to married daughters; the dowry and wedding gifts were their share in familial wealth.[54]

From an economic perspective, the tenuous state of Jewish survival in medieval Germany no doubt lent the inheritance issue an increasing urgency. If they could help it, no parent would consider taking a bride who lacked a dowry for their son, no matter how beautiful the maiden. While Jewish law assured orphans a dowry, Jewish fathers in Germany felt obliged to guarantee a significant additional sum for their daughters in case the parents died before the daughter was married off. According to Rabbi Moses Mintz (German; fl. mid-fifteenth century), this concern for securing their daughters' marriageability seems to have been the motivating factor behind an ordinance "in these regions" to use inheritance contracts.[55] Typically, fathers gave unmarried daughters contracts valued at up to one half a male's portion in the estate.

---

52. Me'ir ben Baruch of Rothenburg, quoted in Mordecai ben Hillel ha-Kohen, *Sefer Mordekay 'al Baba' Batra'* 584, 599. Similar contractual gifts *mortis causa*, aimed at shifting inheritances as well as making endowments to the Church, were in use in Germanic society from the Frankish period throughout the Middle Ages. See Rudolf Huebner, *A History of Germanic Private Law*, Francis Philbrick, trans., (Boston: Little, Brown, 1918), pp. 744–45.

53. Huebner, *A History of Germanic Private Law*, p. 730. Huebner notes that in rural regions the preference of sons over daughters was maintained during the Middle Ages and until modern times. Daughters of nobles were forced to renounce their rights to an inheritance upon their marriage (Huebner, p. 749). By the age of Protestantism, married daughters among the ruling classes and lesser nobility had no rights of inheritance (see Paula Fichtner, *Protestantism and Primogeniture in Early Modern Germany* [New Haven: Yale University Press, 1989], pp. 8, 20).

54. S.D. Goitein, *A Mediterranean Society*, vol. 3 (Berkeley: University of California Press, 1978), pp. 281–82.

55. Moses Mintz, *She'elot u-teshubot rabbenu Mosheh Minẓ*, Yonatan Domb, ed., vol. 1, (Jerusalem: Machon Yerushalayim, 1991), no. 47b, p. 211. There does not seem to have been a fixed form of contract in contemporary use although Mintz does make specific reference to a "half a male's portion" contract (see below, n. 65). On the history of such contracts

Once married and the dowry paid, Jewish brides and their husbands typically held an inheritance contract promising them a portion in her father's estate—ranging from half a male's portion to a full share in the assets.[56] While such inheritance contracts brought little immediate relief to a nascent family, they were another means of guaranteeing that capital would be available to the couple in the future and made an eligible daughter far more attractive to the prospective husband's family, which also had to contribute to making the newlyweds an economically viable unit.

Like their spiritual forebears in fifteenth-century Germany, Polish Jews also attempted to secure a portion of their estates for their daughters.[57] Not only did Polish Jews have precedents in their own tradition for such arrangements; they lived in a society where there was more equitable distribution of assets among offspring than there was in much of Europe. Although a few of the wealthiest families in the Polish-Lithuanian Commonwealth received from the Sejm the right to assign all immovable property to their eldest sons, women generally had substantial property rights in Poland.[58] Under the influence of Hungarian law, the long-term trend to-

---

and other attempts to inherit daughters, including those by Sephardic and Karaite communities, see Simhah Assaf, "Le-she'elat ha-yerushah shel ha-bat," in *Festschrift zum siebzigsten Geburtstage von Jakob Freimann* (Berlin: Rabbinerseminar zu Berlin, 1936), pp. 11–13. Also see Yuval, *Ḥakamim be-doram,* pp. 29–32, as well as his "Ha-hesderim ha-kaspiyyim shel hanisu'in be-Ashkenaz be-yemey ha-beynayyim," in *Dat ve-kalkalah,* Menahem Ben Sasson, ed.,(Jerusalem: Shazar Center, 1995), pp. 199–207, who discusses the Ashkenazic model in greater detail and cites examples of pre-sixteenth-century accords. Yuval emphasizes the importance of such contracts in mid-fifteenth-century marriage agreements and argues that, in all likelihood, the arrangement existed already in the fourteenth century.

56. Mintz, *Responsa,* no. 45, p. 192, dated 1469. Many medieval legal systems postponed the rights of half-brothers and sisters to full blooded siblings in a number of ways (See Huebner, *A History of Germanic Private Law,* p. 730).

57. Halkhic inheritance law was not only being challenged in the sphere of women and their rights. Among fifteenth-century French Jews living in Italy, the custom was to ignore the halakhic rule that the firstborn male receive a double portion. Jews, like Italians in general, granted every son an equal portion. See Colon, *Responsa,* no. 8; Christiane Kapisch-Zuber, *Women, Family, and Ritual in Renaissance Italy,* Lydia Cochrane, trans., (Chicago: University of Chicago Press, 1985), pp. 45, 284.

58. On the debate among the upper classes in sixteenth-century western Europe regarding primogeniture, see Joan Thirsk, "The European Debate on Customs of Inheritance, 1500–1700," in *Family and Inheritance: Rural Society in Western Europe, 1200–1800,* Jack Goody, et al., eds. (Cambridge: Cambridge University Press, 1976), pp. 177–91. Polish magnates seeking such rights—and the newly rich were particularly interested in doing so—

wards granting women greater inheritance rights continued in Polish law in the seventeenth century with daughters as a group, no matter how many they were, receiving one-quarter of noble estates as inheritances.[59] The laws of many towns went even further, granting daughters and sons equal rights of inheritance.[60]

By the sixteenth century, Polish Jewry also achieved a broad and equitable system of distribution of familial assets. However, as will be shown, Jews followed their own traditions in this regard and do not appear to have depended upon models in Polish society for enhancing women's inheritance rights. In general, Polish Jews continued the trend of Italian (French) and German Jewry to grant daughters inheritance contracts but perceived distinct disadvantages to the agreements that had been used in previous generations:[61] those agreements granted daughters no rights to assets acquired by their fathers after the date of the contract or to improvements made on the assets by male siblings; fathers could transfer assets held at the time of the agreement at will, thereby reducing the value of a daughter's share;[62] and

---

seemed to be concerned about securing their family's wealth and power for future generations. Such privileges were given very begrudgingly by noblemen and were granted but seven times between 1550 and 1648. Ordinances granting these rights excluded women from succession in all but extreme situations. Land covered by such an entail was effectively removed from circulation since it could not be sold, let alone used as part of a dowry. See A. Mełen, "Ordynacje w dawnej Polsce," *Pamiętnik Historyczno-Prawny* 7.2 (1929): 42, and Juliusz Bardach, *Historia państwa i prawa polski do roku 1795*, vol. 2 (Warsaw: Państwowe Wydawnictwo Naukowe, 1957), pp. 173–74.

59. Juliusz Bardach, Boguslaw Lesnodorski, and Michal Pietrzak, *Historia państwa i prawa polskiego* (Warsaw: Państwowe Wydawnictwo Naukowe, 1987), p. 236.

60. Wacław Soroka, "Main Instituttions of the Polish Private Law, 1400–1795," in *Polish Law Throughout the Ages*, W. Wagner, ed., (Stanford: Hoover Institution Press, 1970), p. 84. Soroka adds that daughters shared equally in the inheritance of maternal assets that were intestate.

61. Isserles labeled such contracts "half a male's portion contracts" (see below, n. 65). None of the texts that he quotes use this phrase but rather the term "inheritance contract." See Jacob Molin, *She'elot u-teshubot ha-Maharil*, Yitzchok Satz, ed., (Jerusalem: Machon Yerushalayim, 1979), no. 88; Jacob Weil, *She'elot u-teshubot Mahar"i Vveyil* (Jerusalem: Tif'eret ha-Torah, 1988), no. 109; *Dinim ve-halakot* 16, 27; Colon, *Responsa*, no. 78; Isserles, *Darkey Mosheh*, Eben ha-'ezer 108.2. Other fifteenth-century sources, however, do refer to the contract as a "half a male's portion contract." See, for example, Jacob Molin, *Shu"t Maharil ha-ḥadashot*, Yitzchok Satz, ed., (Jerusalem: Machon Yerushalayim, 1977), no. 164, p. 228 (the language of the questioner).

62. Molin, *Responsa*, no. 88, p. 161, ruled it improper for a father to convey to his wife property that he had already promised to daughters in an inheritance contract.

creditors of an estate and unmarried daughters, who had to be supported from proceeds of the estate, had proceeding liens on the assets, further weakening a married daughter's position.[63] Dissatisfied with these provisions, sixteenth-century Ashkenazic Jewry developed what came to be called the "half a male's portion" contract.

According to its terms, fathers typically assumed a debt to their daughter(s)/son(s)-in-law of one thousand "golds"[64]—not payable, however, until a moment before a father's death.[65] Until that moment, the father had usufruct of the funds and could spend them as he pleased.[66] However,

---

63. See Moses Isserles, *Darkey Mosheh ha-shalem ḥoshen misphat*, H.S. Rosenthal, ed., (Jerusalem: Machon Yerushalayim, 1979–1983), vol. 2, 281, pp. 155–57; *Shulḥan 'aruk*, Ḥoshen mishpaṭ 281.7. Both Mintz, *Responsa*, no. 22, and Molin, *Responsa* (new), no. 155, p. 212, wrote that daughters only have a share in what is left after all creditors are paid.

64. Numerous types of gold coins were circulating in Poland in the 1550s including gold talers and ducats. The insistance on gold coins may have been an attempt to protect daughters from the ramifications of any depreciation in the value of silver coinage.

In Lvov in 1555 an unskilled worker made approximately 1.5 grosz per diem. There were about 52 grosz in a gold ducat and about 32.66 grosz in a gold taler at the time. A "pail" of beer cost about 3 grosz in Lvov in that year (see Stanislaw Hoszowski, *Ceny we Lwowie w XVI i XVII wieku* [Lvov: J. Mianowski, 1928], pp. 155, 176, 246–47). For examples of prices in the early seventeenth century, see below, pp. 138.

65. The contract called for the debt to be paid a moment before the father's death because no one can obligate himself to do anything after his death. These fifteenth-century inheritance contracts could be construed as debts or gifts depending on how the contract was worded (Molin, *Responsa* [new], no. 164, p. 229).

I hesitate to accept Molin, *Responsa* (new), no. 155, p. 211, as a fifteenth- century example of the debt contract that became commonplace in sixteenth-century Poland (i.e., half a portion or 1,000 golds). The relevant section appears to be the interpolation of a sixteenth-century copyist ever anxious to clarify matters in British Museum Hebrew MS. Add. 27,111 (Margoliouth 575) for readers (see Satz's introduction, p. 13). Among his changes was the rewriting of the word *zehubim* ("golds") to "ducats" when *zehubim* seems to have been the standard rabbinic phrase of Molin's time and place (Satz, no. 164, n. 2; a responsum in which the copyist failed to convert one such reference). Ducats were also not the local currency although they may have been in circulation. If one accepts Yuval's tentative suggestion (*Ḥakamim be-doram*, p. 29) that Rabbi Zalman ha-Kohen of Nürnburg, the questioner in no. 155, explained the inheritance contract to Molin (surprising in itself) by referring to the custom of Poland in the first half of the fifteenth century, the matter becomes even more difficult. Poland was still without known halakhic leadership at that time and was an unlikely site for halakhic innovation. It would seem that the copyist may have been explaining to his sixteenth-century readers what an inheritance contract was by inserting a brief comparison to what he thought they might be familiar with, that is the "half a male's portion contract" of sixteenth-century Poland.

66. The contract was not unique to Poland. Rabbi Me'ir Katzenellenbogen wrote that such contracts were used in Italy (*She'elot u-teshubot Maharam Paduv'ah* [Venice, 1553], nos.

when the father died, daughters could present the beneficiaries, usually the surviving sons, with a claim for one thousand golds. The "half a male's portion contract" offered beneficiaries the option of either paying the debt or giving their sister(s) one half of a son's portion in the estate.[67] Since one thousand golds was more than the entire value of most estates, it was in the sons' best interests to give their sister(s) half portion(s).[68]

45, 51). Joseph Katz received a question from Moravia where it was the custom to promise such a contract to prospective sons-in-law and deliver it just before the wedding (*Responsa*, no. 2, p. 14). The contract was still in use in Moravia in the mid-seventeenth century (Krochmal, *Responsa*, nos. 95, 96, 114; responsum no. 114 discusses a single mother who left such a contract for her daughter). A seventeenth-century copy of a contract from Germany appears in Samuel ben David ha-Levi, *Naḥalat shib'ah* (Amsterdam, 1667), no. 21, pp. 69a-70a; see too Jacob Margolis, *Seder ha-geṭ*, Yitzchok Satz, ed., (Jerusalem: Machon Yerushalayim, 1983), pp. 321–22. Samuel ben David ha-Levi observed that in Poland only fathers wrote inheritance contracts while in Germany the custom was that both mothers and fathers gave their daughters "half a male's portion contracts" (n. 1).

67. An illustration. Jew A leaves an estate valued at 500 golds after all debts are paid and assets calculated. A has three children. The oldest child, B, a daughter, and two younger sons, C and D. Before his death A indebted his estate to B for 1000 golds using a "half a male's portion contract." With A's death, C and D have a choice. They can either pay 1000 golds to B, which is more than the value of the entire estate, or they can give B a half portion. Whether B gets 125 golds and C and D 187.5 golds each or whether B gets 100 golds and C and D 200 each remains unclear. (The latter seems to have been the practice in Molin, *Responsa* [new], no. 155, p. 212.)

The notion of daughters receiving half a male's portion is not unique to Judaism. According to the Qur'anic legal principle of *ta'sīb*, a son's portion is twice that of a daughter's. See N.J. Coulson, *Succession in the Muslim Family* (Cambridge: Cambridge University Press, 1971), pp. 41–42. Whether the Jewish community was influenced at some earlier time by the Muslim model remains to be investigated.

68. Katz, *Responsa*, no. 74, pp. 169–70, noted that scribes generally wrote 1,000 golds in these contracts because that was more than enough to encourage the sons to give their sister half a portion. This amount continued to be used in Moravia at least until the mid-seventeenth century (Krochmal, *Responsa*, nos. 95, 96, 114), although scribes in the Lvov region in 1630 did not know how much to write in the contract. In that year the community in Żółkiew ruled that the sum stipulated in a contract should depend on the amount daughters received as dowries. A man who gave his daughter up to and including 400 golds should write 200 golds in the "half a male's portion contract;" from 400 to 1,000 golds, 500 golds; 1,000 to 1,500, 1,000 golds; and for any amount above 1,500 golds a scribe should write 2,000 golds in the "half a male's portion contract" (Cygielman, *Yehudey Polin ve-Liṭa'*, p. 505). It would appear that the ordinance of Żółkiew was not attempting to write in an unattainable amount and insure the daughter one half a male's portion but rather to guarantee a fair settlement based upon the family's station in life.

The essential legal difference between what was called the "half a male's portion contract" and the inheritance contract of earlier generations was that the new contract transformed daughters into creditors of the estate whose claims preceded those of beneficiaries (but not those of other creditors).[69] If sons granted their sisters half a male's portion, as they invariably did, daughters were guaranteed rights to distributions from all movable assets of the estate, no matter when they were acquired. Daughters were also entitled to a portion of assets due the estate but not yet realized.[70] Nevertheless, there were limitations. The contract specifically excluded daughters from receiving land and books, and sons could pay off creditors with movable property even though there were ample real estate assets. This was, however, a provision of limited importance in Polish-Jewish society, where few people owned substantial amounts of real estate.[71]

Without a long tradition to provide precedents for this sort of estate arrangement,[72] Polish rabbis had to settle a number of legal uncertainties surrounding the "half a male's portion contract": Did daughters have rights to assets in their grandfathers' estates if their fathers predeceased their grandfathers?[73] Did a prospective son-in-law who had been promised a

---

69. Isserles, *Shulḥan ʿarukh*, Ḥoshen mishpaṭ 281.7. See too Mintz, *Responsa*, no. 22; Katz, *Responsa*, no. 37, pp. 113–14; Natan Kahana, *Sefer she'elot u- teshubot dibrey renanah*, I. Herskovitz, ed., (Brooklyn, N.Y.: n.p., 1984), no. 49, pp. 214–15.

70. Isserles, *Shulḥan ʿarukh*, Eben ha-ʿezer no. 108.3.

71. Isserles, *Darkey Mosheh*, Eben ha-ʿezer no. 113.5; *Shulḥan ʿaruk*, no. 113.2; Kahana, *Responsa*, no. 49, p. 214. Samuel ben David ha-Levi explained that books and land were not included in the contract because people did not want items that were generally passed down from generation to generation to be lost from the family (*Naḥalat shibʿah*, p. 73b, n. 6; see too Luria, in Isserles, *Responsa*, no. 4, p. 17; Wettstein, "Qadmoniyyot," pp. 607–608, a last will and testament from Cracow, 1647). The custom had fifteenth-century antecedents; see Molin, *Responsa* (new), no. 164, pp. 228, 231. See, however, Mordecai ben Hillel, *Baba' Batra'* 599 where books and land were specified among the assets that the son-in-law was to receive. A clause could be inserted into the contract requiring that the daughter have living children for it to be valid— presumably an attempt by fathers to prevent assets from leaving the family. See, for example, Isserles, *Shulḥan ʿaruk*, Eben ha-ʿezer 90.1.

72. Writing in mid-seventeenth century Moravia, almost a full century after the issue began to be discussed in Polish rabbinic sources, Krochmal wrote that "there is no custom" regarding the "half a male's portion contract" (*Responsa*, no. 114).

73. Katz, *Responsa*, no. 1, p. 7. The assumption was that although not inherited during the father's lifetime, legally speaking the grandfather's estate "passes through" the father to the grandchildren. The grandfather's legacy should therefore be considered an asset of the father's estate in which the daughters have a right to half a male's portion.

"half a male's portion contract" at the signing of the engagement contract have the right to inherit from the bride's father if the latter died before the wedding when the contract was to have been delivered?[74] Could contracts be bought and sold while the father was still alive and, if so, could sons who had bought a sister's contract decide to pay themselves as bearers of the debt one thousand golds upon their father's death, leaving no assets in the estate and effectively disinheriting their other sisters?[75] In these cases rabbis were being asked to clarify aspects of contracts that contradicted the spirit—if not the letter—of the halakhah.

When halakists confronted any new phenomenon, they sought a familiar halakhic model as a legal frame of reference. Once rabbis were able to bring the inheritance contract into the orbit of previous halakhic thought, they could scrutinize it like any other legal matter, using precedents and familiar analysis. For example, to decide whether a daughter had rights to assets in her paternal grandfather's estate based upon an inheritance contract that she held from her deceased father, Polish rabbis found a talmudic source in the following:[76]

> If a son sold some of his father's assets while the father was alive and then [the son] died, his son [i.e., the grandson] may take [the assets that were sold away] from the buyers.[77]

Samuel ben Me'ir (ca. 1080/85–ca. 1174), the French rabbi whose commentary on this passage is the standard exegetical work, explained:

> For example, Reuben sold the portion that he expected to receive as an inheritance (*ra'uy*) from Jacob his father and then Reuben died during Jacob's lifetime. Then Jacob died, and afterwards Hanoch, Reuben's son, comes and takes away the goods that Reuben his father sold from Jacob's possessions from the buyers because they [the goods] are only an expectancy and had never come to Reuben that he should be able to allow the buyers to obtain

74. Katz, *Responsa*, no. 2, p. 14.

75. Katz, *Responsa*, no. 8, p. 31.

76. The claim was brought by the son-in-law on the basis of his wife's contract. Her father had predeceased the grandfather by six years (Katz, *Responsa*, no. 1, p. 12). Although no date is given, the case was debated in the 1550s. One of the correspondants was Rabbi Me'ir Katzenellenbogen, who wrote to Joseph Katz just after the burning of the Talmud in Italy (1554).

77. B.T., *Baba' Batra'* 159a.

legal rights over them. And just like an expectancy cannot be mortgaged so too it cannot be sold as we learn in tractate *Bekorot* 52b . . .[78]

Both in the Talmud and in the later commentary, the issue revolved around whether a father could alienate the rights of beneficiaries from property that he had expected to receive but never did. Could a father assign unalienable rights in his own father's estate to his daughters before he actually received the assets himself?

Isserles could not come to a decision solely on the basis of rabbinic texts: earlier authorities had arrived at no clear conclusion regarding the sale of an expectancy. Following the opinion of Me'ir of Rothenburg, Isserles declared that since the law remained in dispute, it rested upon the claimant (here the daughter) to produce evidence supporting her claim.[79] Luria also understood the laws of a creditor's rights to expectancies to favor the sons in this matter.[80]

Both jurists could have ended the discussion right there, leaving daughters without rights in their grandfather's estate. However, each continued his independent inquiry by turning to the language of the contract to prove that the daughter did have a right to inherit a portion of her grandfather's estate. The contract promised the daughter a share in "expectancy like in property already held in possession" and while, according to the halakhah, expectancies (or any other future) cannot be sold and therefore cannot be assigned to daughters, no one doubted that contractual conditions could be made with regard to expectancies. The father had the right to declare that if the sons wished to be free of the debt, they would have to include the daughters in the division of any future inheritance.[81] The language of the contract, then, became the determining legal factor—in part, because it best expressed the intentions of the father. That it violated the intention of Masoretic legislation and awarded daughters a share in inheritances was irrelevant.

---

78. The standard convention for naming parties in rabbinic legal cases is to use the names of the patriarch Jacob and his family.

79. Isserles, *Responsa,* no. 3, pp. 8–9.

80. Luria, *Responsa,* no. 49, pt. 1. That both Luria and Isserles resorted to the language of the contract to prove their points did not prevent them from arguing over their talmudic conclusions. These discussions almost take on a life of their own, independent of the narrow legal matter at hand (see Isserles, *Responsa,* no. 8; Luria, *Responsa,* no. 49, part 2 [both of Luria's responsa appear in Isserles's collection as well, nos. 4 and 71]).

81. Luria, in Isserles, p. 17; Isserles, *Responsa,* no. 3, p. 9. Isserles had four other proofs that relate to the language of the contract and the intent of the father (pp. 10–13) that he used to deflate the arguments of Joseph Katz, who believed that the daughter had no portion in the expectancy.

Joseph Katz faced the same problem as Luria and Isserles. Like them, he could not muster an indisputable conclusion from rabbinic literature concerning expectancies. He even suggested that expectancies were not the issue at hand.[82] Ultimately, for Katz too the matter hinged on what he believed to be the intent of the contract. Did it include such an unusual possibility as a father predeceasing his parent or not? Katz thought not. Yet he argued that even if all his assumptions were incorrect and the father specified that if he predeceased his father his portion of the grandfather's estate should be included in the inheritance contract, the daughter/son-in-law would still not receive the money.

> Who could know how much their grandfather had when the half a male's [portion] contract was written or before the death of their father [when this amount] was an expectancy for their father. Because certainly, whatever their grandfather earned after the death of their father is not [part of an] expectancy with the death of their father [and] is not included in this condition [i.e., the inheritance contract . . . and it is only a] questionable expectancy.[83]

As Katz understood the matter, even a specific condition in the inheritance contract granting daughters rights to their grandfather's assets did not give them a claim to what their grandfather acquired after his son's death. This meant that the exact value of the expectancy at the time of the father's death had to be determined—a virtually impossible task when, as Katz pointed out, a person's net worth could change if he picked up a penny in the street. With the value of the expectancy uncertain, the burden of proof fell on the daughter to determine what her grandfather owned at the time of her father's death. Unable to determine the amount, the assets remained with the sons because the halakhah does not allow money to be collected on the basis of doubt.[84]

While Isserles and Luria both attempted to move this matter from the

---

82. Katz, *Responsa*, no. 1, p. 11.

83. Katz, *Responsa*, no. 1, p. 12.

84. Katz sent his opinion to Rabbi Qalman of Worms (d. 1560), who was the rabbi in Lvov and a sage of the older generation, and to Rabbi Qalman's son-in-law, Rabbi Eliezer ben Manoaḥ, both of whom concurred with him. He also corresponded with Katzenellenbogen, who disagreed with him on this matter. According to Katz, Katzenellenbogen finally wrote to him that he should not rely on his opinion now because "in our great sins, the wells of Talmud are not in his hand." As Katz pointed out, Katzenellenbogen was writing at the time of the burning of the Talmud in Italy (1554).

realm of expectancies into the field of contract law, Katz's fear of taking money from someone in a case of legal doubt prevented him from exploring new possibilities.[85] In principle, however, Katz was not opposed to daughters receiving inheritances, as a dispute that arose regarding a "half a male's portion contract" revealed.

Katz was asked about a case involving a wealthy father who wanted to follow the common custom and commit himself to paying his daughters one thousand golds when he and everyone else knew that half a male's portion of his estate would be worth much more than one thousand golds. In his responsum Katz indicated that this problem arose a number of times, presumably at the insistence of angry daughters who knew that they were being squeezed out of what they and the community recognized as their fair share of their father's wealth. Without quoting a single rabbinic source, Katz demanded that wealthy parents obligate themselves to leave their daughters a sum much larger than half a male's portion of their assets (and, needless to say, greater than one thousand golds). Maintaining that the idea behind such contracts with the one thousand golds figure was to insure their daughters half a male's portion, he argued that violating the spirit of the contract in effect destroyed its legal basis and flew in the face of what society had established as equitable treatment for daughters.[86] Thus halakhah was used as the mode of argumentation in this instance and not as the legal basis of the custom. In other words, Katz was using the language of the law to set social policy.

While Katz attempted to protect the integrity of the "half a male's portion contract," he did not always try to guarantee daughters an inheritance. He ruled that two sons who bought one of their three sisters' contracts with their father's blessing could opt to pay themselves the one thousand golds when their father died and leave little for their remaining sisters.[87] For Katz

85. Years later the matter had yet to be resolved. A rabbi wrote to Me'ir ben Gedaliah that while he and his colleagues sided with Luria (Isserles's responsa were not published until 1640 and were likely not widely known), a minority of people who thought of themselves as scholars claimed that one may not decide a debate between such halakhic titans and that the assets must remain with the sons since money cannot be collected on the basis of doubt. Me'ir ben Gedaliah himself generally sided with Katz in this regard (*Responsa*, no. 14).

86. Katz, *Responsa*, no. 74, pp. 169–70.

87. Katz, *Responsa*, no. 8, pp. 31–34. The father was present and formally agreed to the sale of the contract, knowing full well, Katz assumed, that the sons would choose to enrich themselves at the expense of their sisters.

the halakhah was quite clear in this matter: sons who had a contract that gave them the option of paying the debt or giving their sisters half a male's portion could choose as they pleased without regard for the financial loss they would inflict on their sisters.

Katz rejected the daughters' contention that the entire contract was but a legal fiction intended to insure them a half a male's portion and that the father's intent should be followed in settling the claim. Supporting the integrity of the debt contract and the sons' right to decide whether to pay their sisters or share the inheritance with them, he claimed that written words are legal determinates, not nebulous intentions. Ironically, in ignoring the role of intent, Katz rejected the very concept upon which he had relied to force wealthy fathers to write larger sums in their contracts in the previously cited case. Yet if he had not dismissed the idea here, the contract would arguably have ceased to have been a debt contract (since sons no longer had a choice of what to do) and would have reverted to becoming an inheritance contract with all its concomitant drawbacks.

As in the case of the grandfather and grandchildren discussed above, Katz was reluctant to transfer money from one party to another without a clear halakhic basis for doing so.[88] He demonstrated no inclination to explore opinions that might protect the daughters' interests.[89] Quite the contrary. He sought to show that the textual interpretations of the tosafists countered such possibilities and went so far as to try to preclude any rehabilitation of such ideas by others.[90]

Katz concluded this section of his responsum with a telling legal suggestion.

---

88. Upon the death of any father, all assets came into the possession of the sons according to the law of the Torah. Debts and obligations against the estate could then be presented to the sons for payment.

89. Katz was unwilling to follow the view of the one authority, Rabbi Samuel ben Isaac ha-Sardi (1185/90–1255/6), who ruled that one must be concerned with the ramifications of one's actions on others, particularly since, in Katz's view, the tosafists and Mordecai ben Hillel had precluded any textual support for ha-Sardi's position. Katz argued, albeit somewhat weakly, that in the case of a "half a male's portion contract" even Sardi himself might have supported the rights of the sons.

90. Ha-Sardi's view remained a distinct practical possibility since not only did ha-Sardi concur with the view of one of the great talmudists of the Middle Ages, Rabbi Moses ben Nahman (Nahmanides; 1194–1270), but Jacob ben Asher quoted ha-Sardi, as well as the tosafists, in his code of law (*Ṭur,* Ḥoshen mishpaṭ 66.24). Katz surmised that because Jacob ben Asher cited the tosafists last he sided with their view.

> And even if the [claims] would be equal, nevertheless, one must rule to preserve the inheritance [law of] the Torah. And if there is no certain proof for this, there is a hint of it in the tosafists who write . . . "that in all instances we prefer to follow [the] inheritance [law] of the Torah."[91]

In a case of doubt, then, Katz stood firmly on the side of the Torah, even if it served only as an ancillary argument. While he supported what seemed to be an almost universal desire among Polish Jews to insure that their daughters received an inheritance, he was unwilling to reinterpret the Talmud, test the limits of halakhic thought vis-à-vis contemporary social values, or create legal technicalities that might expand daughters' rights. There was likely only limited pressure for him to do so. The basic social need had been accommodated within the rubric of the law.

All attempts to grant daughters an inheritance not only violated the verse, "If a man dies and has no son then you shall pass his inheritance to his daughter" (the verse implied to the rabbis of the Talmud that if he has a son you may not do this; Numbers 27.8), but ignored the talmudic statement of Samuel to Rab Judah the Learned,

> Do not be among those who transfer inheritance even from a bad son to a good son because no one knows what issue [lit., "seed"] will come from him and much more so from a son to a daughter.[92]

It seems that a piece of talmudic advice—as opposed to legislation—could not withstand the pressures of changing social values that had come to demand that daughters have a share in an inheritance—for whatever reason. Nevertheless, there were those who grasped for some way to defend the custom in light of this talmudic passage.

In the fifteenth century, Moses Mintz tried to justify the use of inheritance contracts by comparing them to the Talmud's enactment of the "male children's marriage contract." Just as the latter was instituted in order to encourage fathers to dower their daughters generously and thus make them more attractive to suitors, so too, Mintz argued, the inheritance contract of his day was made to foster marriages. In light of this, Mintz argued, the statement of Samuel could be set aside.[93]

---

91. *Tosafot,* B.T., *Ketubbot* 91b; Katz, *Responsa,* no. 8, p. 33.

92. B.T., *Ketubbot* 53a.

93. Mintz, *Responsa,* no. 47 (end).

The desire to encourage marriages, however, was not always a valid explanation in sixteenth- and seventeenth-century Poland. When a wealthy Cracow Jew, Todros Kozuchowski, lay gravely ill in 1647, he decided to increase the amount to be given to his sons-in-law in the "half a male's portion contracts" that they already held.[94] Such a gift could do little to enhance the eligibility of his married daughters but would appear to have been a simple act of affection, a gesture not unknown even in the most patriarchal societies.[95] Samuel ben David ha-Levi was well aware that as the second half of the seventeenth century began, "half a male's portion contracts" were no longer a form of enhancement for eligible daughters. He suggested that fathers gave their sons-in-law such contracts for their married daughters' benefit. When sons-in-law would see that they were considered "almost" like sons by their in-laws they would love their wives "at all times."[96]

The above examples demonstrate how the changing values of sixteenth-century Jewish society in the realm of inheritance law were accommodated with contracts that conformed to the letter of the law but had no regard for legislative intent. The biblical law calling for estates to pass exclusively to male heirs (when they existed) was effectively circumvented by debt agreements endorsed by the most outstanding Polish rabbis. Although such arrangements strictly adhered to the rules of the halakhic system, Polish rabbis were, without doubt, altering Jewish tradition.

Maintaining Personal and Communal Probity

Beyond monetary considerations and the need to protect disadvantaged members of society, other concerns moved jurists to reexamine the halakhah. The need to preserve the personal reliability of a large group of Jews led Moses Isserles to assume perhaps one of the boldest legal positions of

---

94. Kozuchowski also used the "half a male's portion contract" to leave money to his wife. In order to protect her interests, he stipulated that the increased gifts to his sons-in-law would be null and void if anyone challenged her contract in court (Wettstein, "Qadmoniyyot," pp. 609–10). On Kozuchowski, see Bałaban, *Dzieje Żydów w Krakowie*, pp. 188–89. According to Bałaban, Kozuchowski died in 1648.

95. In medieval Egypt, where the patriarchal system ruled, Jewish fathers were known to leave daughters a token of their affection (Goitein, *A Mediterranean Society*, vol. 3, pp. 281–82).

96. Samuel ben David ha-Levi, *Naḥalat shib'ah*, chap. 21, n. 4b, pp. 70b-71a. He also quotes Mintz's explanation.

the period. Isserles was asked whether he was aware of any legal basis for the custom common especially among Moravian Jews to drink the wine of non-Jews, a custom that "no one" tried to stop. If he did not know of a rationale, the question continued, could one be found?[97]

Isserles was not just faced with a legal problem. Failure to find a basis for the custom of Moravian Jews would have created a small fissure in the sixteenth-century Jewish community. During this period Moravian Jews supplied Poland with a portion of its kosher wine, but because these merchants themselves drank non-kosher wine, Polish Jews could not believe their claims that the wine they were shipping was kosher.[98] In order to reestablish the suppliers' halakhic integrity, Isserles had to articulate a halakhic rationale for their practice. Once some source existed, even if halakhicly incorrect and unknown to most Jews, Moravian Jews would no longer be considered to be flouting the law but simply relying on a mistaken source.[99] Removed thereby from the category of sinners, they would not be suspected of misleading other Jews. The problem lay in finding a source.

Isserles had to wrestle not with just one prohibition against imbibing the wine of non-Jews, but two. One was a biblical injunction against deriving any benefit from *yeyn nesek*, wine used specifically for idolatry.[100] The second concerned *stam yeynam*, the wine of non-Jews or kosher wine that had been touched by a non-Jew.[101] As part of an effort to prevent Jewish men from having sexual intercourse with non-Jewish women and ultimately

---

97. Isserles, *Responsa*, no. 124, p. 484. The question has been abridged and reformulated by Isserles. This responsum was omitted from the Amsterdam (1711) edition and all susequent editions of Isserles's responsa until it was reinserted by Siev. On the removal of the responsum see Elisheva Carlebach, "Rabbi Moses Hagiz: The Rabbinate and the Pursuit of Heresy, Late Seventeenth–Early Eighteenth Centuries," (Ph.D. diss., Columbia University, 1986), pp. 84–85. Ben Sasson has presented a somewhat different approach to this responsum. See his *Hagut*, pp. 22–25.

98. *Bekorot* 4.10 states, "This is the general rule: whoever is doubted regarding a matter may not judge or give testimony regarding it." See too *Bekorot* 5.4 which Isserles also alludes to.

99. Isserles specifically stated that even if he could find an allowance, not every drinker of non-kosher wine would be aware of it. Isserles assumed that Moravian Jews simply followed the example of their fathers—who, Isserles assumed, must have had an allowance—and therefore were not true sinners (pp. 485–86). See Isserles, *Shulḥan 'aruk*, Ḥoshen mishpaṭ 34.4, who ruled that someone who sins due to a mistake is still considered a reliable witness.

100. B.T., *'Abodah zarah* 29b based on Deuteronomy 32:38.

101. *'Abodah zarah* 2.3, B.T., *Shabbat* 17b. The tosafists (B.T., *'Abodah zarah* 29b) suggested that, unlike the bread and oil of non-Jews that were only prohibited to eat, *stam yeynam* was totally prohibited because of its similarity to *yeyn nesek*.

coming to worship their gods, the rabbis made a separate ordinance prohibiting drinking and benefiting from the latter. To clear the Moravians, then, both prohibitions had to be addressed.

Isserles began his search in somewhat of a quandary. If he were to offer a halakhic basis for drinking non-kosher wine, sinners would have support for their practice and continue to sin. If he remained silent, he feared that sinners "in every place" would reason that if these Jews drink non-kosher wine and nothing happens to them, why should they not do the same? Besides, they would say, if it is not permitted, why are Jews drinking it at all? Faced with a similar no-win situation, the first-century tanna Rabbi Johanan ben Zakka'y decided to deal with the halakhic issue at hand despite apprehensions that sinners would misperceive his answer.[102] This talmudic precedent made it imperative that Isserles respond.

According to the Talmud, the third-century Babylonian rabbi, Rab, believed that a one day old non-Jewish child who touches wine renders it *yeyn nesek.* The tosafists explained that Rab's contemporary, Samuel, disagreed and allowed Jews to use and drink wine touched by young non-Jews since they were too young to understand the nature of libation.[103] Rabbi Isaac ben Samuel of Dampierre (d. ca. 1185; known by the acronym *RiY*), one of the leading tosafists, reported that Samuel's position was not only accepted by two earlier legists but was to be found in the *tosafot* written by students of his uncle Jacob Tam—implying that Jacob Tam himself accepted the more lenient view. The tosafists added that Samuel ben Me'ir, Jacob Tam's brother, and Rabbi Judah ben Nathan (eleventh-twelfth centuries; known by the acronym *RiYBaN*), cited in the name of their teacher, Rashi, earlier responsa permitting Jews to benefit from wine touched by non-Jews. Their assumption was that since contemporary non-Jews generally did not perform libations for idol worship, their touch was like that of a one day old child and Jews were not prohibited from deriving benefit from the wine.

The combination of Jacob Tam's opinion and that of Rashi and his students was most perturbing to Isaac of Dampierre, who spelled out the implications in a letter to his uncle. The wine of non-Jews had suddenly become permitted in all respects including consumption!

> Come and see that because of you and your [grand]father and your brother,

---

102. B.T., *Baba' Batra'* 89b.

103. B.T., *'Abodah zarah* 57a, *tosafot* on 57b.

> the touch of a non-Jew on wine has become permitted to the world even to drink. Because your brother, Rabbi Samuel, ruled in the name of your [grand]father, our teacher Solomon, that the non-Jews in this time are considered like a one day old baby and you rule regarding a one day old baby like [the talmudic rabbi] Samuel who said that [a mere babe] does not make *yeyn nesek* that would become prohibited even to drink.[104]

Confronted by his nephew in this way, Jacob Tam vigorously denied the lenient view, attributed it to an over-eager student, and assured Isaac of Dampierre that he believed Rab's view to be correct. *Yeyn nesek* was prohibited to drink.

Isserles was well aware that all authorities accepted Jacob Tam's corrected opinion and he too accepted it, expecting others to do so as well. Yet it was the rejected first opinion, the work of the mistaken student, that became the basis of Isserles's decision. Moravian Jews who drank the wine of non-Jews, Isserles claimed—without any textual basis or even hearsay to this effect—must have been relying upon a tradition of their fathers that the first opinion of Jacob Tam was correct. Isserles thereby created a source upon which Moravian Jews could rely—even though it was a mistaken one and most likely unknown to most, if not all, Jews who drank non-kosher wine. Yet with this source to justify their behavior, drinkers of non-kosher wine were no longer deemed sinners but simply mistaken. If they took an oath, they could be trusted when they claimed that the wine they were delivering was kosher.

Having "legally" solved the problem of *yeyn nesek*, Isserles had yet to explain the separate rabbinic ordinance against drinking *stam yeynam.* In large part, this had already been accomplished by the tosafists who had historicized and explained that benefit from *stam yeynam* was prohibited only when there were many idol worshipers who performed libations. But when idolatrous libations do not exist, as was the case in twelfth-century France, it was enough for *stam yeynam* to be like the oil and bread of non-Jews that the rabbis prohibited to eat but allowed one to derive benefit from.[105]

Isserles suggested that Moravian Jews followed the tosafists and, since there was no fear of libation in contemporary times, considered *stam yey-*

---

104. *Tosafot,* B.T., *'Abodah zarah* 57b. The issue of *yeyn nesek* often occupied the creative energies of the tosafists. See Soloveitchik, "Can Halakhic Texts Talk History?," pp. 152–96.

105. This position was rejected by Asher ben Yehi'el (*Beyẓah* 30a) and his son, Jacob (*Ṭur,* Yoreh de'ah 123).

nam to be like the bread of non-Jews. He proceeded to posit that due to a scarcity of potable fluids, Moravian Jews were able to draw an analogy between the bread of non-Jews, which the Jerusalem Talmud permitted people to eat because of a food shortage, and *stam yeynam.*[106] Moravian Jews believed that because of need they could drink *stam yeynam.*[107] As for the necessity of a rabbinic conclave to allow the drinking of wine as occurred with respect to bread, Isserles, using the method of the tosafists, contended that perhaps the rabbis never made an ordinance prohibiting drinking *stam yeynam* when there was little else to drink.[108]

Well aware that his argument was weak at best and fearful of its ramifications, Isserles warned readers that he was only trying to find a possible allowance for the actions of Moravian Jewry and that no one should rely on him.

> . . . And even more so in those places that do not have the custom to permit it [*stam yeynam*], for they have the truth in their hands that it is forbidden. It is forbidden [for them] to change and everyone who breaks through the fence, a "snake" (a play on a Hebrew acronym for various forms of rabbinic excommunication) of the rabbis will bite him since anyone who violates their words deserves death.[109]

In sum, Moravian Jews were mistaken in drinking *stam yeynam.* For practical purposes, however, Isserles was willing to assume that they were not disregarding the law, an assumption he substantiated according to the rules of the halakhic system with little or no regard for objective facts.

Isserles was not the only Polish rabbi of his day to deal with this problem. Solomon Luria also tried to find some allowance that would permit

---

106. See J.T., *'Abodah zarah* 2.9, 41d.

107. Without doubt, there was a shortage of potable fluids in sixteenth- century Europe. Safe drinking water was scarce although malt and beer were relatively "germfree" because of the care exercised to prevent souring during production. See Joseph Strayer, ed., *Dictionary of the Middle Ages* (New York: Scribner, 1982–1989), s.v. "Brewing," by Robert Multhauf. Even if the carefully selected water used in brewed liquids proved to be bacteriologically infected, the heating and boiling (if hops were used) of the water before mashing and the alcohol produced during fermentation removed much of the danger of infection. The resulting drink was also quite resistant to the growth of bacteria (H. S. Corran, *A History of Brewing* [Newton Abbot: David and Charles, 1975], pp. 30, 35). Isserles, however, appears to have been quite willing to assume that malt too was in short supply in Moravia.

108. See *'Eduyyot* 1.5.

109. Isserles, *Responsa,* no. 124, p. 487.

110. Also see Joshua Höschel, *Responsa,* pt. 1, Yoreh de'ah 16.

people to trust the kashrut claims of those who drank non-kosher wine.[110] Unlike Isserles, Luria made no attempt to provide a legal basis—however flimsy—for drinking *stam yeynam.* Instead, he focused on trying to validate the oaths of those who drank such wine. Like Isserles, however, Luria was forced into an exegetically radical position to solve a practical problem. In the midst of a discussion of what type of sinners were acceptable as ritual slaughterers, Luria wrote,

> And the later authorities wrote that this is the law [concerning] whoever neglects the bans of the congregation that made a ban that no one should ritually slaughter except the known slaughterer and someone disobeyed and slaughtered. His slaughtering [i.e., the meat] is prohibited because he is similar to someone who is suspect in this matter until he accepts repentance. However, it appears [that] whoever is suspect regarding *nesek* [i.e., he drinks *stam yeynam*] may testify regarding the wine if he takes an oath regarding it because he does not stand sworn from Sinai. He is lenient in *stam yeynam* which is only [a] rabbinic [decree]. In particular now, because of our great sins, the fence of Israel has been broken open in a number of places regarding *stam yeynam,* intentionally and unintentionally, until it has become as if it is permitted in the eyes of the masses. And someone who prevents [himself] from drinking it, they will think of him as haughty or stupid. And because of this we do not say that [those who drink it] are suspect with regard to an oath. And so I ruled in practice only [I required] that they impress upon him well and explain the oath very well in order that there not be found falsehood and deceit.[111]

The Mishnaic rule in such matters was quite specific: "Whoever is doubted regarding a matter may not judge or give testimony regarding it" (*Bekorot* 4.10). Those who drank *stam yeynam* should not have been allowed to testify with respect to kosher wine for they had violated their Sinaitic oath to observe the commandments that, according to tradition, all Jews were sworn to at Mount Sinai.

To rehabilitate the testimony of such people, Luria allowed them to take an oath that their wine was kosher. The problem was that violators of an oath, even a symbolic oath, invalidated their oaths in all matters. Luria's solution was to explain that the oath taken by the Jewish people at Sinai was

111. Luria, *YSS, Ḥullin* 1.6.

112. See B.T., *Shebu'ot* 21a, 22b, 23b. Rabbi Nissim ben Reuben Gerondi (B.T., *Nedarim* 8a) tried to limit the idea even further by explaining that the Jews only swore to laws that were clearly stated in the Pentateuch and did not require rabbinic interpretation.

only to observe biblical, not rabbinic, laws.[112] Since drinkers of *stam yeynam* "only" violated a rabbinic prohibition, they had not violated their Sinaitic oath. Therefore their declarations could be believed.

Faced with a serious communal problem, Luria was willing to rely on the psychological impact that an explanation of the oath would have on the supplier of the wine. Luria believed that with clear knowledge of what he was swearing to God about, no one would dare lie.

Despite their exegetical gymnastics, in the long term Luria and Isserles did not succeed in liberalizing the qualifications of kosher wine merchants. In the 1630s Joel Sirkes in Cracow as well as Jewish leaders in the Lvov region were certifying as "trustworthy in the making of kosher wine" individuals who specifically bound themselves to the halakhah before rabbinic authorities. Since only such people were deemed reliable, importers of kosher wine took these individuals with them on their trips to Hungary so that they would certify that the wine being made and brought to Poland was indeed kosher.[113] Dealers themselves would not be believed.

It is not surprising that in the mid-sixteenth century rabbinic leniency—assuming that all Jews could be trusted until it was known that they were sinners (*ḥezqat kashrut*)—did not continue with regard to *stam yeynam*; in certain regions the taboo associated with its consumption had begun to wither.[114] In a responsum Luria lamented that it was the "disgrace of the Ashkenazim" that they did not look askance at anyone who drank non-kosher wine in a non-Jew's hotel.[115] Solomon ben Judah Leybush wrote that (presumably Polish) Jews had started to ignore this prohibition despite the efforts of earlier legalists to guard against their doing so.[116] The problem was not unique to wine. By the late sixteenth century rabbis enjoined

---

113. *She'elot u-teshubot ge'onim batra'ey*, no. 13; Sirkes, *Responsa* (new), no. 29, written by Rabbi Menahem Ashkenazi of Rymanów in 1636, and no. 30, written by Sirkes's student, Yehuda' (Leb ben Jacob Katz?). Also see Joshua Höschel, *Responsa*, pt. 2, no. 26, with respect to a shipment of wine from Austria.

114. Isserles himself believed that the practice of believing Jews based on their *ḥezqat kashrut* was not in accord with the letter of the law. See Moses Isserles, *Sefer darkey Mosheh ha-shalem me-Ṭur Yoreh de'ah* (Sulzbach, 1692), no. 119.1. On *ḥezqat kashrut* see *Enẓiqloppedyah talmudit*, vol. 14, s.v. "*ḥezqat kashrut*," pp. 26–27.

115. Luria, *Responsa*, no. 72; see above, pp. 39–40.

116. Solomon ben Judah Leybush, *Responsa*, no. 139, p. 36. Solomon believed that unless there was the potential for significant financial loss, jurists had to be stringent in matters of *stam yeynam* to prevent any further erosion in public observance.

Jews from buying foodstuffs that could possibly be non-kosher (i.e., almost anything but fruits and vegetables) from anyone not specifically known to be trustworthy.[117] As David ben Samuel ha-Levi commented regarding this change, "It is proper especially since we see the deterioration of the generations, and the generations have not grown better."[118]

The erosion in public observance prompted rabbis and laymen to tighten controls over the production and delivery of kosher wine. Solomon Luria noted that rabbis in "Russia" proclaimed that the wine of a Jew may not be drunk until "important" witnesses (i.e., those beyond reproach) testified that the provider of the wine was reliable.[119] In 1595 the community in Cracow ordered that the rabbi, together with three duly appointed laymen should investigate all matters where there was a fear of non-kosher wine ". . . and be stringent with all the stringencies in the world as befits this time to fence in the breaches in the unguarded fields . . ."[120] Me'ir ben Gedaliah wrote that he had used all the punishments and bans that he could muster to prevent people from drinking *stam yeynam*, apparently without success.[121]

These efforts by Polish rabbis to stem religious backsliding caused a significant hardship for at least one Jewish community in southern Poland. In an undated responsum, Me'ir ben Gedaliah was asked by the rabbi of Cracow what to do about the community of Rymanów, which was not obeying the decree of the "scholars of the generation" made at the most recent fair, enjoining Jews from dealing in *stam yeynam*. Called to Cracow and warned about their non-compliance, leaders of the Rymanów community explained that they were unable to obey the decree because wine was, and historically had been, the basis of their trade with the neighboring Hungarians, who regularly paid their debts with wine.[122] Jewish residents of Rymanów ar-

---

117. See Falk, *Qunṭeres*, p. 2b, who required Jews who made cheese and butter on farms to come to the rabbi of the town for certification before beginning to sell their goods. Merchants at fairs required a certificate from the rabbi of their home region. Also see Bałaban, "Die Krakauer Judengemeinde-Ordnung," p. 357.

118. David ben Samuel ha-Levi, *Ṭurey zahab*, Yoreh de'ah 119, n. 2.

119. Luria, *YSS, Ḥullin* 1.36.

120. Wettstein, "Qadmoniyyot," p. 595. Also see Bałaban, "Die Krakauer Judengemeinde-Ordnung," pp. 305–6. In 1603 the Jewish community of Frankfurt also took steps to prevent Jews from purchasing wine from non-Jews. See Finkelstein, *Jewish Self-Government*, p. 260.

121. Me'ir ben Gedaliah, *Responsa*, no. 50.

122. Isserles, following earlier authorities, specifically allowed Jews to accept *stam yeynam* as payment for their debts from non-Jews (*Shulḥan 'aruk*, Yoreh de'ah 123.1 and 133.1 with the gloss of Shabbetay ben Me'ir ha-Kohen 133, n. 4).

gued that they could not simply move elsewhere in order to avoid the problem: the local noble was known to be cruel and would not let them leave his territory. Moreover, they maintained, this was an old problem that had been brought before Rabbis Isserles, Isaac ha-Kohen, Joseph Katz, and Solomon ben Judah Leybush[123] (respective heads of the rabbinic court in Cracow, under whose jurisdiction Rymanów fell), each of whom had allowed the Jews of Rymanów to continue to deal in *stam yeynam* after considering the extenuating circumstances.[124]

Me'ir ben Gedaliah was also reluctant to hinder the Jews of Rymanów in their attempts to make a living. Although he prohibited them from purchasing *stam yeynam* for profit, he did allow them to accept it as a means of payment if their debtors were unable to pay in cash or some other form of barter, as Isserles had allowed in the *Shulḥan 'aruk.*[125] Aware that some of the rabbis in Cracow would not be pleased by a decision that countered rabbinic efforts to eradicate the consumption of non-kosher wine in the Jewish community, Me'ir ben Gedaliah justified his position by proving that the prohibition against dealing in *stam yeynam* was rabbinic in origin and that there was a tradition of lenience in the prohibition when it was necessary to help Jewish communities support themselves. He made it clear, however, that he had a record of being strict in upholding the prohibition against drinking *stam yeynam.*

Despite the best efforts of Polish rabbis—the ruling in Rymanów notwithstanding—Jewish merchants continued to trade in the wine. A student wrote to Joel Sirkes that he had done as his teacher told him and had not forgotten to warn those suspected of trading in *stam yeynam* with "all the intimidations" and he "hopes to God" that the people will change.[126]

As for the community of Rymanów, not only did they continue to deal in *stam yeynam* but they tasted it too (without swallowing it), as they had for some time, with the blessing of a younger colleague of Me'ir ben Gedaliah, Rabbi Samuel of Przemyśl, who felt compelled to find a halakhic

123. See Solomon ben Judah Leybush, *Responsa*, no. 139, p. 36. On Solomon ben Judah Leybush in Cracow see Herskovitz's unpaginated introduction to the collection.

124. Me'ir ben Gedaliah, *Responsa*, no. 50. The responsum is undated. Also see *PVAA*, no. 852.

125. See above, n. 122.

126. Sirkes, *Responsa* (new), no. 30.

127. *She'elot u-teshubot harrey qedem*, I. Herskovitz, ed., (Brooklyn, N.Y.: n.p., 1988), no. 15, p. 249. An unknown rabbi asked Samuel of Przemyśl to concur with his lenient view. On Rabbi Samuel of Przemyśl, see Lewin, *Me-boqer le-'ereb*, pp. 117–19, 127–28.

rationale for their practice and help them make a living.[127] Yet Samuel of Przemyśl's lenience may have contributed to future problems for the local rabbi in Rymanów, Menahem Ashkenazi. In 1636 Ashkenazi was faced with a case involving wine merchants who had taken loans from Polish nobles in order to travel to Hungary and produce kosher wine for local consumption. During production, the wine was very likely touched by a non-Jewish worker while he was removing a piece of wood that he had dropped into a barrel of the wine.

Ashkenazi was asked to determine if the wine was still kosher. If he said it was not, the merchants would face severe financial loss. Ashkenazi, however, was hesitant to show lenience, for reasons that he spelled out in a letter in which he sought the advice of his teacher, Sirkes.

> . . . And I did not want to decide this matter . . . in order not to be lenient in the eyes of the laity because they are not "sons of Torah" and they will come, God forbid, to break through an opening fenced in by the great rabbis who placed a ban here in the holy community on the drinker and dealer in *stam yeynam* and particularly since those who break through have multiplied and they drink [*stam yeynam*] in private although not in public and the custom of their fathers is in their hands and it is [therefore] difficult to separate them [from drinking *stam yeynam*]. And many who drank before the ban as they pleased are suspected today of drinking in private and even though they guard themselves today not to drink it in public, my heart tells me that they are suspect in this sin and therefore I did not want to teach them leniency here. And even though it is known to me and the rest of our nation that the man, Solomon Duqler, owner of the wine, is careful about the prohibition of drinking *stam yeynam* like one of the ordained and therefore it is a meritorious act [miẓvah] . . . to say . . . that the wine is permitted . . .[128]

Ashkenazi knew that a means of permitting the wine could be found, and he knew the halakhic ideal was to be lenient. "We do not investigate carefully [*medaqddeqin*] *yeyn nesek*," stated Rabbi Judah in the Jerusalem Talmud.[129] Nevertheless, Ashkenazi feared the social ramifications of lenience. Because earlier bans against *stam yeynam* had not been taken seriously, he worried that allowances would be abused. He was more concerned at this time with upholding tradition in the community, even if an upstanding individual had to suffer severe financial hardship because of it.

128. Sirkes, *Responsa* (new), no. 29.

129. J.T., *Sanhedrin* 4.8, 22b.

Ultimately, Ashkenazi's fears about his community were dismissed by Sirkes, who wrote elsewhere regarding *stam yeynam* that "we are very lenient regarding it in this time" (i.e., legists were lenient in adjudicating such matters).[130] Joshua Höschel observed that society ("*ha-rabbim*") did not normally ignore this prohibition.[131] Apparently, the problems of Rymanów, where dealing in *stam yeynam* was important for the the local Jewish economy, do not appear to have been common in mid-seventeenth century Poland.

Thus there seems to have been no consensus in the matter. The law prohibiting *stam yeynam* was central to Jewish life and self-definition in the Diaspora. Legists used the rules of the halakhic system to interpret the law and meet what they perceived to be the religious needs of their communities. When its observance was lax, the machinery of halakhah was engaged to foster greater piety.[132] When religious demands resulted in real economic and communal hardship, rare was the rabbi who would not attempt to reinterpret the halakhah.

Unlike looking at women or Sabbath weddings in time of need, rabbis made no consistent attempt to find allowances for the consumption of *stam yeynam* nor did they suggest that it might be preferable that people disregard the rabbinic law of *stam yeynam* inadvertently rather than do so knowingly—as the rabbis of the Talmud at times suggested with respect to other laws.[133] Isserles tried to expound a rationale for those Moravian Jews who drank non-kosher wine but he never suggested that his argument—using a faulty source to solve a practical problem—be used as a precedent. Over the next generations Polish rabbis continued to confront the problem of Jews drinking non-kosher wine by being restrictive in their halakhic rulings with respect to *stam yeynam.* However, as in other areas of the halakhah, such severity tended to soften in the face of human suffering.

---

130. *She'elot u-teshubot ha-ge'onim batra'ey,* no. 13; Sirkes, *Responsa* (new), no. 32.

131. Joshua Höschel, *Responsa,* pt. 1, Yoreh de'ah 16.

132. Jacob Katz, in "Hirhurim 'al ha-yaḥas beyn dat le-kalkalah," *Tarbiz* 60 (1991): 108–9, has argued that because matters of kashrut played such a central role in Jewish self-definition they were much more resistant than other areas of Jewish law to economic pressures.

133. See B.T., *Shabbat* 148b.

5

The Acquisition of Leases

From approximately 1550 until the early seventeenth century, the growth of the Polish economy was stimulated in large part by the Vistula grain trade, which was dominated by members of the nobility who had the financial wherewithal to ferry their grain surpluses along the Vistula and Bug Rivers to the international market in Gdansk. The vast majority of Polish producers, peasants and tenant farmers who were primarily subsistence growers, did not directly participate in the trade but, as a result of it, enjoyed a significant improvement in local terms of trade.[1]

Disposable income acquired by the nobility from the grain trade was not consistently invested in means of production but used instead for personal consumption, directly or indirectly.[2] Poland did not expand and develop its economic base but remained a supplier of raw materials ever dependent on foreign markets. When, around 1620, slower population growth, a significant increase in western grain output, and cheaper grain from Russia resulted in a decline in western demand for Polish grain, the Polish economy began to falter.[3] Perhaps it could have weathered the effects of dwindling

1. See Witold Kula, *An Economic Theory of the Feudal System: Towards a Model of the Polish Economy 1500–1800*, Lawrence Garner, trans., (London: NLB, 1976), pp. 125–26. Relying too heavily on the words of the early seventeenth-century anti-Jewish author Sebastjan Miczynski, Schiper, *Dzieje handlu żydowskiego*, pp. 71–77, presented Polish Jews as very active in the Gdansk trade, as well as all international commerce, up to 1648. While some Jews participated in the grain trade in this period (see Sirkes, *Responsa* [old], no. 27; *taqqanot* of Rabbi Meshulam of Cracow [1590], first published by Isaiah Sonne, "Taqqanot shel issur Shabbat ve-yom ṭob," *Ḥoreb* 2 [Fall 1935]: 237–46, and reprinted by Halperin in *PVAA*, p. 486), many more purchased surpluses from minor producers for sale in regional markets (also see Cygielman, *Yehudey Polin ve-Liṭa'*, Supplement, p. 8). The concept of Jews as secondary merchants is developed by Hundert, "Security and Dependence," pp. 140, 204.

2. See Kula, *An Economic Theory of the Feudal System*, p. 51. See, however, William Dwight Van Horn III, "Suburban Development, Rural Exchange, and the Manorial Economy in Royal Prussia 1570–1700," (Ph.D. diss., Columbia University, 1987), pp. 407–10, who questions just how much cash nobles actually had to spend on consumer goods and points out that contemporary farm management handbooks "urged parsimony."

3. See Jan De Vries, *The Economy of Europe in an Age of Crisis, 1600–1750* (Cambridge: Cambridge University Press, 1976), pp. 56–57; Maria Bogucka,"Zboże rosyjskie na rynku

grain exports, but it suffered other economic setbacks in the second quarter of the seventeenth century as well. Reduced exports meant that grain flooded domestic markets, lowering prices and returns for all producers. The exploitation and devastation of peasant agriculture by the nobility further pressured domestic markets. These and other factors led to bouts of double digit inflation and a monetary crisis in the 1620s that helped send Poland into a deep and extended economic slide that was only aggravated by the Cossack revolts (1648–1651) and the Swedish invasions (1655–1658).[4]

As elsewhere, Jewish communities in Poland were not insulated from general economic developments. Communal leaders, empowered by both tradition and the halakhah, attempted to regulate the internal Jewish market and to deal with the repercussions of economic trends on their communities. In some instances, such as when they imposed restrictions on the hoarding of food, leaders acted in consonance with the values of the Jewish Prophets.[5] In other areas, however, solutions of lay leaders to contemporary economic problems were often at odds with the halakhah.

One of the important sources of income for Jews, particularly those living in the eastern and developing sections of Poland during the sixteenth and first half of the seventeenth centuries, was the *arenda* (pl. *arendy*), a lease that for a stipulated sum gave a lessee rights to operate and enjoy the income from whatever was leased, be it a mill, tavern, or salt mine.[6]

---

amsterdamskim w pierwszej połowie XVII wieku," *Przegląd Historyczny* 53.4 (1962): 620–21. On the extent of the economic decline in both rural and urban Poland see Jerzy Topolski, "La régression économique en Pologne du XVIe au XVIIe siècle," *Acta Poloniae Historica* 7 (1962): 35–45.

4. See Zbigniew Wójcik, "Poland and Russia in the 17th Century: Problems of Internal Development," in *Poland at the 14th International Congress of Historical Sciences in San Francisco*, Bronisław Geremek and Antoni Mączak eds., (Wrocław: Ossolineum, 1975), pp. 116–17.

5. Amos 8.4–5,7; B.T., *Baba' Batra'* 90b with the comments of Samuel ben Me'ir; *Shulḥan 'aruk*, Ḥoshen mishpaṭ 231.25; Bałaban, "Die Krakauer Judengemeinde-Ordnung," pp. 357–58.

6. On *arendy* and choosing an *arendar* see Rosman, *The Lords' Jews*, pp. 106–47. Although Rosman focuses on the eighteenth century, much is germane regarding the earlier period as well. Also see Baron, *A Social and Religious History of the Jews*, vol. 16, pp. 265–78, and Hillel Levine, *Economic Origins of Antisemitism*, (New Haven: Yale University Press, 1991), pp. 61–74. Similar leases existed in fifteenth-century Poland (see, for example, Cygielman, *Yehudey Polin ve-Liṭa'*, pp. 339–40, 340–41).

Arendy, which could be on royal or private lands, were usually sold to the highest bidder for a three year period.[7] When the lease expired there would be a new bidding process. Stiff competition among contemporary businessmen for profitable leases all but ensured that an arendar rarely held a lease for two successive terms.[8]

While state officials generally left the negotiation and sale of leases on private lands to local custom, rabbinic authorities could not.[9] According to the halakhah, bidding on a lease currently held by another Jew was an infringement of the lessee's rights. Yet if rabbis failed to allow Jews to bid on an arenda held by another Jew, they almost certainly would be allowing a lucrative source of income to slip away, not only from an individual but from the community: depending on the nature of the arenda, a Jewish arendar could provide other Jews with jobs and make purchases from Jewish suppliers and artisans. A profitable arenda thereby had a positive ripple effect on the local Jewish economy and increased the local Jewish community's tax revenues. Needless to say, if the arenda went to a non-Jewish bidder, the Jewish community would enjoy fewer benefits.

In 1546 a dispute over an arenda broke out between two groups of Jews competing to buy a lease in Lithuania. About three years before the squabble erupted, a local Jew (called "Simeon" by the rabbis in order to protect his identity) and his associates bought an arenda to produce and sell liquor on a noble's estate for three years. In order to manage the arenda, Simeon left the town where he lived and moved to the area where he held the arenda. According to Simeon's account of the events as related by his antagonist (called "Reuben," the source of all information about this dispute), sometime before the contract expired, Simeon heard that a group led by Reuben was negotiating to purchase the arenda for the next three years. Simeon believed this to be a clear violation of the halakhic prohibition of encroachment (*hassagat gebul*).[10]

---

7. The three-year term for an arenda was codified by Sigismund I in 1523 (*Volumina Legum* vol. 1, 422–23).

8. In Podolia, around the year 1600, lessees rarely held a lease to term as competitors tried to displace current arendars by outbidding their contracts (see below, p. 116).

9. Custom rivaled and supplemented legislation in Poland until the country was partitioned in 1795. "In our kingdom, not only written enactments but also age-old customs are to be observed in many localities," read the 1552 edict of Sigismund. See Peter Siekanowicz, *Legal Sources and Bibliography of Poland* (New York: Praeger, 1964), pp. 6–9.

10. Technically, the prohibition of *hassagat gebul* applies only to property in the Land of Israel (Deut. 19.14), a problem addressed by Luria in responsum no. 89.

Simeon went to the noble and town elders who had to authorize the sale of the arenda and negotiated with them until they agreed to renew his contract. According to Simeon's statement, however, the frustrated Reuben did not give up his pursuit of the arenda and lobbied Queen Bona Sforza's (1494–1557) scribe, who influenced the queen to order the town council to reassign the arenda to Reuben and his group.[11]

Reuben countered that he had never intended to encroach on Simeon's arenda, although he reminded the judge that it was the local custom to bid on an arenda while someone else held it. Indeed, Reuben claimed that others had done this to him and his associates when they had held a liquor arenda sometime earlier. Reuben explained that now he and his consortium had been called by town leaders and the local judge—as a trustworthy witness could testify—and told that the council was prepared to sell them the arenda. Apparently, the council feared that another individual was about to buy the arenda directly from the noble for a higher price and a bribe, without the necessary consent of the town council.[12] Excluded from an imminent deal, town leaders looked to strengthen their hand.

Reuben and associates agreed to purchase the arenda, and a contract was drawn up, signed, sealed, and delivered to him. At this point the council asked to see the contract again and, when Reuben gave it to them, they refused to return it unless each council member was given the customary and appropriate "consideration." While they assured Reuben that no one else would be able to buy the arenda, they were resolute in declaring that the contract would remain in a council member's private strongbox until Reuben paid the outstanding "debt." Eventually, the two groups arrived at a mutually agreeable sum.

According to Reuben, at this point Simeon and his associates tried to bribe the noble and offered to raise the price of the arenda if he would agree to sell it to them. Pleased with the sweetened proposal, the noble requested that the council not return the contract to Reuben.

---

11. Queen Bona Sforza maintained an active presence in Lithuania, where she owned large tracts of land. Her ongoing "interference" in the affairs of others earned her the enmity of the *szlachta*. See *Polski słownik biograficzny*, Władysław Konopczynski et al., eds., (Cracow: Nakład Polskiej Akademii Umiejętnośći, 1935–), s.v. "Bona Sforza," by Władydsław Pociecha.

12. According to Lithuanian statutes, even though an arenda was a private contract, it had to be signed by three witnesses who were members of the *szlachta* (Zygmunt Gloger, *Encyklopedia staropolska ilustrowana*, with an introduction by J. Krzyzanowski, [Warsaw: Wiedza Powszechna, 1972], s.v. "*arenda*").

Reuben and his associates went before the Jewish communal leadership and warned Simeon and his associates not to cause them damage or cause the "consumption of Jewish money in the hands of non-Jews."[13] Yet, according to Reuben, Simeon continued his efforts until the noble convinced a few of the town council members to cancel their agreement with Reuben, a fact that Reuben claimed to be able to corroborate with independent testimony. In the presence of the noble, Reuben responded by warning council members who had been wooed by the noble that if they canceled the contract he would be forced to inform the queen. Their reported response: "What can we do? These Jews offered a higher price," a sentiment echoed by the noble himself. To add insult to injury, Reuben complained that not only would the council not return the contract, but council members would not even repay the bribes that they had accepted from him and his associates.

At some point Queen Bona Sforza's scribe visited the town to hear the complaints of the townspeople against the noble and the town council. Reuben and his associates were among those who presented grievances and complained about the high cost of bribing the council if one wanted to hold an arenda. The scribe not only recorded the information but rebuked the council for its handling of the matter. Again, council members defended themselves by asserting that another Jew had offered more money for the arenda—adding that the noble had ordered them to take it because the higher price would benefit the royal fisc. An argument then broke out between the council members assembled before the scribe. Some cried out that the second agreement was invalid because it had been made without the knowledge of the whole council and had been sealed with a stolen town seal. The scribe dutifully recorded all that transpired before him and reported it to the queen. Bona Sforza ruled that the council must write a new arenda for Reuben and return the bribes that they had taken from Reuben's consortium. The council complied with the royal order and the contract was sealed with the seal of the council, the noble, and the local diet.[14]

The Queen's ruling did not put an end to the dispute. The litigants subsequently brought the matter before Rabbi Isaac ben Bezalel (d. 1576),

---

13. The Talmud expresses concern about the "consumption of the money of Israel," but does not raise the issue of "in the hands of non-Jews" (see B.T., *Sukkah* 56b; *Ḥullin* 56a; *Bekorot* 40a).

14. Luria, *Responsa,* no. 35.

head of the yeshiva and rabbinic court in Włodzimierz. Ignoring Reuben's petition that he choose a colleague familiar with the customs of the locale where the events had transpired to sit together with him on the matter, Isaac ben Bezalel judged alone.[15] After hearing both sides, he declared that since Simeon held the arenda when Reuben made his offer for the lease, Reuben was guilty of encroachment. Isaac ruled that Simeon would hold the lease on the basis of the contract already written in Reuben's name—presumably out of deference to the royal ruling. In addition, he ordered Reuben to pay the difference in cost between what Simeon ultimately had to pay for the arenda and what it would have cost him had Reuben not interfered.

Although judges were not obligated to explain the basis of their decisions to laymen, Isaac ben Bezalel told Reuben that he had a responsum from Eleazar ben Judah of Worms stating

> Be careful and do not encroach upon your friend nor take his livelihood. And if one bought merchandise or coins from the authorities and someone else should come and offer more [for it] in order to take it from his friend, this may not be forgiven and he is called wicked and there is no thief like him. And if he will not listen to the voice [of communal authority, he] should be separated and ostracized until he "repairs" his offense.[16]

Dissatisfied, Reuben appealed the case to Solomon Luria, who at the time was a young rabbi in his native Lithuania.

Luria showed little deference for the opinion of a colleague whose approbation he himself had sought on occasion.[17] Instead, he took Isaac ben Bezalel to task for not heeding the talmudic dictum, "Do not judge alone because no one may judge alone except One" (*Abot* 4.10), words that Mai-

---

15. Reuben based (or was advised to base) his plea on Maimonides, *Code of Law*, Laws Concerning Sales, chap. 26, nos. 7–8, and others who ruled that in matters of sales, everything depends on local practice.

16. The citation seems to be the language of an ethical work rather than that of a responsum. Urbach, *Ba'aley ha-tosafot*, pp. 407–8, suggests that Eleazar may have used the same language in a responsum discussing encroachment that he uses in his *Hilkot teshubah* (Laws of Repentance) where this passage appears with minor variants (*Sefer ha-roqeaḥ ha-gadol* [Jerusalem: Ozar Haposeqim, 1967], no. 28). Perhaps Isaac ben Bezalel did not quote a responsum (*teshubah*) of Eleazar ben Judah, as Reuben thought, but rather a portion from *Hilkot teshubah* as a means of rebuking his behavior.

17. Luria, *Responsa*, nos. 1, 15, each of which concludes with the approbation of "Isaac ben Bezalel who lives in Włodzimierz."

monides considered a "command of the rabbis."[18] Further, Luria chided Isaac for deciding a case based on a comparison between an earlier ruling, that is, Eleazar ben Judah's decision, and the case before him. Luria maintained that this was in clear violation of a talmudic prohibition against comparing cases to arrive at a decision if there was a great sage in the land.[19] Even if Isaac ben Bezalel had conducted a full review of the sources, Luria would have rejected his conclusion. No judge had the right to rule if his teacher was alive (and apparently Isaac's teacher was still living), even if both sides agreed to accept his verdict. As far as Luria was concerned, Isaac ben Bezalel was too eager to rule and in this instance was "a fool, wicked, and haughty." Luria thus disqualified him as a judge before even considering his legal arguments, for only outright repudiation of his judicial authority would invalidate all his "perversion[s] of the law" if Luria failed to refute definitively even one of them in the course of his responsum.

It is worth noting that the very principles that Luria forwarded to repudiate Isaac ben Bezalel disqualified Luria himself from acting as arbiter. A young rabbi with senior colleagues, a man whose teacher was apparently alive and well, an arbitrator whose ruling was sought by only one of the litigants, Luria appeared to be in no position to consider the case. Well aware of his predicament, Luria offered a simple solution: he was not about to decide the law but simply to quote what had already been stated by the great scholars of the past, something that a student may do even during his teacher's lifetime. It took Luria twenty-three printed pages simply to quote the law.[20]

Before addressing the specific question of Reuben and Simeon, Luria sought to clarify the operative legal principle in this case: encroachment on someone's livelihood (*mehapek ba-ḥararah shel ḥabero*; lit., "one who is turning over [examining] a cake of his fellow"—and someone else comes and takes it from him).[21] Thoroughly outlining the scope of the law—so thor-

18. Maimonides, *Code of Law*, Laws Concerning the Sanhedrin, chap. 2, no. 11. No one doubted that an expert could judge alone, especially since both sides had agreed to accept his verdict. Nonetheless, Maimonides and Moses of Coucy (see *Sefer miẓvot gadol* [Jerusalem: S. Monson, 1961], positive commandment no. 97) as interpreted by Luria believed that ideally a judge should not act alone but as part of a tribunal.

19. B.T., *Yebamot* 109b.

20. Luria, *Responsa*, no. 36.

21. B.T., *Qiddushin* 59a.

oughly that many years later when he discussed the matter in his talmudic commentary he was satisfied to copy portions of this responsum verbatim—Luria attempted to demonstrate that the law had very limited parameters.[22] He argued that the overwhelming majority of Ashkenazic authorities had accepted the view of Jacob ben Me'ir Tam that the laws of encroachment do not apply to ownerless property (*hefqer*) or to a "find," something not to be acquired anywhere else. A possible voice of dissension from Samuel ben Me'ir was restricted by Luria to a specific circumstance leaving Rashi and a few, but significant, authorities as rejected supporters of a broader definition of the category.[23]

Luria further limited the applicability of the law by claiming that even if a case should arise in which someone was guilty of encroaching on another person's livelihood, he cannot be coerced into returning what he has taken from his victim. As for Eleazar ben Judah's statement that "if he will not listen to the voice [of communal authority, he] should be separated and ostracized until he 'repairs' his offense," that is to say until he pays back the person whom he has wronged, Luria correctly pointed out that this concerned someone who had taken something from his friend after the friend had already purchased it.[24] Encroachment on a potential purchase, in this case the rights to the lease during the next term, was not covered by Eleazar's statement.

Although Luria may have convincingly established his legal position regarding the inapplicability of encroachment laws, historical facts contradicted his thesis. Mordecai ben Hillel had noted in the name of the eleventh-century French scholar, Rabbi Joseph Tub Ellem, that there were Jewish communities that forced a Jew who had encroached on a *ma'arufi'a* (the medieval institution through which a Christian granted a Jew the right to manage his business affairs, a right that Jewish communities considered

---

22. Luria, *YSS, Qiddushin* 3.2. Luria was not the only one to think that his treatment of the matter was extensive. In his gloss to *Shulḥan 'aruk*, Ḥoshen mishpaṭ 237, Shabbatay ben Me'ir ha-Kohen simply referred his reader to this responsum (among others) for an in-depth treatment of the matter (n. 1). Also see Haym Soloveitchik, *Halakhah, kalkalah, ve-dimmuy 'aẓmi* (Jerusalem: Magnes, 1985), p. 80, n. 62.

23. According to Luria, the limitation of Samuel ben Me'ir's view had already been suggested by Joseph Colon (*Responsa*, no. 118) leaving it for Luria to try to prove Colon's point.

24. Luria himself defended and invoked Eleazar ben Judah's dictum in a case of encroachment (*Responsa*, no. 89). See below, p. 109, n. 40.

to be a monopoly) to return what he had taken.[25] If the Ashkenazic tradition had left an opening for encroachers to be compelled to return their gains, Luria quickly closed it not only with halakhic reasoning but by citing the halakhic masters of his age.

> Our teacher and our rabbi, Rabbi Qolonimos, whose honor rests now [i.e., lives] in Brest Litovsk, in sitting with the judges and all the great debaters, fine golden jewels [i.e., scholars], who are there with him agreed, and these are the words of the great one, "and in these regions we have not found our hands and feet to judge the laws of ma'arufi'a."

Thus although rabbinic scholars of the past may have decided such issues, leading rabbis in sixteenth-century Poland did not feel qualified to do so.

Although Luria's conclusion removed the possibility of corrective action being taken against someone who bid on an arenda currently held by another Jew, it did not efface the Talmud's denouncement of such people as "wicked."[26] Again, Luria attempted to limit the talmudic statement. The Talmud stated that "if someone else *came* and took it [emphasis added]" from his friend he was wicked. Luria implied from this that only if the competitor came and took it was he condemned. However, if the lessor initiated the search for another lessee, then the competitor had every right to bid on the lease. To bolster his view, Luria cited Rabbi Isaac of Évreux (first half thirteenth century), who ruled that

> it is prohibited for a teacher to hire himself to a householder who [already] has another teacher in his house so long as the teacher is in his house. Since the teacher is employed there, the teacher [seeking work] should go elsewhere to be hired *unless the householder says* that he does not want to retain his [present] teacher [emphasis added].[27]

Someone who heard that the employer/lessor was looking for another employee/lessee and decided to compete for the position was not "wicked."

25. Mordecai ben Hillel, *Baba' Batra'* no. 515; *Hagahot Maymoniyyot*, Laws of Neighbors 6.8. Also see *Teshubot Rabbenu Gershom me'or ha-golah*, Shlomo Eidelberg, ed., (New York: Yeshiva University Press, 1955), no. 70, pp. 162– 63, and Me'ir ben Baruch, *Responsa* (Prague), no. 815. For an explanation of *ma'arufi'a* and its origins, see Shlomo Eidelberg, "'Maarufia' in Rabbenu Gershom's Responsa," *Historia Judaica* 15.1 (April 1953): 59–64.

26. B.T., *Qiddushin* 59a.

27. See *Tosafot, Qiddushin* 59a. The identification of "our master, Rabbi Isaac," as Isaac of Évreux is made by Urbach, *Ba'aley ha-tosafot*, p. 632, n. 48.

Although Luria advanced other arguments to support his position, the key to his response is embedded in the following:

> And the most important matter in my eyes, since we find it there in tractate *Baba' Batra'* (54b), [is that] possessions of non-Jews are like ownerless property [*hefqer*] etc. These words apply when there is no law of the government [*dina' de-malkuta'*] that says that land cannot be bought without a contract but if there is a law of the government etc., [then this is] no[t the case]. And Maimonides added in [his] explanation in his Laws of Original Acquisition, chapter 1, number 15, "This rule applies [only where there is no established law of the king]. But where there is a judgment and law of the king that one does not acquire land unless one writes a contract or pays the price or [does] anything similar, we follow the law of the king because we judge monetary matters according to the law of the king."[28]
>
> *A maiori ad maius* here, what a man commonly buys from the city leaders [in such matters] we follow the law of the government. And it is known in the entire kingdom that we buy [the right to] farm taxes or their equivalent and liquor and other rights in the town with an arenda contract and based on this they judge [matters]. And they are also accustomed to sell [the arenda] before the term of the first [holder of an arenda] expires and they sell it to a second person because many people seek to buy [an arenda] and they are quick to precede [others] and acquire it. And because of this they raise the price [of the arenda] and this is an increment and benefit to their treasuries [i.e., of those selling the arenda] . . . custom is the most important factor with regard to buying and selling. Therefore it appears to me that whoever buys [the right to farm] taxes or similar [rights] from the king, even before their time [i.e., before the previous contract has expired], the purchase is valid and whoever takes it from him [is guilty of] absolute theft and [the right can be] taken from him by a court.[29]

The reality of the marketplace was that people bought and sold arendy while someone else still held them. It is unlikely that Jews made this rule; instead, they probably found the practice to be the custom of the marketplace and accepted it. Simeon most likely bought his arenda from a non-

---

28. Luria's citation of both the Talmud and Maimonides varies from the standard printed texts. In both instances, I have followed Luria's language.

29. Luria, *Responsa,* no. 36. Also see Luria, *YSS, Baba' Qamma'* 10.18, in which Luria quotes his commentary to the third chapter of *Baba' Batra',* no. 153, that not only is the law of a monarch recognized by the halakhah, but so too are the customs and manners of the land (*hanagat ha-medinah ve-nimuseha*). The *YSS* on *Baba' Batra'* is not extant.

Jew in this manner and Reuben probably had indeed lost his the very same way. As Luria poignantly cited from Ecclesiastes 1.9, "There is nothing new under the sun." Simeon knew that this was the custom when he bought his arenda. Unless he was "a fool," he had no reason to believe he should be an exception.

By forbidding Jews to bid on an arenda held by another Jew, Isaac ben Bezalel left Jews on an unequal footing in competing with non-Jews for a lucrative business venture. While he may have meant to protect Jewish arendars, his ruling all but insured that an arenda currently held by a Jew would pass to a non-Jew—with crippling repercussions for Jewish communities. Luria made every effort to undermine the halakhic integrity of Isaac ben Bezalel's response and allow Jews to bid freely for arendy.[30] With his forceful reinterpretations of earlier legal thought, Luria almost proved Isaac ben Bezalel to be the fool that Luria claimed he was. Such an impression was not lost on Joseph Katz, to whom young Luria sent his responsum for comment and a second opinion.

Katz attempted to rehabilitate Isaac ben Bezalel on the basis of a number of assumptions, including the need to validate common practice.[31] Whereas Luria dismissed Isaac ben Bezalel's decision to rule unilaterally, Katz defended the use of a single judge when both parties agreed to accept his decision. Offering a number of proofs to support his claim as well as a refutation of Luria's reading of the Mishnah in *Abot* 4.10, Katz concluded:

> My friend, I have brought many proofs because if it is not so [that a judge may hear a case alone when the litigants agree to his acting as magistrate] we cannot find our hands and legs since this is a daily occurrence.[32]

Indeed, people commonly appeared before an arbitrator, either lay or rabbinic, to decide their cases quickly and unilaterally. If left unchallenged,

30. Luria concluded his responsum by noting that he was called on not only to do justice, but to demonstrate to the public that there is only one Torah. There are not two: one that allows that which appears to be prohibited; and one that prohibits, especially to the poor(?), that what seems to be permitted (see B.T., *Sanhedrin* 100a).

31. In a brief introduction probably written while preparing his responsa for publication some forty years after his reply to Luria, Katz wrote that he never saw Isaac ben Bezalel's ruling (no. 17, p. 52). All his information about the case was based on the information supplied to him by Luria.

32. Katz, *Responsa*, no. 17, p. 54.

Luria's outright rejection of a single judge or arbitrator would have undermined the judicial system of the Polish Jewish community.

Katz also attacked the very crux of Luria's legal argument. Whereas Luria attempted to demonstrate that the vast majority of Ashkenazic jurists followed the opinion of Jacob Tam that severely limited the applicability of the laws of encroachment, Katz believed that most jurists, including Me'ir of Rothenburg—who was aware of both Rashi and Jacob Tam's positions and thus in the best position to decide the law—followed the view of Rashi, who believed that the laws of encroachment apply to ownerless property.[33]

Basing his position on a broad interpretation of Jacob Tam and Rabbi Isaac ben Moses of Vienna (ca. 1180–ca. 1250), Katz challenged the notion crucial to Luria's position: that the law of the land, or in this case the custom of the land, determines the halakhah.[34] Instead, he argued, only a custom that local rabbis have publicly agreed to can abrogate the halakhah. Yet Katz's proof texts hardly proved his point. Jacob Tam, who generally accepted the Jerusalem Talmud's rule that "a custom nullifies the halakhah,"[35] only wrote that there are times when one should not rely on local custom—and offered no practical advice for determining such times.[36] Isaac ben Moses of Vienna offered only one example of when a "custom nullifies the law."[37] Nothing suggests that either of these jurists would have extended their statements to commercial transactions, where custom exercised wide legal authority.

There was no denying Luria's point that Simeon entered this matter aware that current custom sanctioned, if not encouraged, competitive bidding on an arenda while someone else held it. Yet by restricting a halakhicly recognized category such as The Law of the Land is the Law, Katz effectively limited the ability of the marketplace to shape the halakhic process. His broad interpretations of Jacob Tam and Isaac ben Moses demonstrated little concern for the economic fallout of his view on Jews searching for a livelihood.

But even Luria imposed limits on the power of local custom. Although

33. See Rashi's comments to B.T., *Qiddushin* 59a.

34. Katz, *Responsa*, no. 17, p. 58.

35. J.T., *Yebamot* 12.1, 12c.

36. See Mordecai ben Hillel, *Baba' Batra'* 464; also *tosafot*, *Baba' Batra'* 2a. On Jacob Tam and custom see Urbach, *Ba'aley ha-tosafot*, pp. 80–82.

37. Isaac ben Moses' view is cited in Mordecai ben Hillel, *Baba' Meẓi'a'* 366.

he championed free competition in the matter of arenda, he did not believe in unbridled competition that would permit bidders to displace lessees in the middle of their tenure, even if such a practice was sanctioned by ordinances of the local Jewish community. In Luria's opinion, no community had the right to institute an ordinance that contradicted the halakhah, and he believed any encroachment on someone else's livelihood that resulted in an immediate loss by the original lessee was prohibited by the halakhah.

In an undated responsum without allusion to the specific geographic region in which the events took place, Luria agreed to join with other rabbis in condemning the encroachment by Isaac Shernaz(?), David Senderlis(?), and others on a tax collection lease that "Abraham" had held for a number of years.[38] The loss of the lease cost Abraham about 1,500 (no currency is mentioned) in credits that he had extended to debtors and that he had no possibility of collecting once displaced. Contemporary rabbis demanded that those who took Abraham's lease pay his losses. Abraham's competitors, however, seem to have been working well within the parameters of a local ordinance of the Jewish community that allowed unrestricted competition in bidding on leases and that most rabbis accepted as valid. Luria took it upon himself to show that, in this case, Shernaz and his associates were liable because they had violated the halakhah prohibiting encroachment on someone's livelihood.[39]

Based upon the testimony of Abraham, Luria concluded that the competitors had malicious intent, tried "to waste the money of Israel," rejected the admonition of others, ignored their local rabbinic court, and had dealt deceitfully. Luria believed that they deserved to be fined for moral reasons, but he had to find a halakhic rationale in order to punish them legally, and this he could not do. Forced to extrapolate from the curse of Deuteronomy 27.17 against someone who encroaches on his neighbor's property, Luria was left with little more than an implicit proof.[40] Nevertheless, even a fee-

---

38. Luria, *Responsa,* no. 89. Like many of the responsa in the collection, it is unsigned. Whether Abraham held a *czopowe* (see below, n. 45) is unclear. Abraham may have purchased the right to collect a toll.

39. In joining the call for punishment, Luria attempted to preclude a possible counterclaim that the damages inflicted on Abraham were indirect (*gerama'*) and that the purchasers of the lease could not be held liable for such losses.

40. Ironically, one of Luria's halakhic proof texts against encroachment is Eleazer ben Judah of Worm's *Sefer ha-roqeaḥ,* no. 28, the very text cited by Isaac ben Bezalel and rejected by Luria in the previously discussed responsum.

ble halakhic source was enough for Luria to argue against the validity of the *taqqanah* (ordinance) allowing bids to displace an arendar during his term—and to call for punishment of those who placed such bids.

While others countered, according to Luria, that the *taqqanah* was made for political reasons, in particular to maintain good relations with the Polish authorities (*shelom malkhut*), Luria moved to restrict it by claiming—without any historical basis or documentation—that its enactors only permitted encroachment when there was no loss to the current tax collector but only a loss of potential income. Under those conditions, he suggested, encroachment would be halakhicly acceptable.[41] Luria never bothered to prove his premise that an ordinance may not contradict the law; it was axiomatic to him.

As part of Luria's attempt to fix what he believed to be an economic and moral injustice, he all but created a prohibition against stealing someone's source of livelihood. Through comparisons with other legal cases, he used the halakhah as a means of altering the meaning of a *taqqanah*, which, "corrected" by him, could stand alone as the basis for punishing encroachers.

Neither the aforementioned views of Isaac ben Bezalel and Katz—nor Luria's concomitant threat that purchases made while another Jew held an arenda could be summarily reversed—had much if any impact on the marketplace. Bidding wars between Jews continued until communal councils felt compelled to ban Jews from competing for an arenda that a Jew already held. The dispute between Simeon and Reuben erupted in 1546. Sometime before 1596, the Council of Four Lands banned any Jew from trying to lease an arenda so long as a fellow Jew held it, even if the potential buyer only sought to hold the arenda after the present lessee's term expired.[42] In 1623 the Lithuanian Council ruled,

> And now, since we have seen the damages that one causes to his friend in raising the cost of leasing an arenda [by bidding up the price] and destroys his friend's source of income and commits [financial] suicide as well, we

41. Even here Luria could not muster an undisputable proof. He wrote, "And if there is no proof for this there is a hint of it" in the laws of working on the intermediate days of festivals. The rabbis of the Talmud allowed one to work on these days if one would otherwise suffer a loss. However, one may not work if one only loses potential income which is not termed "damage."

42. *PVAA*, no. 32 (1596), which refers to an earlier ordinance promulgating this ban.

> therefore have ordained and agreed that anyone who has held an arenda three years or has a contract for an arenda for three years even though he has not [yet] held it [for three years], his friend may not encroach upon him for as long as he lives.[43]

Sometime later the Council clarified its decree and allowed the holder of an arenda to continue to enjoy protection from competing bids for the lease even if the noble from whom he leased the arenda died and a different noble assumed possession of the estate.[44]

Even those jurists like Sirkes, who accepted Luria's ruling allowing bidding on arendy for the next term, did not question the community's right to grant arendars protection from competition after a number of years of undisturbed possession. On the contrary, Sirkes felt that there was a pressing need for such legislation. Jewish arendars of taverns, for example, operated according to no real fiscal year, at the end of which all their accounts with non-Jews, malters, distillers, and patrons would be settled before someone else came and took over the arenda. Sirkes reasoned that such

---

43. Sirkes, *Responsa* (old), no. 60. The text appears with some variants in *PH,* no. 73 (1623). The Lithuanian Council allowed a creditor to encroach upon a continually delinquent debtor as a means of punishing the debtor (*PH,* no. 17, [1623]).

44. Such clarifications were not unusual. Joel Sirkes notes that eventually all ordinances regarding arendy ended with the following stipulation:

> The rule that emerges is that it is impossible to clarify and explain all aspects and details of holding an arenda in writing and even what is clearly written can be explained in different ways and therefore all matters of holding an arenda must be judged by judges seated in court according to what appears correct in their eyes and the needs of the time. (Sirkes, *Responsa* [old], no. 60)

The same concept appears in *PH,* no. 87, from 1623. However, in *PH* local leaders are designated to "clarify and explain the ordinance and to show and to understand why the ordinance was originally enacted." *PVAA,* no. 32 (1596), raises this very issue and comes to exactly the opposite conclusion, allowing competitive bidding for an arenda upon the noble's death, even when his direct heir assumes the estate. All question of interpretation were refered to the heads of the Council of Four Lands.

According to Polish law, when an estate was granted to a noble for life by the king, the noble could not pass his rights to his heirs (Ettinger, "Ḥelqam shel ha-Yehudim," pp. 132, 137). The lease therefore terminated immediately with the death of such an owner. The arendar's sole recourse in trying to recover his costs was against the deceased's personal property (Gloger, *Encyklopedia staropolska,* vol. 1, p. 68).

arendars, facing substantial loses from competition, needed the protection of the community.[45]

The Lithuanian Council's ordinance protecting an arendar from competitive bidding was tested in Brest Litovsk in the first half of the seventeenth century. When a particular noble died, the local *qahal* tried to prevent the Jews who currently held the arenda there for the mill and the sale of liquor from renewing it with the new owner. Instead, the *qahal* proposed that it take over the lease in order to provide local residents, the majority of whom were poor, with a source of income. The *qahal* also requested that the rabbinic court restrain the present lessees from trying to counter its bid in order not to raise the price of the arenda.

To support their claim against the present holders of the arenda, the *qahal* produced a document from "about forty years" before that implied that the *qahal* had held the arenda at that time and had chosen to sublease it to three members of the community for one year. The local *pinqas* recorded that the community had also made an ordinance that was later reconfirmed and established "until the coming of the redeemer," that whoever held the arenda must pay fifty Lithuanian *szok* (3,000 Lithuanian *grosz*) annually to the *qahal*, a custom that persisted until the present problem arose.[46] Now, forty years later, the community contended that it had always

45. Sirkes, *Responsa* (old), no. 61. Sirkes refused to extend this logic to those who held the right to collect the *czopowe*, an alcoholic beverage tax imposed by local nobles and often farmed out for collection. Polish law equated the *czopowe* with arendy (see *Volumina Legum*, vol. 3, 397 [1620], 442 [1621]). Jewish communities believed that a Jew holding a *czopowe* posed a serious threat to their physical wellbeing (They feared the reaction of non-Jews who resented Jews lording over them, collecting taxes). In 1580 the Polish Council banned Jews in Great Poland, Little Poland, and Mazovia in the strongest terms from having anything to do with the *czopowe* (*PVAA*, no. 1). Similary, various Jewish communities in the Ottoman Empire banned Jews from custom farming, fearing the ramifications for the Jewish community (see Aryeh Shmuelevitz, *The Jews of the Ottoman Empire in the Late Fifteenth and the Sixteenth Centuries* [Leiden: Brill, 1984], p. 176). Jews in Lithuania, however, continued to hold the *czopowe* with the blessing of the Lithuanian Council (*PH* nos. 4, 73, 82 [all from 1623]).

46. In the sixteenth century, the annual income of a Lithuanian peasant was generally between 300 and 600 Lithuanian grosz (grošis; in the first half of the century a laborer with a work horse could be hired for 1.5 Lithuanian groschen per day). In 1592 a Protestant school teacher, who was obliged to support four poor students as a condition of his employment, was paid 3,000 Lithuanian grosz annually while his two assistants received 1,800 and 900 respectively (Aleksandras Radžius, "Cash Flow in Medieval Lithuania," *The Knight* 12.5 [March–April 1990]: 5).

held the rights to the arenda and had simply subleased them for fifty *szok* annually to whomever purchased the lease from the noble.

The current holders of the arenda countered that such an attempt to block their renewal of the lease was against the *taqqanah* of the Council proscribing Jews from destroying another's source of income. Moreover, they argued, even if the *qahal* had once held the arenda, it had only held it for one year and had subsequently renounced its rights to the arenda—its *ḥazaqah* (claim based on undisturbed possession)—by demanding an annual payment of fifty Lithuanian *szok* from whoever leased the arenda.[47]

Sirkes, the rabbi to whom this problem was addressed, realized that the claim of the current arendars was technically correct. His sympathies, however, lay with the needs of the community and his a priori assumption was that the qahal must receive the rights to the arenda because

> . . . the arenda for liquor [will provide] a living for many people since when the *qahal* leases the liquor [arenda] from the noble there will be bread for many heads of households, everyone will be able to sell liquor in his house . . .

The stark contrast between the wealth of the three current arendars and the poverty of the majority of the community only accentuated the problem.

In order to justify his position legally, Sirkes took liberties with the legal statements of two earlier halakhic authorities and attempted to restrict the rights of communities to enact statutes. He ruled that councils had no right to enact laws that were harmful to the community.[48] If they did, their enactments were void. Sirkes was so certain that the *taqqanah* was not applicable that he ventured to add that even if the first noble were still alive, the *qahal* could prevent the current arendars from renewing their lease. Aware that his argument was halakhicly weak, he tried to demonstrate that the ordinance prevented individuals—not communities—from bidding on

47. The claims are summarized by Sirkes, *Responsa* (old), no. 60.

48. See Eliezer ben Joel ha-Levi, quoted in Mordecai ben Hillel, *Baba' Batra'* 481–82; Colon, *Responsa*, no. 14. While Eliezer ben Joel ha-Levi and Colon only remarked that a community has no right to interfere in matters between individuals (if the community is not affected), Sirkes presented this as the *qahal* can only act "for the benefit of the community"— that is, it can take no action that is not in the community's best interests. His atypical looseness with the sources further points to his desire to find an allowance in the case before him.

arendy held for a number of years: the statute was written in the singular, not the plural.

Sirkes sought other ways to strengthen his position. Even if the Council's ordinance could be found to apply to communities, Sirkes argued that it could be nullified because the needs of the community are considered a religious matter (*dabar mizvah*), a legitimate basis for dissolving vows (acceptance of the ordinances was viewed as a vow), even those of the community. "We have no greater religious precept," he wrote, "than giving the many a livelihood."

Free from the restrictions of the Council, the community could pursue the liquor arenda but not the less lucrative lease for the mill. According to Sirkes, the community remained bound by the ordinance with respect to the mill even though income from the mill would certainly have lessened the hardships of at least some poor people in the town. Sirkes's previous arguments that the language of the ordinance did not include a community and that the Council could not make ordinances to the detriment of a community vanished. Having solved the most pressing issue, he was content to let the community fall back under the jurisdiction of the national Council's statutes. His halakhic probing was intended to solve a particular problem. He was careful not to set a precedent that was potentially devastating to Jewish national self-government.

A different approach to reconciling the ordinances of the communities and halakhah was taken by Me'ir ben Gedaliah of Lublin, who was asked by a colleague whether members of the Jewish community were free to bid on an arenda that a Jew had held for a number of years but which he now had to abandon when both the noble and his creditors forced him to leave town.[49] Responding briefly because of his responsibilities at the yeshiva at the beginning of the term, he first states that there is room to consider whether encroachment is even applicable to an arenda, according to the halakhah. Nevertheless, since the custom "in these states" was to prohibit encroachment, he accepted that an arenda becomes the undisputed property of the holder.

Unlike Luria, who rejected an ordinance at odds with the halakhah,

49. Me'ir ben Gedaliah, *Responsa*, no. 62. Both the reformulated question sent by Rabbi Abba' Segel and the response are undated. However, Me'ir ben Gedaliah notes that the arendar went to Cracow to lobby his cause. This most likely took place before 1609, when the royal court left Cracow.

Me'ir ben Gedaliah, without challenging the legitimacy of the statute, chose to determine how the halakhah responds to the reality created by the ordinance. As in any other case, he tried to locate a parallel talmudic source that could be used to establish precisely when someone loses rights to his property.[50] Having found the source, he ruled by extension that if it was clear that the current arendar could not possibly hold his arenda, or if he renounced it, whoever can buy the arenda can keep it since if another Jew does not seize the opportunity, the noble will sell it to a non-Jew or keep it for himself.

Me'ir ben Gedaliah reinforced his position with a precedent from the responsa of Joseph Colon, who stressed that the current holder of a monopoly must renounce his rights or clearly resign himself (*ye'ush*) to never being able to exercise them before someone else may acquire them.[51] Although Me'ir ben Gedaliah accepted the notion that an arenda became the property of its holder, he did not allow a disenfranchised arendar to sell his arenda.[52] Once separated from his property, the lease holder lost all rights to it.

After presenting his halakhic opinion, Me'ir ben Gedaliah informed his questioner that he had spoken with the head of his community, Solomon the doctor, whom he held in great personal esteem. According to Solomon, the ordinance required that whoever took over the arenda must pay the original arendar an unspecified sum.[53] Me'ir ben Gedaliah said no more. Not attempting to integrate the ordinance into his halakhic opinion or decide between them, he left it to the questioner to reconcile the contradic-

---

50. B.T., *Baba' Qamma'* 116b with the comments of Rashi. Me'ir ben Gedaliah works with the opinion of Rab Ashi.

51. Colon, *Responsa*, no. 132.

52. Me'ir ben Gedaliah was quite aware that Colon allowed the holder of a monopoly to sell his rights if he could not use them. However, Me'ir ben Gedaliah rejected the possibility by differentiating between the cases. In Colon's example there was no breach in the relationship between the Jew and the person that he bought the monopoly from and therefore the Jew still had rights to the monopoly. Here, however, the arendar was spurned by the local noble, which in effect severed the Jew's rights to the arenda. In addition, if another Jew did not come and pay for the arenda, the noble would simply rent it out to a non-Jew. It would be lost to the first arendar, making it all the more similar to the talmudic case cited by Me'ir ben Gedaliah, where the owners cannot retrieve the item.

53. Also see Me'ir ben Gedaliah, *Responsa*, no. 111. On Dr. Solomon, who enjoyed special royal privileges, see Mathias Bersohn, *Tobiasz Kohn* (Cracow, 1872), pp. 46–47, and Mattahias Zunz, *'Ir ha-ẓedeq* (Lvov, 1874), in his notes on pp. 10–11.

tion between the halakhah and the ordinance. He himself made no effort to do so. To him they remained two separate realms.

Communal ordinances and halakhic opinions notwithstanding, the lucrative nature of arendy constantly tempted Jews to bid for them even when another Jew already held the lease. One final example is from Benjamin Slonik, writing sometime after 1590 (likely from Podhajce, about sixty miles southeast of Lvov).[54] He complained:

> It is a daily occurrence that we see the lawless people of the generation (periẓey ha-dor) when they see that one holds an arenda and makes some profit [from it] they immediately jump before the nobles and purchase that very arenda and cause great damages to the current holder of the arenda.[55]

Slonik was asked to adjudicate a case in which a Jewish arendar appeared to have leased a town from its owner (*arenda miejska*; since private towns were viewed as property, they could be bought, sold, and pawned). The owner then pawned the town to another noble from whom the Jew, Reuben, bought it and held it for almost ten years. In the final year of Reuben's lease, a non-Jew came and bid on the town/arenda. To protect himself, Reuben agreed to hold it in partnership with the non-Jew for one year, at the conclusion of which the owner of the town redeemed his land, only to pledge it again to yet another noble, a transaction negotiated by Reuben.[56]

In lieu of a fee for his negotiating services, Reuben asked the new noble not to raise the price of the arenda above the five hundred "golds" annual fee that he had always paid—a request that the noble acquiesced to verbally. But Reuben's non-Jewish partner had different ideas: he bid the arenda up to 700 golds, a difference that the noble could not overlook.[57] Sensing that the non-Jew was up to no good, Reuben decided to call his bluff. He went to the noble and told him, "My lord, I certainly do not want to cause you

54. Ettinger dates this responsum to the early seventeenth century ("Ḥelqam shel ha-Yehudim," p. 137). The only actual clue to its date is Slonik's quotation of the responsa of Joseph Katz. The responsa appeared in Cracow in 1590.

55. Slonik, *Responsa*, no. 28.

56. Negotiations were considered part of an arendar's functions. See Ettinger, "Ḥelqam shel ha-Yehudim," p. 136.

57. According to Reuben, the noble was willing to forgo a difference of one hundred golds but no more.

such damage. If the non-Jew will give you seven hundred, I forgive [your promise] and you [may] give the arenda to the non-Jew."

The noble called the non-Jew to inform him of his success and to draw up the lease, only to find that the non-Jew did not have the money. Enraged, the noble forced him to hold the arenda with Reuben, but at a cost of 350 golds for the non-Jew and only 250 for Reuben. Unable to pay even this reduced amount, the non-Jew came begging to Reuben for help.

Holding the upper hand, Reuben was not quick to negotiate a settlement. But during the time he was trying to pressure the non-Jew further, Simeon and Levi, two other Jews, came and bought the non-Jew out, leaving Reuben to cry encroachment.

Laymen accosted by eager competitors looked for legal protection not only to halakhot prohibiting encroachment—which they seemed to have known little about—but to communal ordinances on the matter. Reuben was no exception. He argued to Slonik that his competitors had not only violated the laws of encroachment but also

> the ordinance that exists in this region that every Jew who holds an arenda, even though his term has expired, nevertheless no Jew may lease that arenda until the first Jew has left it for at least six months. And anyone who violates this ordinance, they will pronounce an excommunication on him [that will be in force] until he will place the arenda in the hands of the [current] holder and the [competitor] will pay all damages from his pocket in addition to other fines.[58]

In addition, Reuben brandished a letter from the head of the local rabbinic tribunal, warning competitors not to encroach on his lease.

Simeon and Levi countered by openly disputing the meaning of the communal ordinance regarding arendy, arguing that it did not apply in this case because Reuben held only half an arenda from the new noble. They also claimed that since the non-Jew had held half the arenda for a year, Reuben had relinquished all claims to the monopoly. In matters of ordinances, laymen apparently believed they had the right to interpret aggressively the intention of the framers of the law.

Among Reuben's retorts was a charge based on the comments of the non-Jew to other Jews that Simeon and Levi had put him up to bidding on the arenda in the first place. If true, Simeon and Levi may have been at-

58. Slonik, *Responsa*, no. 27.

tempting to circumvent the ordinances of the region and not just trying to get revenge as Reuben believed. Undoubtedly anguished, Reuben concluded his case saying, "I relied on the law of our Torah together with the ordinance that they [my competitors] would not encroach on my property."

Slonik did not consider the merits provisions of the ordinance in his responsum. Following the approach of his teacher Luria, he analyzed the question according to a number of halakhic criteria. His ultimate concern, however, seems to have been protecting Reuben's livelihood.[59] Reuben had dedicated himself to this arenda, giving up all other pursuits. On the assumption that he would control this lease for as long as the owner of the town lived, he had even moved to the noble's town—where no other Jews lived. Thus he would suffer a serious loss of income if he were removed from even half the arenda, whereas newcomers presumably had other sources of current income they could continue to pursue.

Perhaps nothing epitomizes Slonik's eagerness to guarantee Reuben's source of income more than his explanation of why the year-long partnership with the non-Jew did not halakhicly sever Reuben's claim that the arenda was his livelihood—even though Slonik himself acknowledged that break:

> And if you will say that I have already written earlier that as soon as the non-Jew purchased the arenda Reuben's rights expired and this was no longer his livelihood, one can say that this only applies if the first [i.e., Reuben] did not seek to buy the arenda from the non-Jew, but since [Reuben] made such efforts until he brought the non-Jew into his net [a reference to B.T., *Baba' Batra'* 21b, one of the talmudic precedents used by Slonik in this encroachment case], [the arenda] returned and awakened to become his livelihood and the partners have encroached upon Reuben's livelihood and have taken the non-Jew from his net and bought the arenda from him. Therefore, without doubt, the partners are obligated to return the arenda to Reuben.[60]

Slonik's use of the term "returned and awakened," familiar in the laws of forbidden foods, to refer to economic rights is without talmudic precedent.[61] Further, his entire attempt to broaden Reuben's claim to the

---

59. This is not to exclude Slonik's desire to set an example and fine those who constantly bid against Jewish arendars, as described above.

60. Slonik, *Responsa,* no. 27.

61. The term usually refers to problems of forbidden mixtures such as foods. See *Enẓiqloppedyah talmudit,* vol. 13, s.v. "ḥozer ve-ni'ur," pp. 23–54.

arenda is suspect. While Reuben actively sought to recapture the total arenda, there is no disputing that during the previous year he received no income from the half that was in the hands of the non-Jew. To claim, on the basis of a non-applicable rule, that the whole arenda again became Reuben's livelihood just because he had been seeking it was at best illusionary.

Not simply applying the letter of the law here, Slonik was trying to protect the income of a Jew who claimed to have no viable economic alternatives. However, the need to protect Reuben's income was not a recognized and clearly formulated halakhic criteria, easily invoked to dismiss other halakhic arguments and the claims of Simeon and Levi. Slonik had to find some other halakhicly plausible argument to prove his case. In at least one instance this forced him to stretch a point. Most obvious in Slonik's entire discussion, however, is that the very communal ordinance whose meaning was disputed by the parties was of no significance in his legal thought. Perhaps he believed the halakhah was the only legitimate way to solve legal questions.

6

Bills Payable to Bearers

Fernand Braudel has surmised that "as soon as men learnt to write and had coins to handle, they had replaced cash with written documents, notes, promises and orders."[1] Making payments with specie when money meant coins—the first quasi-bank note is thought to have been issued by the Bank of Stockholm in 1661—was a great inconvenience if nothing else. Coins were bulky, heavy, of unreliable value, time-consuming to count, and dangerous to carry.

Although the documents that replaced cash only represented specie and as such were inherently an extension of credit, there is little evidence that merchants were able to develop a system of circulating credit—that is, the ability to transfer notes payable from one person to another—before the early 1400s in England and before 1500 on the Continent.[2] Previously, merchants could transfer bills of debt; but whoever accepted such notes assumed a considerable risk: the bearer of a transferred note generally had no legal recourse against the original borrower if he refused to pay. Roman law, which strongly influenced medieval commercial law in western Europe, dictated that there was only a contractual relationship between debtors and creditors.[3] A borrower was only required to pay the very person who lent him funds.[4]

---

1. Fernand Braudel, *Civilization and Capitalism 15th-18th Century*, vol. 1, *The Structures of Everyday Life*, Siân Reynolds, trans., (New York: Harper and Row, 1981), pp. 471–72.

2. John Munro, "Die Anfänge der Übertragbarkeit: Einige Kreditinnovationen im Englisch-Flämischen Handel des Spätmittelalters (1360–1540)," in *Kredit im Spätmittelalterlichen und Frühneuzeitlichen Europa*, Michael North, ed., (Köln: Bohlau, 1991), pp. 57–59, and Abbott Usher, *The Early History of Deposit Banking in Mediterranean Europe* (Cambridge, Mass.: Harvard University Press, 1943), pp. 98–99.

3. On how, when, and why Roman Law came to influence western European legal systems, see Paul Vinogradoff, *Roman Law in Medieval Europe*, 3d ed., with a Preface by F. de Zueleta (Oxford: Clarendon Press, 1961).

4. Huebner argued that pure bearer clauses (a condition such as "payable to the holder of this letter" as opposed to a power of attorney statement) may have appeared in debt notes in the Germanic lands as early as the tenth century but did not last (Huebner, *A History of Ger-*

The views of medieval Christian jurists also posed an obstacle to the free transfer of notes. Canonists construed the bearer as at best nothing more than an agent for the principal (the original lender). A principal's death extinguished the rights of the purchaser of any outstanding note and left the latter with no legal recourse to collect the note.[5] The presence and consent of debtors were necessary to effect a legally enforceable transfer of a loan.[6]

The first record of promissory notes that passed freely from hand to hand without any documentary evidence of transfer gaining legal acceptance comes from the London Mayor's court of 1436.[7] The verdict in the case of *Burton v. Davy* firmly recognized the bearer's right to collect an outstanding debt and must have reassured English merchants who, by the late fifteenth century, displayed no doubts about the right of a bearer to act as principal.[8] In the Low Countries, a judicial verdict ignoring the medieval line of thought and granting bearers of notes the rights of principals was issued in Antwerp in 1507 and was followed by similar decisions in Bruges

---

manic Private Law, pp. 570, 572). The existence of such notes was disputed by Raymond De Roover, *L'evolution de la lettre de change XIVe-XVIIIe siècles* (Paris: A. Colin, 1953), pp. 88–89, who believed that even such "pure" bearer clauses required a power of attorney.

5. Carl Freundt, *Das Wechselrecht der Postglossatoren*, vol. 2, (Leipzig: Duncker and Humblot, 1909), pp. 25–32, discusses the attempts of the post-glossators to grapple with the endorsed note and the status of the bearer.

6. On possible rationales for the need for the presence and consent of debtors, see M. M. Postan, "Private Financial Instruments in Medieval England," *Vierteljahrschrift für Sozial- und Wirtschafts- Geschichte 23* (1930), pp. 50, 55; and Stanley Bailey, "Assignment of Debts in England from the Twelfth to the Twentieth Century," *The Law Quarterly Review* 48 (1932): 548–49.

7. Frederick Beutel, "The Development of Negotiable Instruments in Early English Law," *Harvard Law Review* 51 (1937–1938): 819–21; Bailey, "Assignment of Debts," pp. 264–65, maintained that as early as the late thirteenth century, the rights of bearers with little to prove their claim beyond possession of a note were recognized by English merchant courts meeting at local fairs. However, John Munro, "The International Law Merchant and the Evolution of Negotiable Credit in Late-Medieval England and the Low Countries," in *Banchi pubblici, banci privati e monti di pietà nell'Europa preindustriale, Atti della Società Ligure di Storia Patria*, nuova ser., vol. 31 (Genova: Società Ligure di Storia Patria, 1991), pp. 58–59, argues that such credit was not truly assignable. Munro maintains that it is "more prudent" to assume that those who presented such bonds for payment were simply agents of the principal.

8. Munro, "The International Law," p. 75, notes, "Although this is the first extant law case to recognize that the bearer, as an assignee, had the full rights of a principal in a commercial bill, the official record of the court, relying on *custom*, does not suggest any conscious innovation on its part."

(1527), Dordrecht, and Utrecht. Official recognition of bearer clauses was conferred on March 7, 1537 by an ordinance of Charles V.[9]

The easy transfer of bearer notes, that is, promissory notes payable to the bearer rather than an individual specifically named on the note, spread into Dutch legal codes in the 1570s and became part of French economic life in the seventeenth century, just prior to entering German legal codes. Even though bearer notes had been known in England for some time, by the end of the sixteenth century they had yet to gain universal recognition in the King's courts, which did not recognize the transfer of negotiable instruments until the seventeenth century and in Common Law courts not before 1704.[10] In southwestern Europe, where many small businessmen used deposit and exchange banks for trade, there was much less pressure to develop a form of circulating credit.[11] As a result, in Italy, for example, Roman Law prevailed into the seventeenth century in this regard.[12]

In Poland, bearer notes were in use already in the fourteenth century. Just as in western Europe, however, the holder of such a note had to prove that he had purchased the note from its previous owner or possessed it through a power of attorney before he would have enforceable legal rights to its value.[13]

The detailed legal and economic developments that took place in Poland

---

9. Usher, *The Early History*, p. 99. Also see De Roover, *L'evolution de la lettre de change*, p. 96, who notes that the 1537 ordinance applied only to bills of debt and letters obligatory that were passed from hand to hand among merchants. The rest of the population enjoyed no such rights.

10. Beutel, "The Development of Negotiable Instruments," p. 839.

11. Herman Van der Wee, "Monetary, Credit and Banking Systems," in *The Cambridge Economic History of Europe*, vol. 5, E. E. Rich and C. H. Wilson, eds., (Cambridge: Cambridge University Press, 1977), p. 301.

12. Freundt, *Das Wechselrecht*, vol. 2, p. 15, notes that such notes appeared in the last quarter of the sixteenth century but were only legally recognized in the first half of the seventeenth century. The greatest resistance to the transfer of notes came not from lawyers but from commercial and banking circles that had to adjust to the impersonal character of commerce created by transferable notes (De Roover, *L'evolution de la lettre de change*, p. 90).

13. Rafal Taubenschłag, "Skrypty dłuzne z klauzula 'na zlecenie' i 'na okaziciela' w średniowiecznem prawie polskiem," *Czasopismo prawnicze i ekonomiczne* 30 (1936): 89–91. Notes payable (bills bearing the name of the creditor and not a bearer or order clause) were transferable simply through sale (pp. 88–89). Also see Bardach, *Historia państwa i prawa polski do roku* 1795, vol. 1, p. 509.

with regard to bills payable have yet to be charted. By the late sixteenth century, however, Polish, Latin, and Hebrew documents discuss a bearer note called a "*membrana*" in Polish (pl. *membrany*) that displayed distinct commercial and legal advances over bearer notes of the fourteenth century.[14]

The sixteenth-century membrana was a piece of paper signed on one side by the borrower. On the reverse side, opposite his name, that borrower, whether an individual or a *qehillah*, could, but did not have to, write in how much money he owed and when the debt would be due.[15] The note, which took but seconds to draw up, was then given to the lender, whose name was not written on it.[16] The great economic advantage of this note was that it could be passed from hand to hand without endorsement or any other formal form of transfer or the explicit knowledge or agreement of the

14. Etymologically, *membrana* is a Latin word meaning "parchment" but as early as 1397 in Poland the term signified a debt bill written on parchment that was used by both Christians and Jews (see Przemysław Dąbkowski, *Rękojemstwo w prawie polskiem średniowiecznem*, Towarzystwo Naukowe we Lwowie, Archiwum Naukowe, section 1, vol. 3 [Lvov: Towarzystwo do Popierania Nauki Polskiej, 1904], p. 240; *PVAA*, pp. 545–46, s.v. "memram"). See too Taubenschłag, "Skrypty dłuzne z klauzula," p. 87, who quotes the case of Daniel the Jew who lent money with a parchment membrana ("quod membranam seu pergamenum") to a non-Jew in 1414. The precise character of the bill is unclear although it would seem not to have been a "pay to the bearer" note.

Based on surviving Hebrew documentation, the word first appeared in Hebrew in the 1595 ordinances of the Cracow Jewish community published by Bałaban, "Die Krakauer Judengemeinde-Ordnung," p. 335. The word appeared again a few years later in Mordecai Jaffe's *Lebush 'ir Shushan* (Cracow, 1598), no. 48. Phillip Bloch, "Der Mamran, der jüdisch-polnische Wechselbrief," in *Festschrift zum siebzigsten Geburtstage A. Berliner's*, A. Freimann and M. Hildesheimer, eds., (Frankfurt: J. Kauffmann, 1903), p. 53, lists the various Hebrew spellings of the word. On sixteenth-century use of the term "membrana" in Polish sources and various spellings, see *Słownik polszczyzny XVI wieku*, Maria Mayenowa, ed., vol. 13 (Wrocław: Zakład Narodowy im. Ossolinskich, 1981), p. 275.

15. See, for example, Bernard Weinryb, *Texts and Studies in the Communal History of Polish Jewry* (New York: American Academy for Jewish Research, 1950), p. 41, discussing membrany issued by the Jewish community in Poznań in 1630 to an individual (no. 103a) and to the Jewish community in Glogów (no. 104). Further examples can be found in Avron, *Pinqas ha-kesherim*, nos. 391 (1645), 591 (1648), 631 (1650). Membrany also passed between family members; see Wettstein, "Qadmoniyyot," pp. 611–12.

16. Seemingly similar notes were in use in Lithuania where they were called "notes of admission" (*listami wyznanymi*; see Gloger, *Encyklopedia staropolska ilustrowana*, vol. 3, p. 201).

maker.[17] When the note came due, the bearer could present it for payment with all the rights of the principal. In a society where merchants met one another at fairs and constantly dealt with people who either knew them or knew of them, failure to pay a membrana, even once, could tarnish their reputations and cripple their ability to function in the marketplace.

Membrany also had a significant advantage for lenders. In selling goods on credit, a seller could halakhicly charge a higher price for most goods than he would have if the purchaser paid cash.[18] By adjusting the transaction price according to the length of the loan, the seller/lender was effectively getting around the prohibition against usury.[19] Moreover, membrany could be discounted, allowing holders of the notes to raise cash quickly if they faced a liquidity crisis. This possibility created an informal secondary market in short-term notes.[20] Membrany became so popular that in the mid-seventeenth century one rabbi wrote, perhaps with some degree of hyperbole, that they were traded more often than movable goods themselves.[21]

Yet membrany were not only without precedent in Jewish law, but highly problematic within the halakhic system.[22] They not only contradicted

---

17. Endorsement of notes developed slowly in western Europe, emerging only in the early seventeenth century, quite some time after the notion of transferability had been established. See Van der Wee, "Monetary, Credit and Banking Systems," pp. 326–29, and his "The Medieval and Early Modern Origins of European Banking," in *Banchi pubblici, banci privati e monti di pietà nell'Europa preindustriale, Atti della Società Ligure di Storia Patria,* nuova ser., vol. 31 (Genova: Società Ligure di Storia Patria, 1991), pp. 1169–70. It does not seem to have gained currency among Jewish merchants in eastern Europe during the mid-seventeenth century.

18. Such arrangments were common among merchants in northern Germany, where they were termed "Borgkauf." See Michael North, "Banking and Credit in Northern Germany in the Fifteenth and Sixteenth Centuries," in *Banchi publici, banci privati e monti di pietà nell'Europa Preindustriale, Atti della Società Ligure di Storia Patria,* nuova ser., vol. 31 (Genova: Società Ligure di Storia Patria, 1991), p. 824.

19. See *Shulḥan 'aruk,* Yoreh de'ah 173.1.

20. See *Shulḥan 'aruk,* Yoreh de'ah 173.4. The discounting of short-term bills of exchange first became common in western Europe in Antwerp in the early 1600s (see Van der Wee, "The Medieval and Early Modern Origins of European Banking," p. 1170).

21. Shabbetay ben Me'ir ha-Kohen, *Siftey kohen,* Ḥoshen mishpaṭ 50, n. 7.

22. Abraham Fuss, in "The Eastern European *Shetar Mamran* Re-examined," *Diné Israel* 4 (1973): liii-lv, dispels the notion first suggested by Reuben Margoliouth ("Margaliyyot hayam," *Qol Torah* 2.2 [Fall 1947], p. 10) and accepted by Israel Halperin (*TMM,* p. 53, n. 3) that such notes were already in use among Jews in twelfth-century Franco-Germany. The

Ashkenazic tradition with respect to assignment[23] but, more significantly, violated the halakhic requirement that debts be transferred in the presence of the borrower, the lender, and the transferee (i.e., novation), or through a power of attorney.[24] They also infringed on the talmudic dictum supported by biblical proof texts that loans be made in front of witnesses.[25] Nevertheless, while there is no record of anyone ever asking Polish rabbis about the halakhic acceptability of the membrany, halakhists were asked numerous questions about problems arising from their use.[26] Obviously, the document was so commonly encountered in both Jewish and Polish society that

---

assumption of a questioner writing to Joel Sirkes that membrany were used in thirteenth-century Spain also appears to be without basis (see Sirkes, *Responsa* [old], no. 32; Asher ben Yehi'el, *Responsa*, no. 65.1).

23. See Haym Soloveitchik, "Pawnbroking: A Study in *Ribbit* and of the halakhah in Exile," *Proceedings of the American Academy for Jewish Research* 1970–1971 (38–39): 219 and n. 32.

24. See *Ṭur*, Ḥoshen mishpaṭ 66. The Talmud's attempts to deal with the assignment of debts is discussed in some detail by Shalom Albeck, "Hishtalshelutah shel ha'abarat hobot ba-Talmud," *Tarbiz* 26.3 (April 1957): 262–86. Yet talmudic solutions were not only just as impractical as they had been ever since economies became mobile in character (see Soloveitchik, "Pawnbroking," pp. 217–18); they also involved numerous financial risks. Novation, for example, was not a continuation of a previous debt but the creation of a new one. As such, the new creditor only acquired liens on the debtor's assets from the time of the new loan, not from the time the original debt was incurred. A sketch of the problem in later Jewish law up to the fifteenth century is given in Abraham Fuss, "Assignability of Debt and Negotiable Instruments in Jewish Law," *Diné Israel* 12 (1984–1985): 19–37.

25. See B.T., *Baba' Meẓi'a'* 75b with the comments of Rashi. Unwitnessed loans were allowed if a pawn was used. See Maimonides, *Code of Law*, Laws Concerning Creditor and Debtor, chap. 2, no. 7; Moses of Coucy, no. 93 (positive commandments); Jacob ben Asher, *Tur*, Ḥoshen mishpaṭ 70.1; and Karo, *Shulḥan 'aruk*, Ḥoshen mishpaṭ 70.1. More than a quarter century before the first mention of membrany in Hebrew sources, Solomon Luria noticed that most merchants relied on a debtor's signature as they would have on that of witnesses who had seen the transaction (Luria, *YSS, Ketubbot* 2.25)

26. Use of membrany was not restricted to Poland and Lithuania. By the 1630s it appears to have been common in western Bohemia as well (see Krochmal, *Responsa*, no. 10). The contract may have been found elsewhere under a different name. There is little, however, to support Halperin's suggestion that documents termed "membrana" used in fourteenth-century Moravia (see Emil F. Rössler, *Die Stadtrechte von Brünn aus dem XIII und XIV Jahrhundert* [Prague, 1852], p. 266, no. 573; Bertold Bretholz, *Geschichte der Juden in Mähren im Mittelalter*, vol. 1 [Brünn: R.M. Rohrer, 1934], p. 132, n. 2; *TMM*, p. 53, n. 3) had the same character as the debt notes used by sixteenth- and seventeenth-century Polish Jews.

the permissibility of their use was taken for granted by everyone, including the rabbis themselves.[27]

Before they could deal with membrany, rabbis first had to decide what constituted a halakhicly valid document, although logically one can assume that if the marketplace developed membrany it also determined what was and what was not a valid contract. Mordecai Jaffe was adamant in demanding that, in order to prevent possible forgeries, the amount owed by the debtor be written on the reverse side of the paper, either by the debtor or by the creditor in the debtor's presence, exactly opposite the debtor's signature. According to Jaffe, since people kept such sheets signed and ready for use, a membrana presented for collection bearing only the debtor's signature had to be temporarily voided until the facts surrounding its issue could be determined, no matter who brought the membrana to court. No one, Jaffe assumed, would consciously let what amounted to a blank check in his name circulate in the marketplace.[28]

Jaffe was so convinced of his logic that he declared this to be a "great working legal assumption" (*ḥazaqah gedolah*), even stronger than the assumptions that the rabbis of the Talmud used to decide legal questions regarding the transfer of money from one person to the other. He even tried to find a talmudic support for his assumption in the general rabbinic prohibition of leaving too much space between one's signature and the terms of a contract.[29] If the rabbis were concerned about improper additions to an itemized contract, they certainly would have rejected a membrana signed on only one side. Their silence about such a blank contract was precisely what Jaffe used to make his case; it was so obviously prohibited that the

---

27. Me'ir ben Gedaliah, *Responsa,* no. 22, an undated responsum, stated that according to the laws of "their courts" (i.e., Polish courts), the simple transfer of a bill of payment from hand to hand made the bearer of a note the principal.

28. Jaffe noted that merchants sent signed membrany with trusted colleagues to fairs, where the colleague would act as an agent and fill in the amount of the debt before buying goods for the sender. Said Jaffe,

> and who would believe any man to give him a contract that he could write on it whatever he might want. Such a person is nothing but a simpleton who believes everyone and everything (see Prv. 14.15) or is out of his mind and should be included among idiots. And the actions of such a man are meaningless. (Jaffe, *Lebush 'ir Shushan,* no. 48)

29. B.T., *Baba' Batra'* 161a-162a.

rabbis did not even have to mention it.[30] He did not openly admit the possibility that the rabbis were silent on the matter because they had never considered it.

Joshua Falk, who most likely wrote in Lvov just a few years after the publication of Jaffe's work, responded to Jaffe by noting that some lenders would not accept a membrana unless it was blank on the reverse side so that they could add their costs, some of which were unknown at the time of the transaction, to the total amount of the loan. By leaving the second side blank, a creditor insured that he could fill in the total amount due when it was finalized.[31] A needy borrower could hardly refuse such a demand.

In the 1620s and 1630s, a significant minority of merchants in Cracow, and probably at the fairs too, continued to give creditors signed membrany without filling in the amount to be paid. While some rabbis shared Jaffe's concerns about the practice, the market obviously did not and, ultimately, it controlled the manner of use of the contracts.[32] Rabbis only exercised authority over membrany transactions when something went askew and the parties involved appealed their cases.

An undated responsum reveals that Joel Sirkes was asked whether there was any basis in rabbinic literature for collecting a membrana in court or whether the practice was wholly based on ordinance and custom. After all, the membrana was not a halakhicly recognized contract. Sirkes responded by trying to suggest some halakhic standing for the document. He turned to a responsum of Moses Nahmanides, who wrote that a signatory to a contract that he cannot read is responsible for the performance of all conditions in the contract on the assumption that he signed the contract relying on what other people told him it meant.[33] So too, Sirkes suggested, in the case

---

30. A claim could be made that a bearer should be believed because he could have written in much more than he claimed when presenting a blank membrana. Jaffe rejected this premise. In Jaffe's view such a claim would be like a mere possibility in the presence of witnesses who are capable of establishing the facts (*miggo bi-mqom 'edim*). Sharp critiques of Jaffe's halakhic arguments were made by David ben Judah in his *Sefer migdal David* (Prague, 1616), pp. 28b-30a, a work intended "to save the great scholars [Karo and Isserles] from the complaints of Jaffe who comes to destroy the truth" (p. 2b).

31. Joshua Falk, *Sefer me'irat 'eynayim*, 48, n. 1.

32. Sirkes, *Bayit ḥadash,* Ḥoshen mishpaṭ 48. Also see Shabbetay ben Me'ir ha- Kohen, *Siftey kohen,* Ḥoshen mishpaṭ 69, n. 17, who, together with his father, agreed with Jaffe but added, quoting Sirkes, that, based on ordinances of the communities, the custom was not to do so.

33. Quoted by Karo, *Beyt Yosef,* Ḥoshen mishpaṭ 45.1. Also see 68.6.

of a membrana. A debtor signed a document agreeing to follow the creditor's interpretation of the note and any riders that he may attach to it. Moreover, since the debtor knew that the creditor would circulate the note, it was as if the debtor had written a bearer clause in the contract insuring that he would pay whoever presented the note, even though the bearer received it without power of attorney. The debtor also implicitly agreed not to claim that he only had a personal encumbrance to the original creditor.[34] Yet Sirkes could not deny that without witnesses to establish that a loan took place, a debtor had the halakhic right to come to court and claim that he paid the note or that he had never issued the membrana. Legally speaking, a membrana without witnesses remained little more than a piece of paper. Even the debtor's own signature was legally worthless.

With nothing to recommend the practice halakhicly, Sirkes wrote very plainly that according to the halakhah one cannot collect a debt on the basis of a membrana. The only legal sources that granted creditors the right to collect with a membrana were the ordinances of the leaders of the community (*taqqanat ha-manhigim*) that declared that a membrana should have the status of all proper debt contracts, effectively usurping the debtor's rights in halakhah.[35]

Interestingly, despite the inherent halakhic invalidity of the contract, contemporary rabbinic authorities not only accepted the authority of communal statutes regarding membrany but sought proof texts to support the custom of using them. Joshua Falk, for example, applied the words of Jacob ben Asher to the matter:

> We follow the language that is usually written in contracts, even though it is not according to the statutes of the rabbis but [according to] the language

---

34. See Israel Isserlein, *Sefer terumat ha-deshen* (1882; reprint, Bene Beraq, Israel: n.p., 1971) no. 331, in which a non-Jew is said to have borrowed from a Jew and agreed to obligate himself to his creditor and whoever may present the debt (as, Isserlein adds, was often the custom in such contracts used among non-Jews). In such circumstances Isserlein ruled that the debt can be transferred from hand to hand because a bearer clause makes it as if the presenter's name is written in the contract.

35. Sirkes, *Responsa* (old), no. 32. Precisely when and where the leaders of the Jewish community first made such an ordinance remains unknown. However, the following appears in the 1595 ordinances of the Jewish *qahal* in Cracow.

> Membrany have all the stringencies, even the most stringent aspects of holographs in the world, and he [the bearer] may rely on all powers of the contract [as if] the borrower gave him this power (Bałaban, "Die Krakauer Judengemeinde-Ordnung," p. 335).

> that laymen customarily use in that place, and even if it is not written [properly] we judge it as if it is.[36]

Sirkes too was willing to follow what he considered to be a ruling made for the benefit of trade (*taqqanat ha-shuq*).[37] Like the second-century scholar Rabbi Me'ir, each of these jurists recognized a role for communal ordinances in the halakhic process and for custom in matters of contracts.[38]

The extent to which rabbis were willing to be guided by the rules of the community with respect to membrany was tested in the following case: Simeon issued membrany to a number of people to cover his borrowings. When the bills payable came due, Reuben, who held two of Simeon's membrany, and Levi, who held one of Simeon's notes, came to collect from Simeon. Unfortunately for all concerned, Simeon did not have the means to pay back the entire debt.

Such a situation was not unknown in halakhic literature. Numerous medieval authorities had ruled in such cases, and the law according to Jacob ben Asher was that creditors without prior rights must divide a debtor's assets equally. No matter what the size of any one debt, each creditor possessed an equal lien on those assets. If creditor A was owed 100 *zloty*, creditor B 200 *zloty*, and creditor C 300 *zloty*, then the debtor's assets were to be divided equally among all three creditors until creditor A's lien was satisfied. The remaining assets would be divided between B and C until each had received 200 *zloty*, leaving creditor C to rummage for his remaining 100 *zloty* from whatever the debtor had left.[39] This division of assets, however, was not the custom in Cracow or at any of the fairs in Lublin and Jaroslaw during the 1620s and early 1630s.[40] In those places, and likely throughout Poland and Moravia, the division of assets was made on the basis of the

36. Falk, *Sefer me'irat 'eynayim* 45, n. 5 quoting from *Tur*, Ḥoshen mishpaṭ 42.21 (also quoted by Karo). In his gloss, Isserles adds, "And this is the law regarding ordinances of the community or a matter that is the custom of the town" (*Shulḥan 'aruk*, Ḥoshen mishpaṭ 42.15). See, however, Shabbetay ben Me'ir ha-Kohen, *Siftey kohen* 42, n. 36.

37. See Sirkes, *Bayit ḥadash*, Ḥoshen mishpaṭ 48. See too *Bayit ḥadash*, Ḥoshen mishpaṭ 69, n. 9, where Sirkes writes that if the local Jewish leadership makes an ordinance that signed but not witnessed agreements are valid, they are halakhicly binding.

38. B.T., *Baba' Mezi'a'* 104a according to the interpretations of Rashi, the tosafists, Asher ben Yehi'el, and others. See too Karo, *Beyt Yosef*, Ḥoshen mishpaṭ 42.21.

39. *Tur*, Ḥoshen mishpaṭ 104.11.

40. And likely both before and after. See Krochmal, *Responsa*, no. 15, who says that there was no dissension in this matter.

number of contracts. Each contract that a creditor held entitled him to one share in the division of a debtor's property. In the case cited above, Reuben would have received two portions for every one that Levi collected.

Faced with this situation, Sirkes spent the bulk of a responsum dealing with this issue reaffirming the halakhah: assets should be divided on the basis of people, not contracts, since the debtor-creditor relationship is a personal one, not simply a contractual one. A debtor obligates himself to each creditor equally, irrespective of the number of contracts or amounts of the loans. Yet in the last few lines of his responsum Sirkes wrote,

> The custom is now [with respect to] membrany, that one may give it to his friend without a power of attorney and anyone who presents it can collect with it. There was an ordinance of the leaders of the region that collection be made according to the number of contracts. And from this it became common that the judges have the custom to rule thus [i.e., according to the number of contracts] *but not according to the law at all* [my emphasis].[41]

Thus although contemporary practice was to ignore the halakhah and follow the ordinance, Sirkes did not attempt to speak out against the custom or to ground it in the framework of the halakhah. He tacitly accepted it just as the jurists, scholars, and heads of the academies who attended the fairs did.[42] Only one rabbi sometime before 1648—someone whom Menahem Mendel Krochmal labeled "a great one in our generation"—was known to have spoken out against the custom in the hope of reinstating the halakhah. The anonymous rabbi ruled in a case that came before him that creditors should divide the debtor's assets according to their number, not their contracts.

The stance of this unnamed rabbi was opposed by Krochmal, who was already living in Moravia at the time.[43] If this rabbi was correct, Krochmal no doubt reasoned, how had he himself—who had been an associate (*senif)*

---

41. Sirkes, *Responsa* (old), no. 35.

42. Krochmal, *Responsa*, no. 15, writes that the heads of the yeshivas, jurists, and scholars attending the fairs knew of this custom and did not question it.

43. Joshua Höschel, *Responsa*, pt. 1, Ḥoshen mishpaṭ no. 10, which appears to be a question sent to Joshua Höschel by Krochmal, who was living in Prostejov (Prossnitz) at the time and who presents his own view in this matter. No reply from Joshua Höschel is noted. Krochmal came to Prostejov in 1646 and left for Mikulov (Nikolsburg) in 1648. This text parallels Krochmal, *Responsa*, no. 15, which appears to be a later and more clearly presented refutation of this anonymous rabbinic authority, but the earlier text includes novel critiques of the custom.

of the Cracow court and periodically the same at the fair courts—and all his illustrious teachers and all the elders of Cracow allowed courts to rule against the law? Failure to justify the custom would leave not only Krochmal and his contemporaries as mistaken judges but, no less important, would sully the name of his teachers. Krochmal, a student of Sirkes, set out to prove that dividing assets according to contracts was not only based on communal ordinances but was what the halakhah demanded.

In the course of his description of the use of membrany, Krochmal revealed other ways in which the contracts functioned in contradiction to the halakhah. While the halakhah gave priority to earlier contracts (a contract dated January 1, 1615 that came due on February 1, 1616 had a prior lien on assets than a contract dated July 1, 1615 that came due on March 1, 1616), Krochmal said that all membrany presented for payment had equal claims, irrespective of the dates of the contracts.[44] According to Krochmal, this custom was initiated by merchants for the good of the marketplace (*taqqanat ha-shuq*)—before it received the approbation of the rabbis. But Krochmal was not out to justify this practice here, but rather to defend the division of assets according to contracts.

Krochmal differentiated between the classic form of loan, in which creditors divided assets according to their numbers, and loans made with a membrana. When a borrower received money from a lender and wrote a contract in which he stipulated that he would repay a particular lender, he did not just obligate himself financially; he created a personal bond between himself and his creditor. Should the debtor borrow from any number of parties and write similar contracts, he legally obligated himself to each creditor named in each contract. Because of that personal bond between debtor and creditor, if the debtor did not have the cash to pay his debts, his assets were divided according to the number of creditors. Each creditor had an equal, personal lien on the debtor's property—even if one creditor had six contracts while another had but one.

Membrany, however, were based upon a different kind of relationship. Written without names in order to facilitate their easy transfer, they represented not a bond between debtor and creditor, but rather a bond between the debtor and the note.[45] The debtor knew that the lender himself would

---

44. A parallel ordinance was made by Jewish leaders in Moravia in 1650 at Gaya. See *TMM*, no. 225.

45. According to Krochmal in Joshua Höschel, *Responsa*, pt. 1, Ḥoshen mishpaṭ no. 10, inherent in each note is a lien on the debtor's property.

not collect with the membrana, but would pass it on to other merchants. He therefore obligated himself not to the provider of funds but to the note itself. In effect, the bearer came to collect with an empowered note.

The argument, based on the assumed thought processes of the debtor at the time of the loan, is inherently illogical or perhaps more precisely, "ahalakhic." A debtor cannot create a contractual relationship with anything but a human. He cannot designate that his property belongs to a contract but only to the holder of the contract. If witnesses had signed the membrana, then perhaps Krochmal could have followed the logic of Asher ben Yehi'el and suggested that the witnesses would have acquired the rights for the ultimate bearer. A membrana, however, had but one signature—that of the maker.

Likely mindful that this argument would not suffice, Krochmal tried a second approach. Since membrany were easily transferable, in theory, a bearer holding two notes could easily sell one to a second party before coming to court and thus reduce his exposure to potential loss. He would receive money for the sale of the note and, if the halakhah was to be strictly followed, he would divide equally with the other creditors on the basis of their number. Krochmal reasoned that when a creditor came to court with multiple contracts in his hands, we should consider what he could have done to circumvent the problem and consider it as if he had done it. Thus each contract must be viewed as a separate lien on the debtor's property. It is as if each one was in someone else's hands, even though the bearer of the notes did not actually transfer his notes or claim that he could have done so.[46]

The idea of viewing what could have been done as legally accomplished was not a creation of Krochmal's imagination, but had been suggested in another context by Asher ben Yehi'el and had been accepted and codified by his son, Jacob.[47] However, Krochmal acknowledged that a counterclaim could be raised from a discussion of the tosafists, suggesting that such a fictional transfer would be objectionable since it caused a loss to the other creditors.[48] Yet, Krochmal maintained, other creditors would not be suffer-

46. According to Krochmal, one cannot make this claim unless one actually has multiple contracts. If a creditor held a note for one hundred *zloty*, he cannot claim at the time of collection that he should be considered a bearer of multiple contracts because he could have written four notes for twenty-five *zloty* each (see B.T., *Baba' Batra'* 172a).

47. Tur, Ḥoshen mishpaṭ 119.

48. See *Tosafot*, B.T., *Ketubbot* 109b.

ing true losses since the creditor with multiple membrany always had the right to assign the contracts before coming to court. If he did exercise the option, other creditors would be in exactly the same position now that the court fictitiously exercised his option for him.[49]

Krochmal offered yet a third argument in support for the custom of dividing according to contracts, this time by going to the mind of the lender. Drawing a syllogism between a talmudic case that allowed a creditor to accept one note for two transactions or two notes for one transaction,[50] Krochmal argued that the number of contracts determined the number of loans and concomitant liens on a debtor's assets. When the first contract was paid off, one lien was dissolved. The others, however, remained intact until each contract was settled, even if all the contracts were issued at the same time. According to Krochmal's understanding of the talmudic case, in accepting numerous notes, creditors assumed that they had separate liens. Otherwise, why would anyone have accepted multiple contracts when one contract would not only be easier but in the creditor's best interests? The whole purpose of multiple contracts was to give the lender numerous liens on a debtor's assets and, in the case of membrany, allow him to collect according to contracts. That no other exegete made such a connection between the talmudic case and loans in general, especially in light of the generally accepted conclusion that loans are collected according to number of creditors and not according to the number of contracts, shows the extent to which Krochmal was searching for a source with which to buttress his position. That he had to defend his final approach with a number of assumptions unarticulated by the Talmud only under-

49. In Joshua Höschel, *Responsa*, pt. 1, Ḥoshen mishpaṭ no. 10, Krochmal cited the position of his opponent who quoted Jacob ben Asher's rejection of the possibility that a creditor known to be bearing a valid and an invalid debt note, one larger than the other, may collect from the larger on the assumption that he could have burned the smaller one before entering court (*Ṭur*, Ḥoshen mishpaṭ 31). Therefore, the unknown rabbi argued, rabbis cannot view membrany as having been transferred after they are presented in court. Krochmal responded that no such proof can be derived from a case in which one of the two contracts was known to be a forgery.

50. B.T., *Baba' Meẓi'a'* 104b-105a. The annonymous rabbi had used this very talmudic text to argue that if one could collect according to contracts, why did the Talmud not stress this idea as practical advice for all creditors. Krochmal responded that the Talmud was only dealing with the most common of cases offering good advice for the lender in one instance and for the borrower in another.

scores that he himself knew that this was not a totally convincing halakhic argument.[51]

Krochmal was well aware that if he took his discussion to its logical conclusion, not only should membrany be collected based upon their numbers but so should all contracts, including ones with witnesses and with the name of the creditor spelled out on the notes—that is, notes that could not be transferred without legal formalities. If Krochmal had failed to draw this conclusion, he would have faced a rather striking anomaly: creditors with universally recognized halakhic contracts would have been at a disadvantage compared to those holding membrany when collecting debts. Creditors holding contracts with witnesses would collect according to the number of creditors, while those holding membrany would collect according to contracts. Krochmal dispelled this possibility. All contracts were to be treated equally and bearers could collect according to contracts, a concept that he claimed he could prove had he wished to take the time to do so. The talmudic case of creditors collecting according to their number only applied when creditors each had one contract. No one could dispute, Krochmal maintained, that multiple contracts gave bearers multiple liens.

In practical terms, Krochmal's justification was of little importance. He only justified legally what was already being widely practiced. In terms of jurisprudence, however, Krochmal's efforts were of greater significance. His a priori assumption was that his teachers and colleagues could not possibly have been violating the halakhah. Since almost everyone, including Krochmal himself, was deciding disputes on the basis of an ordinance/practice that clearly did violate it, he assumed there must have been another meaning to the law. The issue was no longer simply whether to recognize the authority of the ordinances. In order to justify the behavior of his teachers and colleagues, Krochmal was prodded into severely narrowing the scope of the halakhah regarding dividing assets according to creditors. Ironically, because of their actions, ordinances became a source with which the halakhah had to be reconciled, rather than one that had to be reconciled with the halakhah.

---

51. Krochmal's rabbinic antagonist had at least one argument that Krochmal did not address in the responsum. Krochmal's colleague allowed that the halakhah generally permits the division of loans (e.g., converting a loan for 100 *zloty* into two loans for fifty *zloty*) if both creditor and debtor agree. Yet, he argued, in the case of an insolvent debtor this must not be allowed because it may be damaging to other creditors (B.T., *Baba' Batra'* 172a; Isserles, *Shulḥan 'aruk*, Ḥoshen mishpaṭ 53.1). Based on an opinion of the tosafists (*Baba' Mez.i'a'* 20a), Krochmal rejected fears of collusion between debtor and creditor except when such collusion would result in an immediate loss to other creditor(s).

7

Bankruptcy and Those Who Fled Their Creditors

While membrany were both convenient and popular, they were, as discussed above, an unsecured form of credit. Pawns offered creditors greater security, but the cumbersome pledges they involved defeated the purpose of easily transferable bearer notes. Although pawnbroking did not disappear, it essentially remained a form of consumer credit that supplied the needs of small borrowers. Merchants, on the other hand, did not go to pawnbrokers to meet their ongoing credit needs.

Those who extended loans to merchants had always assumed some risks. Without insurance, fire or theft could decimate the assets of any borrower in an instant. Further, even in the best of times, not every business venture was successful and since real property was generally scarce, few borrowers had the means to collateralize their loans. Even if delinquent debtors had assets, they often tried to conceal them from creditors, which only delayed the recovery of the loan and increased the cost of doing so.[1]

The perils of unsecured loans were exacerbated in early seventeenth- century Poland when the country endured a long monetary crisis that peaked from 1620 to 1623. Polish specie, which had a higher metal content than currency in western centers, was taken out of the country by speculators or as payment for western goods, while debased western currency entered the Polish economy as payment for grain.[2] Polish currency was debased from 0.67 grams of silver in 1604 to 0.30 grams in 1623.[3] As in contemporary

1. See, for example, Katz, *Responsa*, nos. 62 (p. 149), 75 (p. 171); Sirkes, *Responsa* (old), no. 38. The idea of concealing assets was likely just as old as the idea that creditors might try to seize a debtor's assets.

2. Maria Bogucka, "The Monetary Crisis of the XVIIth Century and its Social and Psychological Consequences in Poland," *The Journal of European Economic History* 4, no. 1 (Spring 1975): 139.

3. Van Horn, "Suburban Development," pp. 406–7. On the debasement of currency in German lands see Fritz Redlich, *Die deutsche Inflation des frühen siebzehnten Jahrhunderts in der zeitgenössischen Literature: Die Kipper und Wipper* (Köln: Böhlau, 1972), pp. 11–13.

Germany, inflation raged; in Lublin in 1602, 64 chicken eggs cost 5 *grosz*, in 1607 10 *grosz*, and in 1629 40 *grosz*, before falling back to 24 *grosz* in 1633–1634.[4] The mean price of one barrel of beer in Lvov rose from 72 *grosz* in 1585 to 90 *grosz* in 1602 to 210 *grosz* in 1629.[5] While peasants were insulated from the economic fluctuations by their custom of barter trade and their ability to be largely self-sufficient, salaried workers, whose wages did not keep pace with inflation, bore the full brunt of price increases. An unskilled laborer working in Lvov made 3 to 5 *grosz* daily from 1600 to 1620.[6] Not surprisingly, workers went on strike in various towns to protest the growing difficulty of making ends meet.[7] Jews, together with financiers, forgers, minters, and speculators, were popularly blamed for economic woes that they too endured.[8]

Coupled with the monetary crisis of the early seventeenth century was the devastation of peasant agriculture by nobles attempting to increase grain production on their lands. Peasants, many of whom were enserfed laborers, were required to increase the number of days per week that they served the manor as well as to reduce the area of demesne land that they cultivated for their own needs.[9] This economic crippling of the peasantry had a ripple effect on the growth of local manufacturing and artisan production, eliminating many potential buyers of regional finished products. Towns suffered further when nobles anxious to insulate themselves from the rising prices of western finished goods lifted import tariffs. Their attempts to lure foreign merchants to Poland and increase the volume of imported goods in the country did nothing to promote local economic interests.[10]

---

4. See Władysław Adamczyk, *Ceny w Lublinie od XVI do końca XVIII wieku* (Lvov: Instytut Popierania Polskiej Twórczośći Naukowej, 1935), p. 77.

5. Hoszowski, *Ceny we Lwowie*, p. 175.

6. Ibid., p. 244. An unskilled laborer in Cracow in 1595 made between 3 and 4 *grosz* per day, about the cost of a chicken. A mason's apprentice made appoximately 8 *grosz* per day in 1595 (Juljan Pelc, *Ceny w Krakowie w latach 1369–1600* [Lvov: J. Mianowski, 1935], pp. 5, 92, 94, 146).

7. Bogucka, "The Monetary Crisis," p. 146.

8. Ibid., pp. 150–51. See too Janusz Tazbir, "Images of the Jew in the Polish Commonwealth," *Polin* 4 (1989): 21, 24.

9. Labor on estates was generally provided by peasants who in addition to their toil gave about 50 percent of their own production to the lord. See Topolski, "Sixteenth-Century Poland," p. 77.

10. M. Malowist, "The Economic and Social Development of the Baltic Countries from the Fifteenth to the Seventeenth Centuries," *The Economic History Review*, 2d ser., 12, no. 2 (1959): 186–88.

Caught in the midst of an extended currency crisis, Polish landowners who depended on the sale of leases for a major portion of their incomes could not immediately increase their revenues to meet their needs. Ever strapped for cash as inflation ravished the purchasing power of their liquid assets, landowners were forced to borrow funds. Many middle and small gentry were ultimately either dispossessed or forced to sell their assets by creditors who were themselves starved for cash.[11]

The Jewish community was also plagued by cases of personal insolvency. An ordinance of the Jewish community in Cracow of 1604 noted that recently "many" (*kammah ve-kammah*) Jews had come before the court claiming that they had no assets with which to repay their creditors.[12] Some claimed interest charges had consumed their capital and profits, an explanation that was, according to the ordinance, very likely true in certain cases.[13] Indeed, short term intra-Jewish interest rates are thought to have reached as high as 50 percent per annum in the first half of the seventeenth century.[14]

---

11. Van Horn, "Suburban Development," pp. 407–8.

12. Schiper attributed the increase in insolvencies in the Jewish community to the desire of Jews for increasingly large deals that necessitated the use of credit. The burden of carrying large amounts of high interest debt, according to Schiper, was simply too great to bear, a view echoed by Paltiel Dickstein, "Taqqanot va'adey Polin ve-Liṭa' 'al ha-borḥim," *Ha-mishpaṭ ha-'ibri* 1.1 (1918): 29. Schiper also cited the decline of western European markets as a problem for Jews in Poland who held notes from western merchants. According to Schiper, the fall of major Jewish businessmen had a ripple effect on "thousands" of Jewish families (*Beyt Yisra'el be-Polin*, vol. 1, p. 181). Majer Bałaban saw the insolvency problems of the 1620s as a result of the exclusion of Jews by the Poles from local commerce and the overdependence of Jews on the fairs, the routes to which were perilous, often resulting in losses to marauders (*Beyt Yisra'el be-Polin*, vol. 1, p. 63). Both historians have failed to look beyond the Jewish community and notice that the entire Polish economy was enduring a severe economic downturn. It is to be expected that a group like the Jews who were involved in commercial transactions and thus had a greater need for credit would also have a higher rate of insolvencies than Poles.

13. Bałaban, "Die Krakauer Judengemeinde-Ordnung," p. 107. The ordinance specifically stated that the community was moved to take action because insolvency and interest charges were draining the assets of the rich. This further underscores that council members, who as taxpayers represented the most affluent sector of society, often made ordinances to protect their own interests.

14. Weinryb, *Texts and Studies*, p. 29, noted that intra-Jewish credit generally cost from 17–25 percent in sixteenth- and seventeenth-century Poznań. Marcus Breger, *Zur Handelsgeschichte der Juden in Polen während des 17.Jahrhunderts* (Berlin: R. Mass, 1932), pp. 31–33, maintained that short term (up to three weeks) interest rates ranged from 33.3 percent in 1639 to 50 percent in 1646.

There were also those who brought financial ruin upon themselves by borrowing money for personal needs such as paying for a daughter's dowry.[15] Others in dire need borrowed money rather than endure the shame of taking charity,[16] although in difficult economic times there was even less chance that such people would repay their loans. While the virulently anti-Jewish philosophy professor of the Jagiellonian University, Sebastyan Miczynski, in a work published in 1618, may have exaggerated the extent of such fiscal ruin among Jewish businessmen, there can be no doubt that Jewish financial failures rose sharply during this period and did not go unnoticed in the Polish community.[17]

Within the Jewish community the ramifications of the problem of personal bankruptcy were particularly acute. Losses not only consumed the pool of capital available for lending but for business ventures in general. If enough capital was drained from the market, the price of credit for all borrowers would invariably rise. The default of debtors also had a domino effect on other businessmen. Those who had sold merchandise to fellow Jews with a debt-for-merchandise agreement would have to absorb the losses, a perilous proposition for those living on the edge of solvency themselves.

Beyond the immediate economic crunch caused by default, there was the potential for an added economic burden on the community if debtors failed to repay loans to non-Jewish creditors. In 1618 a non-Jewish lender sought and received permission from the provincial ruler (*wojewoda*) to force the local Jewish community "to give him justice" after a delinquent Jewish borrower fled from his creditors and left town. When the non-Jew accused the Jewish community of hiding the debtor, the *wojewoda* ordered the leaders of the community to produce the recalcitrant party and demanded that they pay the outstanding debt, associated costs, and damages if they failed to do so before a set time.[18] More significantly, the ruler warned the Jewish community not to harbor thieves and unsavory types (*reyqim*) in their midst. The perception that the Jewish community allowed dishonest busi-

15. *PVAA*, no. 112 (1624).

16. Joseph ben Elijah, *Sefer rekeb Eliyyahu*, p. 12b.

17. Cited by Schiper in *Beyt Yisra'el be-Polin*, vol. 1, p. 180.

18. Jewish communities were often held liable for the debts of insolvent members even after a royal edict against this practice was issued in 1633. See Gershon Hundert, "Jews, Money and Society in the Seventeenth-Century Polish Commonwealth: The Case of Krakow," *Jewish Social Studies* 43.3–4 (Summer-Fall 1981): 268 and n. 68.

nessmen to continue to trade not only threatened to undermine the credibility of Jews in the marketplace but their physical wellbeing as well. As for a delinquent Jewish debtor, if he were caught by the non-Jewish authorities he would be thrown into prison. This, in turn, created an additional burden on the Jewish community since it almost invariably raised funds to ransom (bribe?) its members from Polish jails.[19]

Despite the community's concerns about insolvency, Jewish courts, at least in the time of Luria and Me'ir ben Gedaliah, did not routinely check the credit worthiness of individuals. Credit warnings could turn out to be self-fulfilling prophecies. A rumor that a debtor was experiencing financial difficulties, whether well founded or not, would likely cause all current creditors to press for their money and potential ones to refuse to extend any further credit to a reportedly struggling businessman. The result was likely to be permanent financial ruin for that individual. Thus creditors had to investigate debtors themselves.[20] Personal relationships and a reputation of reliability were crucial to obtaining credit.

Faced with the possibility of a debtor's default, many creditors had little choice but to renegotiate the terms of repayment.[21] Other understandably

19. Sirkes, *Responsa* (old), no. 44. The reformulated question is somewhat mangled. According to Sirkes it seems that the debtor would simply be held in prison. However, in at least one instance addressed to Sirkes, a Jewish debtor felt himself in mortal danger (*piquaḥ nefesh*) from his non-Jewish creditor (*Responsa* [old], no. 13). See too Bałaban, "Die Krakauer Judengemeinde- Ordnung," p. 328, in which the community committed itself to help non-Jewish creditors if a Jew defaulted in order that there be no ḥillul ha-shem (lit., "profanation of God's name"; here, likely a euphemism for damage to the Jewish community). Also see *PVAA*, no. 129 (1624). See too, Rapoport, *Responsa*, no. 9, authored by Heller, where the noble imprisoned a Jewish debtor but eventually released him with two bodyguards to shadow his every move. The community feared that if they knowingly allowed the debtor to flee they would be held responsible for the outstanding debt. Also see Joshua Höschel, *Responsa*, pt. 2, no. 97, where the community was loathe to become involved with an individual's debt to a non-Jew.

20. Me'ir ben Gedaliah, *Responsa*, no. 12, believed that it was impossible for the courts to check on debtors due to subterfuge on the part of debtors. It was also not the court's responsibility. Luria noted that the court could take action to protect creditors if it feared fraudulent conveyances on the part of the borrower (Luria, *YSS*, *Baba' Qamma'* 1.20).

21. Although Israel Treiman, "Majority Control in Compositions: Its Historical Origins and Development," *Virginia Law Review* 24.5 (March 1938): 510–11, noted that respites were so frequently granted in medieval Germany that they fell into disrepute, extension of payment was common in western Europe and was an important factor in the development of local retail trade (see Van der Wee, "Monetary, Credit and Banking Systems," p. 300). Jaffe, *Lebush 'ir Shushan* 128.1, observed that "in these regions" it was common for mer-

anxious creditors seized assets to maximize the return of their own capital without regard for the interests of other creditors.[22] Jewish commmunities felt obliged to protect the interests of all creditors and, beginning in 1595 with the statutes of the Cracow community[23] and followed by the ordinances of local and national councils in Poland, Lithuania, and later Moravia, instituted measures to insure that all creditors threatened by insolvent debtors were treated equally.[24]

The problem of insolvency was not new to Jewish life, although the Talmud had never recognized the continuation of a lien against someone who confronted the court and declared "I do not have any assets." According to talmudic law, the debtor who made such a claim could simply walk away. It was left to the Babylonian rabbis of the seventh century to begin to develop solutions to this problem.[25] Their decisions, together with those of succeeding generations, were codified in Jewish legal texts during the Middle Ages. Such measures, however, were not severe enough to meet the needs of businessmen in sixteenth- and seventeenth-century Poland who wanted to insure the return of their funds.[26] This concern was so strong that eastern Eu-

---

chants, particularly non-Jewish merchants, to grant long extensions and to make "compromise after compromise" with fellow businessmen who failed to repay creditors on time. According to Jaffe, non-Jewish suppliers were interested in the return of their principal and were often willing to forgo accumulated interest charges. Jewish suppliers, Jaffe notes, were generally of a different entrepreneurial temperament and granted shorter extensions while expecting to receive payment of both principal and interest in full. Also see Me'ir ben Gedaliah, *Responsa,* no. 47, an example of restructuring of payments between Jews.

22. Me'ir ben Gedaliah, *Responsa,* no. 11; Slonik, *Responsa,* no. 32. In most countries customs of individual remedies for satisfying creditors existed well before statutes were enacted (see Arnold Ross, ed., *European Bankruptcy Laws,* [Chicago?: Section of International Law, American Bar Association, 1974], pp. 12, 20).

23. Needless to say, the fact that the Cracow ordinances concerning insolvency are the earliest extant documents does not mean that they were the first. They were also not the last attempt of the Cracow community to stem this problem. See Wettstein, "Qadmoniyyot," p. 600, in which in 1604 the community added punishments and stringencies to their ordinances because the problem persisted.

24. *PH,* nos. 21–31, 33 (1623); 117 (1627); 148 (1628); 250 (1631). *TMM,* nos. 228–336 (1650).

25. Menachem Elon, *Ḥerut ha-peraṭ be-darkey gebiyyat ḥob ba-mishpaṭ ha-'ibri* (Jerusalem: Magnes, 1964), p. 40. Elon notes that Rabbi Hai Gaon (Babylonia; d. 1038) instituted a form of excommunication as a means of collecting outstanding debts but this severe method quickly vanished from Jewish jurisprudence (pp. 40–46).

26. Maimonides, *Code of Law,* Laws Concerning Creditor and Debtor, chap. 2, nos. 1–4; *Ṭur,* Ḥoshen mishpaṭ 97, 99.

ropean councils often unabashedly ignored the normative halakhah and instituted statutes that by 1624 openly admitted to violating the law.[27]

For example, in that year the Council of Four Lands concluded their ordinances regarding insolvent debtors by noting that:

> All the ordinances regarding insolvent debtors that the previous [leaders] enacted were for the benefit of the lender. And they made a fence and strengthened [their rules] and uprooted the law of the Torah, as for example, the rule [declaring that once a person is declared an insolvent debtor any assets that he used in a transaction in the last] ninety days [are declared] retroactively [to belong to creditors] or what was ordained [concerning a] woman's marriage contract and creditors, [that the woman] may not collect from movable property even if she collects after her husband's death, and other such matters, we have made this ordinance only for the benefit of creditors who live in our region where our ordinance has spread. However, regarding those who live in other regions we judge them on the basis of our Torah.[28]

The Polish Jewish community consciously and openly ignored the halakhah when dealing with cases of insolvency among its own members. What must be determined is whether Polish rabbis were willing to integrate such lay ordinances into their halakic thought.

Most of the instances in which Polish rabbis left written records of cases involving insolvency had little to do with the ordinances of the community and dealt instead with the legal fallout of bankruptcy in unrelated matters: What name should be written in the bill of divorce given by Joshua ben Moses, who fled from the Lvov region and changed his name because of

---

27. The best overall treatment of the ordinances regarding insolvency in Poland and Lithuania remains Dickstein's, "Taqqanot va'adey Polin," pp. 29–76, although it requires some updating in light of source material published after its composition.

28. *PVAA*, no. 138 (1624). Also see *PH*, p. 279, and *PVAA*, no. 169, calling on those in Lithuania to judge insolvent debtors according to the law "of our holy Torah." Regarding the intentionally limited reach of these ordinances see below, n. 48.

The retroactive voiding of sales made during a suspect period by a debtor who subsequently went bankrupt was an innovation of late thirteenth, early fourteenth-century Italian bankruptcy law to thwart fraudulent conveyances. See Louis Levinthal, "The Early History of Bankruptcy Law," *University of Pennsylvania Law Review* 66 (April 1918): 242. Similar laws protecting creditors against fraudulent conveyances were known in many places including Holland (sixteenth century), England (1571), Scotland (1621), and Lyons (1667). See Ross, ed., *European Bankruptcy Laws*, pp. 13–23.

"money matters?"[29] Can the testimony of a non-Jew be used to allow the wife of David of Gloger, a Jew who fled Poland because of his debts, to remarry?[30] These records attest to the broad ramifications of insolvency in the Jewish community, but shed little light on the attitude of rabbinic leaders to the ordinances.[31]

An exception is a case involving Joel Sirkes, who was the chief rabbi of Cracow—where ordinances regarding bankruptcy dated from at least 1595—when the Council promulgated its ordinances in 1624. In a responsum written sometime after 1650, Sirkes's student, Menahem Mendel Krochmal, reflected on a discussion that he had with his teacher in Cracow about one of the ordinances, probably in the mid to late 1620s.[32] Sirkes was faced with the case of a Jewish merchant from Cracow who sold goods to a Jew from Łęczyca on a debt-for-merchandise basis. Before the debt was due, the trader from Łęczyca became insolvent. To protect his interests, the Cracow merchant, Hirsch Pas, took a letter from Sirkes to the leaders of the community in Łęczyca asserting that Pas had prior rights to the merchandise that he had sold the trader and to whatever the insolvent merchant had received as barter for it. Perplexed, Krochmal asked his teacher whether this was not a violation of the halakhah stipulating that all creditors have equal liens on the assets of an insolvent debtor. Krochmal argued that the only reason that Pas maintained any rights to the original merchandise was because of an ordinance declaring that a creditor may repossess merchandise that he sold to a debtor if it was still in the debtor's hands.[33] The ordinance

29. See Krochmal, *Responsa*, no. 108, dated 1656.

30. Sirkes, *Responsa* (old), no. 94. Elsewhere, in a passing comment, Sirkes noted that people commonly took a different non-Hebrew name when they fled because of money so that they would not be easily found (*Responsa* [old], no. 95). Needless to say, the idea was not new (see, for example, Asher ben Yehi'el, B.T., *Giṭṭin* 34b).

31. See Me'ir ben Gedaliah, *Responsa*, no. 26, who piqued the curious's interest by suggesting that he might have to determine whether a particular statute concerning who has preceding liens on the assets of an estate was correct and just. Ultimately though, he decided that such an investigation was not necessary to forward his particular halakhic argument.

32. See *TMM*, p. 76, n. 4. The discussion seems to have taken place before the publication of Sirkes's *Bayit ḥadash* in the 1630s. Krochmal's responsum was addressed to his son-in-law, Rabbi Gershon Ashkenazi.

33. Cf. *PVAA*, no. 137. According to Roman law, ownership of goods sold on credit transferred to the buyer upon delivery. The only way for the seller to retain title was to make an express condition that ownership not pass to the buyer until he pay in full. These rules appear to have been accepted in all western European countries except England at least until the sixteenth century. By the end of the sixteenth century, French law gave an unpaid seller a

made no provisions for the repossession of any goods other than the very items that the debtor received from the creditor.[34]

Krochmal recorded what he remembered as Sirkes's reply.

> I do not know of the ordinance but replied according to the law because according to the law he should take the available merchandise before other creditors because this debt is a result of this merchandise. And the scholars and leaders of the generation made such an ordinance regarding this for naught, because this is the law and since, based on the law, he has a right to the merchandise itself when it is available, according to the law, he has the same right on what [goods the debtor acquires] with it.[35]

Since Sirkes believed that vendors had the right to seize merchandise sold on credit that remained in the buyer's possession, or any goods received by the buyer in exchange for the merchandise, the ordinance was redundant.

Krochmal debated the issue with Sirkes but remained unconvinced. Krochmal maintained that the supplier in a debt-for-merchandise agreement, as in any loan, did not expect to receive payment from the actual goods that he supplied. Assets given in loans were supposed to be used by the borrower and repayment was expected from other assets. According to Krochmal, once the original transfer between lender and borrower took place, the creditor lost title to the goods that he supplied and only had a claim against the debtor. Sirkes's sources, Krochmal argued, only equated the halakhic status of what was exchanged for merchandise with the merchandise itself; they did not extend that concept to granting a creditor a preceding lien on merchandise that he had given to a now insolvent mer-

---

preferential right to be paid from the proceeds of sale of the goods if the court ordered their resale while they were still in the buyer's hands (Francis de Zulueta, *The Roman Law of Sale* [Oxford: Clarendon Press, 1945], pp. 52–53; Robert Pennington, "Retention of Title to the Sale of Goods under European Law," *International and Comparative Law Quarterly* 27 [1978]: 277–78). Polish law on the issue remains unclear.

34. Krochmal, *Responsa*, no. 117. Also see *TMM*, no. 229 (1650). It remains uncertain whether the ordinance granted the vendor rights beyond the goods themselves. If, for example, the merchandise depreciated in the hands of the buyer did the creditor have the right to collect his loss or did he have to be satisfied with the recovery of his asset? The later possibility would essentially mean that the ordinance called for an annulment of the original sale. See Zulueta, *The Roman Law of Sale*, p. 57.

35. Sirkes repeated his position in his *Bayit ḥadash,* Ḥoshen mishpaṭ 96, n. 23. Also see 108.7, 280.1.

chant. Only the communal ordinance granted the supplier such rights. More importantly, Krochmal was not willing to expand the reach of the ordinance by applying the halakhic concept that what is exchanged for merchandise is like the original merchandise itself. So although Krochmal recognized the authority of the statute, he argued that it must be taken literally. Even an accepted halakhic rule could not be used to broaden a communal ordinance.

Sirkes's professed ignorance of the statute remains shocking. It is almost inconceivable that the greatest halakhic authority of Polish Jewry during the 1620s in the major Jewish center of the age did not know about an ordinance of the Council of Four Lands in a realm of law that had daily applications. Moreover, those in power were seemingly ignorant of the halakhah. If Sirkes was correct and the creditor had halakhic rights to the actual goods, there was no need for such an ordinance.[36] If the halakhah was being enforced in contemporary Poland, or even if it was simply known, would it not have been sufficient to invoke the halakhah itself instead of promulgating a statute?

Although Sirkes claimed to have been unaware of the ordinance allowing creditors to seize available property, he was well aware of the ordinance allowing creditors to imprison insolvent debtors even if they had nothing with which to repay their debts. Drafters of this ordinance had little halakhic material upon which to rely. Isserles had already noted in his commentary to Jacob ben Asher's *Ṭur* and in his glosses to Karo's *Shulḥan 'aruk* that creditors could only force the hand of a debtor who had assets but refused to pay; they had no right to imprison or punish an impoverished debtor.[37] Luria too accepted the view that a poor debtor could not be imprisoned no matter what sort of condition was put in the contract.[38] Jaffe

36. Significantly, Krochmal did not cite precedent to support his view; he was forced to reinterpret sources that prima facie supported Sirkes's position.

37. Isserles, *Darkey Mosheh ha-shalem*, Ḥoshen mishpaṭ 97, p. 160; *Shulḥan 'aruk*, Ḥoshen mishpaṭ 97.15, 30.

38. Luria, *YSS*, *Baba' Qamma'* 8.65. However, Luria noted both here and in his commentary to the *Tur* (Ḥoshen mishpaṭ 97) that Isaac ben Sheshet Perfet allowed the imprisonment of an impoverished debtor if, at the time that he incurred the debt, he had sworn to imprison himself if he failed to pay his creditors, a clause that would invariably increase his credibility with lenders. Isserles incorporated Perfet's opinion into his code (*Shulḥan 'aruk*, Ḥoshen mishpaṭ 97.15). Since the borrower had taken an oath, the halakhah demanded that it be fulfilled.

and Falk ruled similarly.[39] Yet the communities ignored rabbinic precedent—as well as the probability that local communities would have to support the dependents of an imprisoned debtor and even the debtor should he succeed in gaining his freedom.[40] In 1624 the communities agreed that

> If [his assets are] insufficient [to meet his debts, the debtor] will be excommunicated from fair to fair and he will be imprisoned for at least thirty days, and he will not be counted in any matter of holiness (e.g., a quorum in the synagogue), and if he has any [communal] appointment they must remove him until he settles with his creditors . . . And the creditors have the choice whether to imprison him first or excommunicate him first. And all this [is regarding] someone who lost [the money] in the course of business but someone who squandered it and [used it] for his son or daughter's dowry, he is like a thief and should be imprisoned a full year and be disqualified from giving testimony . . .[41]

Although the halakhah prohibited borrowing money for frivolous purposes and warned the borrower not to leave the lender with nothing to collect, it did not sanction prison if the debtor failed to repay the loan.[42] Conversely, a lender was well advised to have nothing to do with a borrower whom he suspected would be unable to repay him because each time the lender pressed the borrower for money he would violate the command of Exodus 22.24, "If you will lend money to any of my people that is poor

---

39. Jaffe, *Lebush 'ir Shushan* 97.15; Falk, *Sefer me'irat 'eynayim* 107, n. 10.

40. See Peter Coleman, *Debtors and Creditors in America* (Madison: State Historical Society of Wisconsin, 1974), p. 250, who noted that even when they were released from prison, those living on the edge of solvency may never have recovered their financial stability and were likely to become public wards.

41. *PVAA*, no. 112. Forcing a debtor who "squandered" his loan to sit in prison for an entire year—where he could hardly work to repay his debt—could only have been a stiff penalty meant to discourage and punish those whose behavior was not in the best interest of merchant lenders. A debtor who tried to make a deal with his creditors could be imprisoned for a year (see *PVAA*, no. 134).

42. Debtor prison was not an innovation of Polish Jewry but was used as early as the fourteenth century in Ashkenaz, although Polish Jewry appears to have been unique in using prison as a punishment for the debtor and not simply as a means of forcing payment of the debt. On the use of prison in Jewish law in general, see Menachem Elon, "Ha-ma'asar ba-mishpaṭ ha-'ibri," in *Sefer yobel le-Pinḥas Rosen*, Haim Cohen, ed., (Jerusalem: Mif'al ha-shikpul, 1962), pp. 171–201. Regarding its use in collecting debts, see Elon, *Ḥerut ha-peraṭ*, pp. 133, 136–37, 176.

among you, you must not be like a collector to him . . . " Rashi, in his commentary to the Pentateuch, explained this to mean that one may not use force to exact payment from a debtor who does not have money. Moreover, God had named Himself protector of those who were oppressed by their creditors without differentiating whether they became poor through business losses or by paying for their children's weddings. ". . .And if he will cry to Me," the Pentateuch concludes, "I will hear because I am merciful" (Exodus 22.26). The Bible makes no distinction as to how a debtor lost the money. Jewish law understood this to mean that no matter how he lost it, a borrower who honestly cannot repay his debt cannot be coerced.

Nor can it be argued that the Council was influenced by practices in the Polish community. The last mention of debtor's prison in Polish sources occurred in 1454, and the institution is thought to have vanished from Polish society by the mid-sixteenth century.[43] Indeed, Polish law was rather lenient with delinquent debtors, calling them to court for warnings a number of times before actually liquidating their assets.[44] It seems that the Jewish community, involved in trade that was so dependent on credit, could hardly gamble with its most important resource, namely cash. The Council of Four Lands did whatever it felt was necessary to protect the assets of lenders and the stability of an important sector of the "Jewish economy," even if it involved the violation of a biblical prohibition.

Sirkes was left to comment rather meekly,

> . . . therefore that they imprison even someone who has nothing with which to pay based upon the ordinances of the communities. They have nothing to rely upon and so wrote Rabbi Isaac ben Sheshet Perfet that it is prohibited to take the debtor bodily and [the community] does not have the power to make this ordinance [and] to violate the prohibition.[45]

---

43. Przemysław Dąbkowski, "Załoga w prawie polskiem średniowiecznem," *Archiwum Naukowe* sect. 1, vol. 2.4 (1905): 477. Dąbkowski pointed out that the use of debtor's prison did, however, continue in other eastern Europe regions, among them Moravia, well into the seventeenth century (pp. 476–77).

44. Bartłomiej Groicki, *Tytuły prawa majdeburskiego* (Warsaw: Wydawnicza Prawnicze, 1954), pp. 108–11.

45. Sirkes, *Bayit ḥadash,* Ḥoshen mishpaṭ 97, n. 28; Isaac ben Sheshet Perfet, *She'elot u-teshubot ha-Ribash* (Jerusalem: n.p., 1968), no. 484, who opposed imprisoning debtors in general but attempted to find support for the imprisonment of debtors with assets who refused to pay.

However, unlike Perfet, a fourteenth-century Spanish and North African rabbi who faced a similar problem, there is no evidence that Sirkes ever confronted the Jewish community regarding the practice.[46] He noted the inappropriateness of their actions, but left no record that he or any other rabbi fought for the rights of debtors or challenged communal leaders about an ordinance that violated the law.[47]

While living in Moravia, Menahem Krochmal was confronted with a case of a debtor who had both local and distant creditors but who had insufficient assets to meet all their claims. Fearing that if they waited they would not receive a complete return of their assets, most of the local creditors attempted to collect whatever they could from the debtor immediately, before the distant creditors could even find out about the situation. Although an ordinance of the Moravian community protected the rights of all creditors, local lenders claimed that Moravian ordinances did not apply to those who lived elsewhere.[48] Naturally, other creditors saw this as an injustice and favored an equitable distribution of assets among all creditors.

In responding, Krochmal approached the case with purely halakhic considerations. He cited his teacher, Sirkes, who ruled that if creditors with equal liens were not present when a debtor's assets were divided, the court should hold their portion until their return. Krochmal agreed that a creditor should not suffer a loss simply due to his absence.[49] Although he dis-

---

46. Perfet noted that he wanted to annul the practice of imprisoning insolvent debtors that he claims was the rule in the Kingdom of Aragon. Community leaders, however, told him that if he did, people would stop lending money. Rabbis in Poland were not alone in facing this problem. The issue arose in Salonika, North Africa, Italy, and Moravia. Yet in these areas one could not imprison a debtor who truly had nothing with which to pay his debt. See Elon, *Ḥerut ha-perat*, pp. 152–209.

47. Elon notes that Heller, in his supercommentary to Asher ben Yehi'el's halakhic commentary on *Baba' Meẓi'a'* (chap. 5, no. 38, n. 2), called for the establishment of "ahalakhic" ordinances such as imprisoning debtors to insure that creditors would continue to lend money. However, whether Heller would have subjected even destitute debtors to prison remains unclear. Heller's commentary, *Pilpula' ḥarifta'*, was published in 1619 (Prague) well before his arrival in Poland in 1631.

48. Krochmal, *Responsa*, no. 118; *TMM*, no. 229 (1650). It was common for authorities to protect the interests of local creditors before those of foreigners just as the Council of Four Lands had done in 1624 (*PVAA*, no. 138). Regarding the limited reach of such statutes see Kurt H. Nadelmann, "Bankruptcy Treaties," *University of Pennsylvania Law Review* 93 (September 1944): 58–59. Nadelmann adds that the tendency to give priority to domestic creditors over foreigners remained very strong in most of Europe until the late seventeenth and into the eighteenth centuries (p. 61).

49. Sirkes, *Bayit ḥadash*, Ḥoshen mishpaṭ 104.2. Also see 99.9.

puted one of Sirkes's proof texts, he offered others to support this view. In so doing Krochmal rejected the validity of the ordinance in the face of the halakhah without ever searching to uncover sources about the nature and limits of communal authority.

His disregard for the ordinances in this case notwithstanding, Krochmal had a particular stake in protecting the statutes of the Moravian communities. Unlike in Poland, disputes over the meaning of communal laws in the Moravian Jewish community were routinely brought to the chief rabbi for interpretation.[50] As chief rabbi, Krochmal played a role in the legislative process and was given the opportunity to reinterpret and expand ordinances or, perhaps, even reject them. A second case demonstrates that he used halakhic rules and rationales in doing so.

In Moravia there was an ordinance detailing how to divide the assets of a debtor who died leaving insufficient assets to pay both his creditors and the *ketubbah* (marriage contract) of his surviving wife. Like almost all the ordinances that dealt with insolvency, this statute was intended to protect creditors from fraud and keep credit flowing in the market even in difficult times. According to the legislation, if a debtor owned real property at the time of his marriage, then on the basis of the marriage contract, a wife had the right to collect up to four hundred gold "rhinish" if she had been a maiden at the time of her marriage, and two hundred if she had been a widow or divorcee—no matter what amount had been stipulated in the marriage contract. She also had rights to all clothing that she brought into the marriage. Creditors would divide the remaining assets. If the debtor had no land at the time of the marriage, the statute decreed that his wife could collect up to one hundred "rhinish" plus her clothing. The remaining assets would be divided among his creditors.[51]

It did not take long for people to find ways to circumvent these regulations. Attempting to protect his prospective wife, an individual could obligate himself to his bride before his marriage for one thousand golds, payable a moment before his death. Then according to the language of the debt agreement, if he were to die with insufficient assets to meet his outstanding obligations, his wife, as a creditor, would have a preceding lien on all assets, since chronologically her debt preceded those of others. She would collect

---

50. Polish rabbis could also be asked to settle intercommunal disputes between the Polish and Lithuanian councils, as they were in 1644 (*PH*, pp. 279–80).

51. *TMM*, no. 235 (1650), Krochmal, *Responsa*, no. 109. The responsum is not dated.

her entire debt and likely exhaust all assets in the estate before other creditors received anything. The couple could thus circumvent an ordinance that had existed in the region "since days of old" with, halakhicly speaking, a perfectly valid contract.

In the case at hand, Krochmal was asked whether such a contract was valid since the ordinance only made rules concerning marriage contracts or whether the intent of the ordinance should be followed to protect creditors and encourage continued lending.

Since the questioner did not specify whether the wife was given both a marriage contract and a debt instrument or just the latter, Krochmal explored both possibilities. If the note involved was not connected to a marriage contract Krochmal sided with the creditors. He reasoned that if the debt agreement was sanctioned, everyone would use such contracts to circumvent the ordinance.[52] Krochmal's overriding concern, like the rationale behind the ordinance, was to protect creditors and keep credit available in the marketplace. The rabbis of the Talmud themselves had tried to expand the rights of creditors, in some instances even ignoring what they believed to be the law of the Torah, in the hope of "not closing the door in the face of lenders."[53] Yet there was no denying that the Moravian ordinance made no specific provisions for debt contracts. Krochmal had to expand the ordinance to apply equally to a note and to the marriage contract itself.

Instead of being guided by the language of the ordinance Krochmal followed its intent.

> Because the essence of the ordinance that they enacted . . . was not to close the door [in the face of lenders], since if she collects her marriage contract and any additional amounts and creditors find nothing from which to collect, they will stop lending. If so, what difference is there between a marriage contract and a debt contract? Even though only a marriage contract is mentioned in the ordinance, nevertheless a debt contract that she has in place of

---

52. Krochmal rejected the idea that merchants would be loathe to give their brides such contracts if it meant that they would unable to receive credit in the future. If some women received them, all women would demand them, and no groom would be able to refuse. Krochmal also suggested that brides would make the receipt of such contracts a condition for bringing a dowry into the marriage. Who could turn down the certainty of a dowry out of concern that creditors might turn him away in the future? Besides, Krochmal added, no one really planned on becoming a debtor (see B.T., *Baba' Batra'* 51a).

53. See B.T., *Sanhedrin* 31a-b; *Baba' Qamma'* 8a. Also see B.T., *Baba' Meẓi'a'* 68a and *Baba' Batra'* 176a.

> a marriage contract is included in the ordinance because if not, what did the scholars accomplish with their ordinance? . . .[54]

If, however, the husband gave his wife both a marriage contract and a note, Krochmal ruled that the note and the marriage contract were both valid and the couple had successfully dodged the ordinance. Krochmal knew that this was an unlikely scenario. Only "one in a thousand" people would assume a debt together with a marriage contract: such a combination would not only leave any heirs with nothing but, if the couple divorced, the ex-wife would still receive money if the ex-husband predeceased her.[55] Krochmal saw little danger to the credit market in declaring that such a situation the debt contract was not included in the local ordinance.

Confronted by those who tried to circumvent ordinances and thereby threaten the credit markets, Krochmal pushed to keep credit available. When there was little threat, as in the case of someone who held both a marriage contract and a debt note, he had little reason to concern himself.[56] Nevertheless, in both instances Krochmal used the language and method of the halakhah in ruling on a communal ordinance.

Although communal ordinances almost always benefited creditors, there was an exception in which the ordinances did more to protect the rights and dignity of a debtor who had not paid his debt than the halakhah did. This was when a debtor died. To trace briefly the halakhic background, Isserles ruled in *Shulḥan 'aruk,* Ḥoshen mishpaṭ 107.2,

> Rabbi Israel of Krems [fourteenth century] writes in the name of Isaac ben Moses of Vienna who wrote in the name of Jacob ben Me'ir Tam and our teacher, Rabbi Simhah [ben Samuel of Speyer]: if Reuben owed Simeon [money] and Reuben died, Simeon may prevent his burial until they [the

54. Krochmal anticipated a number of possible objections to his expansion of the ordinance. Among those that he deemed worthy of a preemptive response was the view of Asher ben Yehi'el that one may not add to an existing ordinance (Asher ben Yehi'el, *Responsa,* no. 54.1). Krochmal argued, however, that even Asher ben Yehi'el would admit that a new occurrence could be subsumed in the original ordinance if its rationale was in harmony with the original ordinance.

55. If the husband were to predecease his first wife, she would not only have received her marriage contract when she divorced but would now receive the one thousand golds upon his death. This would likely leave children without an inheritance and any family from a second marriage destitute.

56. The notion that halakhah adapts in areas under pressure and remains firm in other domains was developed by Soloveitchik, *Halakhah, kalkalah ve-dimmuy 'aẓmi,* pp. 77–78.

> beneficiaries] pay him . . . and if the creditor comes and takes all the deceased's money he is not obligated to bury him [i.e., to pay for the burial].[57]

A long Ashkenazic tradition supported a creditor's right to prevent the burial of a debtor when the deceased's estate owed him money. Joshua Falk tried to limit this tradition to instances where the creditor refused to believe the family's contention, supported by an oath, that the deceased left nothing.[58] Yet in 1624 the Council of Four Lands ruled that family members might bury the debtor themselves without concern for the creditor's halakhic rights.[59] Presumably contemporary notions of respect for the dead outweighed the Council's general desire to protect creditors.

The Jewish community was not unique with its ordinances regarding insolvency. European governments, too, had sought ways to protect creditors' rights. Early European bankruptcy laws were generally designed almost entirely as a remedy for creditors, not debtors.[60] Everyone knew that without credit no economy, be it local, regional, or inter-regional, could function. Everyone also knew that those with money would not lend it unless their risk was minimized.[61] Although the Talmud itself had established the idea

57. Elon suggested that the Jewish community accepted this means of exacting payment from the surrounding twelfth-century Christian community. See *Ḥerut ha-peraṭ*, pp. 238–40 and 241, n. 22, on the latter part of Isserles's gloss, which is not actually found in Isaac ben Moses of Vienna's work.

58. Falk, *Sefer me'irat 'eynayim* 107, n. 10. This and other opinions from the period are cited in Elon, *Ḥerut ha-peraṭ*, pp. 241–44.

59. *PVAA*, no. 128 (1624).

60. See Vern Countryman, "Bankruptcy and the Individual Debtor—and a Modest Proposal to Return to the Seventeenth Century," *Catholic University Law Review* 32.4 (Summer 1983): 810. Debtors were treated like outlaws. In fifteenth- century Spain they wore iron collars "one finger thick," in France a green cap, and in Leyden (1501) and Rotterdam (1519) an insolvent debtor had "to appear and stand before the town house in his undermost garments for three successive days at a spot three or four steps high, each day for one hour, to wit from half past eleven until half past twelve" (see Stefan Riesenfeld, "The Evolution of Modern Bankruptcy Law," *Minnesota Law Review* 31.5 [April 1947]: 441, n. 308b).

61. In 1283 Edward I of England agreed, under pressure from merchants anxious for some form of security, to allow creditors to "sue debtor's bodies" (i.e., imprison them) if they did not repay their debts. The statute specifically stated that the reason for this ruling was that without some legal recourse for collecting their debts, many merchants had refrained from coming into the realm (see Abraham Freedman, "Imprisonment for Debt," *Temple Law Quarterly* 2.4 [July 1928]: 335–36). In Holland the preamble to Charles V's Perpetual E d i c t

of protecting creditors' interests, businessmen's concepts of how to protect the rights of creditors and those allowed according to the halakhah were not always in accord.

In some areas Polish rabbis tried, like rabbis in medieval Franco-Germany before them, to harmonize the law with general business practices. But like all other religious authorities, they could not restructure the marketplace.[62] Even in staunchly Catholic countries such as sixteenth-century Spain and Portugal where churchmen had the support of the political leadership, canonists could not control contemporary business practices. With respect to usury, Catholic scholastics generally accepted the custom of the marketplace and tried to justify legally what had already become common practice.[63] Islamic lawyers too had to make legal accommodations with commercial custom.[64] Lacking practical alternatives, religious leaders could only respond to what was taking place. If they failed to accept contemporary custom they threatened to turn businessmen into sinners and would likely have rendered themselves irrelevant.[65]

Rabbis in medieval Ashkenaz, who were no more able than anyone else to reconfigure business procedures, faced a further complication. Failure to adapt the halakhah to contemporary commercial practice would have effectively sent Jews to Gentile courts, where justice was dispensed according to the law of the marketplace. This would have jeopardized Jewish communal autonomy.[66] Medieval Ashkenazic society, however, did not have Jewish lay

---

expressed the matter somewhat differently. "In order to guard and foster trade debtors must be compelled to pay their debts and must be prevented from evading their liabilities by flight" (quoted in Levinthal, "The Early History of Bankruptcy Law," p. 246). The edict dictated that anyone who left their home with the purpose of defrauding creditors was to be considered as a common thief and, if caught, was to be hanged.

62. On medieval Franco-Germany see Soloveitchik, *Halakhah, kalkalah ve-dimmuy 'aẓmi*, p. 79.

63. See John Noonan, Jr., *The Scholastic Analysis of Usury* (Cambridge, Mass.: Harvard University Press, 1957), pp. 312–13.

64. On several such problems in Muslim jurisprudence, see Abraham Udovitch, *Partnership and Profit in Medieval Islam* (Princeton: Princeton University Press, 1970), pp. 4–12.

65. See Noonan, *The Scholastic Analysis of Usury*, p. 314, regarding Martin Azplicueta (Navarus, 1493–1586), a canonist who advised the Kings of Portugal and Spain and later three Popes, who "would not 'damn the whole world' by too rigorous standards" with respect to usury.

66. Soloveitchik, "Pawnbroking," pp. 214–15. Like Rabbi Solomon Adret in thirteenth-century Spain and sixteenth-century Ottoman authorities, Polish rabbis were not about to

courts that were guided by communal ordinances and general business practices. In seventeenth-century Poland, those who wanted justice according to the rules of the marketplace could summon their adversary before such courts without having to turn to non-Jewish courts. Moreover, the disputes of businessmen, at least with regard to debtor/creditor relationships, would remain in the community since it was far more protective of creditors' rights than Polish law was.

Like rabbis in all periods, Polish rabbis had to address the needs of the marketplace in order to keep the halakhah relevant and maintain the integrity of Jewish communal life. As an essentially intra-Jewish matter, perhaps bankruptcy should have been guided solely by halakhic rules. However, unlike both their predecessors in medieval Ashkenaz and their contemporaries in the Ottoman Empire who suggested numerous halakhicly accceptable ways of meeting the needs of businessmen, Polish rabbis left no literary traces of attempts to develop a means of debt collection that would have met both the demands of creditors and the halakhah.[67] At least in this area, Polish rabbis seem not to have been halakhic activists.

Conclusion

By unabashedly admitting that it was ignoring the demands of the law in specific—but limited—areas, the very communal institutions that were to foster religious observance effectively removed rabbis from an area of contemporary Jewish communal and commercial life and accelerated the community's assimilation of nontraditional values. While halakhists all but unanimously opposed debtor's prison, by the early seventeenth century they had in effect acquiesced to the usurpation of rabbinic authority by communal leaders in this area of law.

Halakhists continued to be asked to adjudicate commercial matters

---

declare the decisions of non-Jewish courts to be the "law of the land" (*dina' de-malkuta' dina'*). Doing so would effectively have meant yielding all control in the area of commerce. See the discussion in Isaac ben Abraham of Poznań, *Responsa,* no. 85, p. 182.

67. While Ottoman rabbis rejected the maritime loans and *cambio* in contemporary use on halakhic grounds, they realized the necessity for Jewish merchants to obtain maritime insurance. They therefore suggested numerous other methods of trying to meet merchants' needs in a halakhicly acceptable fashion. See Stephen Passamaneck, *Insurance in Rabbinic Law* (Edinburgh: Edinburgh University Press, 1974), pp. 183–93.

based on the law, but in areas where the needs of the marketplace were most demanding—insolvency, membrany, and arendy—the community moved forward first and consulted the halakhic system later, if at all. The professed word of God did not have enough of a hold on businessmen to make them seek out and follow halakhic solutions when their livelihoods were at stake. Perhaps merchants presumed that there was some form of legal allowance for what was practiced, although few appear to have bothered to check. "Jewish businesses," like those of non-Jews, were run according to the demands of the marketplace. No merchant was anxious to be legally fettered.[68]

Laxity in religious life was nothing new. No society has ever been able to insure that each and every one of its members is never enticed by the charm of a worldly—but forbidden—pleasure. But the communal acceptance of religious neglect in an Ashkenazic society, even in a limited area, was unique. While communal institutions may have believed that they were acting well within their rights to regulate the marketplace, their disregard for rabbinic views such as with respect to debtor's prison fostered religious neglect in a few, but significant, areas of the law. In a society that ostensibly defined itself in religious terms, they effectively rendered certain aspects of the halakhah irrelevant to daily life.

Perhaps because it flirted with the very self-definition of sixteenth- and seventeenth-century Polish Jewry, nonobservance in ritual matters was neither instituted nor accepted by the community. Quite the contrary. It was fought by rabbis—with the assistance of community councils. In commerce, however, an area with little to lend itself to Jewish self-definition, "nonobservance" or at least the independent direction taken by the lay leadership became the basis of communal legislation and practice. While halakhah remained the focus of Jewish life, it had been nudged from a crucial area of that life.

Polish Jewry continued to be what Jacob Katz has termed a "traditional society" built on the values it had received from the past.[69] But in trying to meet its own very real needs, the community, at times consciously and at times unconsciously, transformed some of those values until they may have been unrecognizable to a Jew from an earlier age.

---

68. Even in medieval Franco-Germany, where laymen did not generally look for ways to be lenient in the law and some did not even avail themselves of precedents and/or decisions that supported lenience, Jewish businessmen did not always surrender an advantage in business even when pressed by the greatest halakhists of the age (see Soloveitchik, "Religious Law and Change," pp. 219–20, particularly n.27, as well as his "Pawnbroking," pp. 224–225).

69. Katz, *Masoret u-mashber*, p. 11.

Bibliography

Manuscripts

Archiwum Państwowe Miasta Krakowa i Województwa Krakowskiego (Public Archive of the City and Province of Cracow), Cracow. Varia 12 (1642–1647).

Archiwum Państwowe Miasta Lublina i Województwa Lubelskiego (Public Archive of the City and Province of Lublin), Lublin.

Księga miasta Lublina, Inscriptiones perpetuitatum civitatis Lublines 129 (1541–1561).

Księgi miasta Lublina 22 (1604).

Biblioteka Czartoryskich, Cracow.

Korzeniowski MS. no. 101.

The Bodleian Library, Oxford. (Examined on microfilm at the Jewish Theological Seminary.)

Neubauer MS. 842 (Opp. 76).

Jewish Theological Seminary Library, New York.

J.T.S. Rabbinics MS. 1542.

Primary Sources

Adarbi, Isaac. *She'elot u-teshubot dibrey ribot.* Sudilakov, 1833.

Asher ben Yehi'el. *She'elot u-teshubot le-Rabbeynu Asher ben Yeḥi'el.* Edited by Yitzhaq Yudolov. Jerusalem: Machon Yerushalayim, 1994.

Ashkenazi, Abraham. *Sam ḥayyim.* Prague, 1590.

Ashkenazi, Eliezer. *Dameseq Eli'ezer.* 2 vols. Lublin, 1646.

_____. *Ma'asey Miẓrayim.* Venice, 1583.

Babylonian Talmud. 20 vols. 1880–1886; Reprint, Jerusalem: Peninim, 1971.

Bałaban, Majer. "Die Krakauer Judengemeinde-Ordnung von 1595 und ihre Nachtrage." *Jahrbuch der Jüdish-Literarischen Gesellschaft* 10 (1912):296–360, 11 (1916): 88–114.

Berechiah Berak ben Isaac Eiziq. *Zera' berak.* 2 vols. Cracow, 1646; Amsterdam, 1662.

Berger, Avigdor. "Teshubot Rabbi Manoaḥ Ha'ndel ba'al *Ḥokmat Manoaḥ.*" In *Sefer ha-zikkaron le-maran Rabbi Ya'aqob Beẓal'el Zolṭey.* Edited by Joseph Buksbaum. Jerusalem: Moriah, 1987, pp. 331–49.

Bersohn, Mathias. *Dyplomataryusz dotyczący Żydów w dawney Polsce na źródłach archiwalnych osnuty (1388–1782).* Warsaw: Edward Nicz, 1910.

Brann, M. "Additions a l'autobiographie de Lipman Heller." *Revue des études juives* 21 (1890): 270–77.

Colon, Joseph. *She'elot u-teshubot ha-Mahariq.* Venice, 1519.

David ben Judah. *Sefer migdal David.* Prague, 1616.

David ben Menasseh ha-Darshan. *Shir ha-ma'alot le-David.* Cracow, 1571.

David ben Samuel ha-Levi. *Ṭurey zahab.* Lublin, 1646.

Delmedigo, Joseph Solomon. *Sefer eylam.* Odessa, 1864–1867.

_____. *Sefer ma'ayan gannim.* Odessa, 1865.

Edels, Samuel. *Ḥiddushey aggadot.* Lublin-Cracow, 1631–1632.

_____. *Ḥiddushey halakot.* Lublin, 1612–1621.

Eleazar ben Judah of Worms. *Sefer ha-roqeaḥ ha-gadol.* Jerusalem: Ozar ha-poseqim, 1967.

Eliezer ben Nathan. *Sefer Ra'aban.* 1926; Reprint, Jerusalem: n.p., 1975.

Falk, Joshua. *Derishah u-perishah (Eben ha-'ezer).* Lublin, 1638.

_____. *Qunṭeres me-ha-Sema'.* Żółkiew, 1833.

_____. *Sefer me'irat 'eynayim.* Prague, 1606.

Gombiner, Jacob. *Sefer shalom bayit.* Edited by I. Herskovitz. Brooklyn, N.Y.: n.p., 1988.

Groicki, Bartłomiej. *Porządek sądów y spraw prawa mieyskich prawa maydeburskeo w Koronie Polskiey.* Warsaw: Wydawnicza Prawnicze, 1953.

_____. *Tytuły prawa majdeburskiego.* Warsaw: Wydawnicza Prawnicze, 1954.

Hanover, Nathan. *Abyss of Despair (Yeven Metzulah).* Translated from the Hebrew by Abraham J. Mesch. New York: Bloch, 1950.

Hayyim ben Bezalel. *Sefer ha-ḥayyim.* Cracow, 1593.

_____. *Vikkuaḥ mayyim ḥayyim.* Amsterdam, 1712.

Horowitz, Abraham. *Yesh noḥalim.* Amsterdam, 1701.

Ishbili, Yom Tob ben Abraham. *Ḥiddushey ha-Riyṭba', maseket qiddushin.* Edited by Abraham Dinin. Jerusalem: Mossad Harav Kook, 1985.

Isaac ben Abraham of Poznań. *She'elot u-teshubot Rabbeynu Yiẓḥaq me-Pozna'.* Edited by Ya'aqob Aharonfeld et al. Jerusalem: Machon Yerushalayim, 1982.

Isaac ben Samuel ha-Levi. *She'elot u-teshubot R. Yiẓḥaq ha-Levi.* Neuwied, 1736.

Isserlein, Israel. *Sefer terumat ha-deshen.* 1882; Reprint, Bene Beraq, Israel: n.p., 1971.

Isserles, Moses. *Darkey Mosheh ha-shalem ḥoshen mishpaṭ.* 2 vols. Edited by H.S. Rosenthal. Jerusalem: Machon Yerushalayim, 1979–1983.

_____. *Darkey Mosheh me-Ṭur Yoreh de'ah.* Sulzbach, 1692.

_____. *Darkey Mosheh Oraḥ ḥayyim.* Fürth, 1760.

_____. *She'elot u-teshubot ha-Rama'.* Edited by Asher Siev. Jerusalem: Feldheim, 1971.

Jacob ben Asher. *Arba'ah ṭurim.* 7 vols. Jerusalem: Me'orot, 1976.

Jacob ben Me'ir Tam. *Sefer ha-yashar le-Rabbenu Tam, ḥeleq ha-she'elot ve-ha-teshubot.* Edited by E. Margoliot and S. Rosenthal. 1898; Reprint, Jerusalem: n.p., 1965.

Jaffe, Mordecai. *Lebush 'ir Shushan.* Cracow, 1598.

_____. *Sefer ha-ḥur.* Lublin, 1590.

Jerusalem Talmud. 1523–1524; Reprint, n.p., n.d.

Joseph ben Elijah. *Sefer rekeb Eliyyahu.* Cracow, 1638.

_____. *Sefer yesod Yosef.* Cracow, 1638

Joshua Höschel ben Joseph. *She'elot u-teshubot peney Yehoshu'a.* 2 vols. Amsterdam, 1715–Lvov, 1860.

Judah ben Samuel he-hasid. *Sefer ḥasidim.* Edited by Jehuda Wistinetzki. With an Introduction by J. Freimann. Frankfurt: Wahrmann, 1924.

_____. *Sefer ḥasidim.* Edited by Reuben Margoliot. Jerusalem: Mossad Harav Kook, 1957.

Judah Leb ben Enoch Zundel. *She'elot u-teshubot ḥinuk beyt Yehuda'.* Frankfurt, 1708.

Kahana, Natan. *Sefer she'elot u-teshubot dibrey renanah.* Edited by I. Herskovitz. Brooklyn, N.Y.: n.p., 1984.

Katzenellenbogen, Me'ir. *She'elot u-teshubot Maharam Paduv'ah.* Venice, 1553.

Katz, Joseph. *She'elot u-teshubot she'erit Yosef.* Edited by Asher Siev. New York: Yeshiva University Press, 1984.

Kayyara, Simeon. *Halakot gedolot.* Vienna, 1810.

Krochmal, Menahem Mendel. *She'elot u-teshubot ẓemaḥ ẓedeq.* Amsterdam, 1675.

Lewin, Louis. *Die Landessynode der grosspolnischen Judenschaft.* Frankfurt: J. Kauffmann, 1926.

_____. *Neue Materialien zur Geschichte der Vierländersynode.* 2 vols. Frankfurt: J. Kauffmann, 1905–1906.

Luria, Solomon. *Ḥiddushey u-bi'urey Maharshal 'al ha-Ṭur.* Jerusalem: Me'orot, 1976.

_____. *She'elot u-teshubot ha-Maharshal.* Lublin, 1574.

_____. *Yam shel Shelomoh (Baba' Qamma').* Prague, 1616–1618.

_____. *Yam shel Shelomoh (Beyẓah).* Lublin, 1636.

_____. *Yam shel Shelomoh (Giṭṭin).* Berlin, 1761.

_____. *Yam shel Shelomoh (Ḥullin).* Cracow, 1633–1635.

_____. *Yam shel Shelomoh (Ketubbot).* Warsaw, 1850.

_____. *Yam shel Shelomoh (Qiddushin).* Berlin, 1766.

_____. *Yam shel Shelomoh (Yebamot).* Altona, 1740.

Maimonides, Moses. *Mishneh Torah.* 6 vols. Jerusalem: Pe'er, 1964–1965.

Margolis, Jacob. *Seder ha-geṭ.* Edited by Yitzchok Satz. Jerusalem: Machon Yerushalayim, 1983.

Medina, Samuel de. *She'elot u-teshubot Maharshdam,* 1862; Reprint, n.p., n.d.

Me'ir ben Baruch. *She'elot u-teshubot ha-Maharam me-Roṭenburg.* Edited by M. Bloch, 1895; reprint, Tel Aviv, n.p., 1969.

Me'ir ben Gedaliah. *She'elot u-teshubot Me'ir me-Lublin.* Venice, 1618.

Meth, Moses. *Sefer mateh Mosheh.* Jerusalem: Ozar ha-poseqim, 1978.

Mintz, Moses. *She'elot u-teshubot rabbenu Mosheh Minẓ.* Edited by Yonatan Domb. 2 vols. Jerusalem: Machon Yerushalayim, 1991.

Molin, Jacob. *She'elot u-teshubot ha-Maharil.* Edited by Yitzchok Satz. Jerusalem: Machon Yerushalayim, 1979.

_____. *Shu"t Maharil ha-ḥadashot.* Edited by Yitzchok Satz. Jerusalem: Machon Yerushalayim, 1977.

Mordecai ben Hillel ha-Kohen. *Sefer Morddekay.* 1880–1886; Reprint, Jerusalem: Peninim, 1971.

Moses ben Jacob of Coucy. *Sefer miẓvot gadol.* 2 vols. Jerusalem: S. Monson, 1961.

Perfet, Isaac ben Sheshet. *She'elot u-teshubot ha-Ribash.* Jerusalem: n.p., 1968.

Pinqas ha-kesherim shel qehillat Pozna' (1621–1835). Edited by Dov Avron. Jerusalem: Mekize Nirdamim, 1967.

Pinqas ha-medinah o pinqas va'ad ha-qehillot ha-ro'shiyyot be-medinat Liṭa'. Edited by Simon Dubnow. Berlin: Ajanoth, 1925.

Pinqas va'ad arba' araẓot. Edited by Israel Halperin. Jerusalem: Mossad Bialik, 1945.

Pinqas va'ad arba' araẓot. Edited by Israel Halperin. Revised by Israel Bartal. With an Introduction by Shmuel Ettinger. Volume 1. Jerusalem: Mossad Bialik, 1990.

Rapoport, Abraham. *She'elot u-teshubot eytan ha-ezrahi.* Ostrow, 1796.

Rössler, Emil Franz. *Die Stadtrechte von Brünn aus dem XIII und XIV Jahrhundert.* Prague, 1852.

Samuel ben David ha-Levi. *Naḥalat shib'ah.* Amsterdam, 1667.

Shabbetay ben Me'ir ha-Kohen. *Sefer geburat anashim.* Dessau, 1697.

_____. *Siftey kohen.* Cracow, 1646–1647; Amsterdam, 1763.

She'elot u-teshubot ha-ge'onim batra'ey. Edited by Löb ben Samuel Zebi Hirsch. Turka, 1763.

She'elot u-teshubot harrey qedem. Edited by I. Herskovitz. Brooklyn, N.Y.: n.p., 1988.

Shulḥan 'aruk. 10 vols. Jerusalem: Tal-Man, 1977.

Sirkes, Joel. *Bayit ḥadash.* Cracow, 1631–1640.

_____. *She'elot u-teshubot ha-bayit ḥadash ha-ḥadashot.* Koretz, 1785.

_____. *She'elot u-teshubot ha-bayit ḥadash.* Frankfurt, 1697. (Two editions published in the same place and same year.)

Slonik, Benjamin Aaron. *She'elot u-teshubot masa'at Benyamin.* Cracow, 1632.

Solomon ben Judah Leybush. *Sefer pisqey u-she'elot u-teshubot Maharash me-Lublin.* Edited by I. Herskovitz. Brooklyn, N.Y.: n.p., 1988.

Sonne, Isaiah. "Taqqanot shel isur Shabbat ve-yom ṭob." *Ḥoreb* 2 (Fall 1935): 237–46.

Taqqanot medinat Ma'hareyn. Edited by Israel Halpern. Jerusalem: Mekize Nirdamim, 1952.

Teshubot hakemey Ẓarfat ve-Lotir. Joel Müller, ed. 1881; Reprint, Jerusalem: n.p., 1967.

Teshubot Rabbenu Gershom me'or ha-golah. Edited by Shlomo Eidelberg. New York: Yeshiva University Press, 1955.

Ulanowski, Boleslaus. "Acta Capituli Plocensis ab anno 1514 ad anno 1577." *Archiwum Komisyi Historycznej* 10 (1916): 129–305.

Volumina Legum. 11 vols. 1859–1889; reprint, Warsaw: Wydawnictwa Artystyczne i Filmowe, 1980.

Weil, Jacob. *She'elot u-teshubot Mahar"i Vveyil.* Jerusalem: Tif'eret a-Torah, 1988.

Weinryb, Bernard. *Texts and Studies in the Communal History of Polish Jewry.* New York: American Academy for Jewish Research, 1950.

Wettstein, P.H. "Qadmoniyyot me-pinqesa'ot yeshanim." *Oẓar ha-sifrut* 4 (1892): 577–642.

Yudolov, Yitzhaq. "Teshubot Maharal me-Per'ag." In *Sefer ha-zikkaron le-maran Rabbi Ya'aqob Beẓal'el Zolṭey.* Edited by Joseph Buksbaum. Jerusalem: Moriah, 1987, pp. 264–96.

Secondary Literature

Adamczyk, Władysław. *Ceny w Lublinie od XVI do końca XVIII wieku.* Lvov: Instytut Popierania Polskiej Twórczośći Naukowej, 1935.

Adelman, Howard. "Rabbis and Reality: Public Activities of Jewish Women in Italy during the Renaissance and Catholic Restoration." *Jewish History* 5.1 (Spring 1991): 27–40.

Albeck, Shalom. "Hishtalshelutah shel ha'abarat ḥobot ba-Talmud." *Tarbiz* 26.3 (April 1957): 262–86.

_____. "Yaḥaso shel Rabbenu Tam le-ba'ayot zemano." *Zion* 19 (1954): 104–41.

Altbauer, Moshé. *Achievements and Tasks in the Field of Jewish-Slavic Language Contact Studies.* Los Angeles: n.p., 1972.

_____. *The Five Biblical Scrolls in a Sixteenth-Century Jewish Translation into Belorussian (Vilnius Codex 262).* Jerusalem: Israel Academy of Sciences and Humanities, 1992.

Assaf, Simhah. "Biṭṭulah shel ketubbat benin dikrin." *Ha-ẓofeh le-ḥokmat Yisra'el* 10 (1926): 18–30.

_____. "Le-she'elat ha-yerushah shel ha-bat." In *Festschrift zum siebzigsten Geburtstage von Jakob Freimann.* Berlin: Rabbinerseminar zu Berlin, 1936, pp. 8–13.

_____. *Meqorot le-toledot ha-ḥinuk be-Yisra'el.* 4 vols. Tel Aviv: Dvir, 1924–1947.

Bałaban, Majer. *Dzieje Żydów w Krakowie i na Kazimierzu (1304–1868).* 2 vols. 1912–1936; Reprint, Cracow: Krajowa Agencja Wydawnicza, 1985–1991.

_____. *Historia i literatura żydowska.* 3 vols. 1925; Reprint, Warsaw: Wydawnictwa Artystyczne i Filmowe, 1982.

_____. *Żydzi lwowscy na przełomie XVIgo i XVIIgo wieku.* 1906; Reprint, Cracow: Orbita, n.d.

Baer, Yitzhak. "Ha-yesodot ve-ha-hatḥalot shel irgun ha-qehillah ha-Yehudit be-yemey ha-beynayyim." *Zion* 15 (1950): 1–41.

Bailey, Stanley J. "Assignment of Debts in England from the Twelfth to the Twentieth Century." *The Law Quarterly Review* 47 (1931): 516–535; 48 (1932): 248–71, 547–82.

Bardach, Juliusz, Bogusław Lesnodorski, and Michał Pietrzak. *Historia państwa i prawa polskiego.* Warsaw: Państwowe Wydawnictwo Naukowe, 1987.

_____. "Gouvernants et gouvernés en Pologne au Moyen-Age et aux temps modernes." *Standen en Landen* 36 (1965): 255–85.

_____. *Historia państwa i prawa polski do roku 1795.* 2 vols. Warsaw: Państwowe Wydawnictwo Naukowe, 1957.

_____. "Le pouvoir monarchique en Pologne au Moyen Age." *Recueils de la société Jean Bodin pour l'histoire comparative des institutions* 21.2 (1969): 563–612.

Baron, Salo W. *A Social and Religious History of the Jews.* Second edition. Volume 16. New York: Columbia University Press, 1976.

Beinart, Haim. "'Ha-siman ha-yehudi' be-Sefarad ve-qiyyum 'ẓav ha-siman' be-yemey ha-melakim ha-qatoliyyim." In *Israel and the Nations Essays Presented in Honor of Shmuel Ettinger.* Edited by Shmuel Almog, et al. Jerusalem: Historical Society of Israel, 1987, pp. 29–41.

Ben Sasson, Haim Hillel. *Hagut ve-hanhagah.* Jerusalem: Mossad Bialik, 1959.

_____. "Taqqanot issurey Shabbat shel Polin u-mashma'utan ha-ḥebratit ve-ha-kalkalit." *Zion* 21 (1956): 183–206.

Berlin (Bar-Ilan), Meyer, and Shlomo Josef Zevin, eds. *Enẓiqloppedyah talmudit.* 22 volumes to date. Jerusalem: Talmudic Encyclopedia Institute, 1947– .

Bersohn, Mathias. *Tobiasz Kohn.* Cracow, 1872.

Beutel, Frederick K. "The Development of Negotiable Instruments in Early English Law." *Harvard Law Review* 51 (1937–1938): 813–45.

Beyt Yisra'el be-Polin. Edited by Israel Halperin. 2 vols. Jerusalem: Youth Department of the Zionist Organization, 1948.

Birnbaum, Henrik. "On Jewish Life and Anti-Jewish Sentiments in Medieval Russia." *Viator* 4 (1973): 225–55.

Blidstein, Gerald. "'Gadol kabod ha-beriyyot'—'iyyunim be-gilguleyha shel halakah." *Shenaton ha-mishpaṭ ha-'ibri* 9–10 (1982–1983): 127–85.

_____. "Individual and Community in the Middle Ages: Halakhic Theory." In *Kinship and Consent.* Edited by Daniel J. Elazar. Ramat Gan: Turtledove, 1981, pp. 215–56.

Bloch, Philipp. *Die General-Privilegien der polnischen Judenschaft.* Posen, 1892.

_____. "Der Mamran, der jüdisch-polnische Wechselbrief." In *Festschrift zum siebzigsten Geburtstage A. Berliner's.* Edited by A. Freimann and M. Hildesheimer. Frankfurt: J. Kauffmann, 1903, pp. 50–64.

Bogucka, Maria. "Polish Towns Between the Sixteenth and Eighteenth Centuries." In *A Republic of Nobles.* Edited and translated by J. K. Fedorowicz, Cambridge: Cambridge University Press, 1982, pp. 138–52.

_____. "The Monetary Crisis of the XVIIth Century and its Social and Psychological Consequences in Poland." *The Journal of European Economic History* 4, no. 1 (Spring 1975): 137–52.

_____. "The Towns of East-Central Europe." In *East-Central Europe in Transition.* Edited by Antoni Mączak, Henryk Samsonowicz, and Peter Burke. Cambridge: Cambridge University Press, 1985, pp. 97–108.

_____. "Zboże rosyjskie na rynku amsterdamskim w pierwszej połowie XVII wieku." *Przegląd Historyczny* 53.4 (1962): 611–26.

Bornstein, Leah. "Ha-hanhagah shel ha-qehillah ha-Yehudit be-mizraḥ ha-qarob me-shilhey ha-me'ah ha-16 ve-'ad sof ha-me'ah ha-18." Ph.D. diss., Bar-Ilan University, 1978.

Brann, Ross. *The Compunctious Poet: Cultural Ambiguity and Hebrew Poetry in Muslim Spain.* Baltimore: Johns Hopkins University Press, 1991.

Braudel, Fernand. *Civilization and Capitalism 15th–18th Century.* 3 vols. Translated and Revised by Siân Reynolds. New York: Harper and Row, 1981–1984.

Breger, Marcus. *Zur Handelsgeschichte der Juden in Polen während des 17.Jahrhunderts.* Berlin: R. Mass, 1932.

Bretholz, Bertold. *Geschichte der Juden in Mähren im Mittelalter.* Volume 1. Brünn: R.M. Rohrer, 1934.

Breuer, Mordecai. "Ma'amad ha-rabbanut be-hanhagatan shel qehillot Ashkenaz be-me'ah ha-16." *Zion* 41 (1976): 47–67.

______. *Rabbanut Ashkenaz be-yemey ha-beynayyim.* Jerusalem: Zalman Shazar Center, 1976.

Brundage, James. *Law, Sex, and Christian Society in Medieval Europe.* Chicago: University of Chicago Press, 1987.

Buber, Salomon. *Qiryah nisgabah.* Cracow: Ha-eshkol, 1903.

Büchler, Adolf. "Seqirah talmudit hisṭorit 'al ha'abarat naḥalah min ha-ben 'al yedey ha-ab." In *The Hebrew University, Jerusalem. Inauguration April 1, 1925.* Jerusalem: n.p., 1925, pp. 77–104.

Carlebach, Elisheva. "Rabbi Moses Hagiz: The Rabbinate and the Pursuit of Heresy, Late Seventeenth—Early Eighteenth Centuries." Ph.D. diss., Columbia University, 1986.

Christian, William A., Jr. *Local Religion in Sixteenth-Century Spain.* Princeton: Princeton University Press, 1981.

Cohen, Esther and Elliott Horowitz. "In Search of the Sacred: Jews, Christians, and Rituals of Marriage in the later Middle Ages." *Journal of Medieval and Renaissance Studies* 20.2 (Fall 1990): 225–249.

Coleman, Peter J. *Debtors and Creditors in America.* Madison: State Historical Society of Wisconsin, 1974.

Corran, H. S. *A History of Brewing.* Newton Abbot: David and Charles, 1975.

Coulson, N.J. *Succession in the Muslim Family.* Cambridge: Cambridge University Press, 1971.

Countryman, Vern. "Bankruptcy and the Individual Debtor—and a Modest Proposal to Return to the Seventeenth Century." *Catholic University Law Review* 32.4 (Summer 1983): 809–27.

Cygielman, S. A. "Shutfut polanit-yehudit be-yiẓur melaḥ mezuqaq be-shanim 1577–1580." *Zion* 51.2 (1986): 211–22.

______. *Yehudey Polin ve-Liṭa' 'ad shenat Ta"Ḥ (1648).* Jerusalem: Zalman Shazar Center, 1991.

Davies, Norman. *God's Playground A History of Poland.* 2 vols. New York: Columbia University Press, 1984.

Davis, Natalie Zemon. "Printing and the People." In *Society and Culture in Early Modern France.* Stanford: Stanford University Press, 1975.

Dąbkowski, Przemysław. *Prawo prywatne polskie.* 2 vols. Lvov: Nakładem Towarzystwa dla Popierania Nauki Polskiej, 1910–1911.

______. *Rękojemstwo w prawie polskiem średniowiecznem.* Towarzystwo Naukowe we Lwowie. Archiwum Naukowe. Section 1. Volume 3. Lvov: Towarzystwo do Popierania Nauki Polskiej, 1904

______. "Załoga w prawie polskiem średniowiecznem." *Archiwum Naukowe.* Section 1. Volume 2.4 (1905): 461–509.

Delumeau, Jean. *Sin and Fear: The Emergence of a Western Guilt Culture.* Translated by Eric Nicholson. New York: St. Martin's, 1990.

De Roover, Raymond. *L'evolution de la lettre de change XIVe-XVIIIe siècles.* Foreword by Fernand Braudel. Paris: A. Colin, 1953.

De Vries, Jan. *The Economy of Europe in an Age of Crisis, 1600–1750.* Cambridge: Cambridge University Press, 1976.

Dickstein, Paltiel. "Taqqanot va'adey Polin ve-Liṭa' 'al ha-borḥim." *Ha-mishpaṭ ha-'ibri* 1.1 (1918): 29–76.

Dinari, Yedidya. *Ḥakmey Ashkenaz be-shalhey yemey ha-beynayyim.* Jerusalem: Mossad Bialik, 1984.

Easterbrook, Frank. "Legal Interpretation and the Power of the Judiciary." *Harvard Journal of Law and Public Policy* 7.1 (Winter 1984): 87–99.

_____. "Method, Result, and Authority: A Reply." *Harvard Law Review* 98.3 (January 1985): 622–29.

Eidelberg, Shlomo. "'Maarufia' in Rabbenu Gershom's Responsa." *Historia Judaica* 15.1 (April 1953): 59–66.

Eisenstein, Elizabeth L. *The Printing Press as an Agent of Change.* 2 vols. Cambridge: Cambridge University Press, 1979.

Elbaum, Ya'aqob. *Teshubat ha-leb ve-qabbalat yessurim.* Jerusalem: Magnes, 1992.

Elon, Menachem. *Ḥerut ha-peraṭ be-darkey gebiyyat ḥob ba-mishpaṭ ha-'ibri.* Jerusalem: Magnes, 1964.

_____. "Ha-ma'asar ba-mishpaṭ ha-'ibri." In *Sefer yobel le-Pinḥas Rosen.* Edited by Haim Cohen. Jerusalem: Mif'al ha-shikpul, 1962, pp. 171–201.

_____. "Power and Authority: Halachic Stance of the Traditional Community and its Contemporary Implications." In *Kinship and Consent.* Edited by Daniel J. Elazar. Ramat Gan: Tutledove, 1981, pp. 183–213.

Erikson, Kai T. *Wayward Puritans.* New York: Wiley, 1966.

Ettinger, Samuel. "Ḥelqam shel ha-Yehudim be-qolonizaẓyah shel Uqr'enah (1569–1648)." *Zion* 21.3–4 (1956): 107–42.

Falk, Ze'ev. *Jewish Matrimonial Law in the Middle Ages.* London: Oxford University Press, 1966.

Feldman, E. "Heykan u-bishbil mi nitaqqnu ha-taqqanot le-issur ha-mela'kah be-Shabbat shel R. Meshulam Feybush me-Qera'qa'." *Zion* 34 (1969): 90–97.

Fettke, Dieter. *Juden und Nichtjuden im 16. und 17. Jahrhundert in Polen.* Frankfurt: P. Lang, 1986.

Fichtner, Paula Sutter. *Protestantism and Primogeniture in Early Modern Germany.* New Haven: Yale University Press, 1989.

Finkelstein, Louis. *Jewish Self-Government in the Middle Ages.* Second printing corrected and emended. New York: Feldheim, 1964.

Fram, Edward. "Jewish Law and Social and Economic Realities in Sixteenth and Seventeenth Century Poland." Ph.D. diss., Columbia University, 1991.

Frank, Mosheh. *Qehillot Ashkenaz u-batey dineyhen.* Tel Aviv: Dvir, 1937.

Fränkel, David. "Diqduqey soferim." *'Alim le-bibliyogerafyah ve-qorot Yisra'el* 1.3 (1935): 112–14.

Freedman, Abraham I. "Imprisonment for Debt." *Temple Law Quarterly* 2.4 (July 1928): 330–65.

Freimann, Abraham. *Seder qiddushin ve-nisu'in aḥarey ḥatimat ha-talmud.* 1945; reprint, Jerusalem: Mossad Harav Kook, 1964.

Freundt, Carl. *Das Wechselrecht der Postglossatoren.* 2 vols. Leipzig: Duncker and Humblot, 1899–1909.

Fuss, Abraham M. "Assignability of Debt and Negotiable Instruments in Jewish Law." *Diné Israel* 12 (1984–1985): 19–37.

_____. "The Eastern European *Shetar Mamran* Re-examined." *Diné Israel* 4 (1973): li-lxvii.

Gajewska, Miroslawa. "Wyposażenie w sprzęty mieszczanskich gospodarstw domowych." *Dom i mieszkanie w Polsce (druga połowa XVII-XIX w.).* Edited by Zofia Kamienska. Wrocław: Zakład Narodowy im. Ossolinskich, 1975, pp. 145–238.

Gieysztorowa, Irena. "Research into Demographic History of Poland. A Provisional Summing-up." *Acta Poloniae Historica* 18 (1968): 5–17.

Gloger, Zygmunt. *Encyklopedia staropolska ilustrowana.* With an introduction by Julian Krzyzanowski. 4 vols. Warsaw: Wiedza Powszechna, 1972.

Goitein, S.D. *A Mediterranean Society.* 6 vols. Berkeley: University of California Press, 1967–1993.

Goldberg, Jacob. "De non tolerandis Iudaeis." In *Studies in Jewish History Presented to Professor Raphael Mahler on His Seventy-fifth Birthday.* Edited by Samuel Yeivin. Merhavia, Israel: Poalim, 1974, pp. 39–52.

_____. *Jewish Privileges in the Polish Commonwealth.* Jerusalem: Israel Academy of Sciences and Humanities, 1985.

Guldon, Zenon and Jacek Wijaczka. "Osadnictwo żydowskie w województwach Poznańskim i Kaliskim w XVI-XVII wieku." *BZIH* 162–163/2–3 (1992): 63–77.

Guldon, Zenon. "Źródła i metody szacunków liczebności ludności żydowskiej w Polsce w XVI-XVIII wieku." *Kwartalnik Historii Kultury Materialnej* 34.2 (1986): 249–63.

_____. *Żydzi i Szkoci w Polsce w XVI-XVII wieku.* Kielce: Wyższa Szkola Pedagogiczna im. Jana Kochanowskiego, 1990.

Gurland, Jonas. *Leqorot ha-gezerot 'al Yisra'el.* 7 vols. 1887–1892; Reprint, Jerusalem: Kedem, 1972.

Halperin, Israel. "Mibneh ha-va'adim be-Eyropah ha-mizraḥit ve-ha-merkazit be-me'ah ha-17 ve-ha-18." In *World Congress of Jewish Studies.* Volume 1 (Summer 1947). Jerusalem: Magnes, 1952, pp. 439–45.

_____. "Re'shito shel va'ad medinat Liṭa' ve-yaḥaso el va'ad arba' araẓot." *Zion* 3 (1938): 51–57.

_____. *Yehudim ve-yahadut be-mizraḥ Eyropah.* Jerusalem: Magnes, 1968.

Historia chłopów polskich. Edited by Stefan Inglot. 3 vols. Warsaw: Ludowa Spółdzielnia Wydawnicza, 1970–1980.

Hoffmann, David. *Der Schulchan-Aruch und die Rabbinen über das Verhältniss der Juden zu Andersgläubigen.* 2nd edition. Berlin, 1894.

Horn, Maurycy. "Działalność gospodarcza i pozycja materialna Żydów czerwonoruskich w świetle lustracji i inwentarzy z lat 1564–1570." *BZIH* 2/82 (April–June 1972): 15–26.

_____. *Powinności wojenne Żydów w Rzeczypospolitej w XVI i XVII wieku.* Warsaw: Państwowe Wydawnicza Naukowe, 1978.

_____. "Spolecznośc żydowska w wielonarodowościowym Lwowie 1356–1696." *BZIH* 157.1 (January–March 1991): 3–14.

_____. *Żydzi na Rusi Czerwonej w XVI i pierwszej połowie XVII w.* Warsaw: Państwowe Wydawnictwo Naukowe, 1975.

Horowitz, E. "'Haknasat kallah' be-geṭṭo Veneẓiyah: beyn masoret le-ḥiddush u-beyn idey'al le-meẓi'ut." *Tarbiz* 56 (1987): 347–71.

Hoszowski, Stanisław. *Ceny we Lwowie w XVI i XVII wieku.* Lvov: J. Mianowski, 1928.

Huebner, Rudolf. *A History of Germanic Private Law.* Translated by Francis Philbrick. Boston: Little, Brown, 1918.

Hundert, Gershon. "An Advantage to Peculiarity? The Case of the Polish Commonwealth." *AJS Review* 6 (1981): 21–38.

_____. "On the Jewish Community in Poland during the Seventeenth Century: Some comparative Perspectives." *Revue des études juives* 142 (July–December 1983): 349–72.

_____. "Jewish Urban Residence in the Polish Commonwealth in the Early Modern Period." *The Jewish Journal of Sociology* 26.1 (June 1984): 25–34.

_____. "Jews, Money and Society in the Seventeenth-Century Polish Commonwealth: The Case of Krakow." *Jewish Social Studies* 43.3–4 (Summer-Fall 1981): 261–74.

_____. "Security and Dependence: Perspectives on Seventeenth-Century Polish-Jewish Society Gained through a Study of Jewish Merchants in Little Poland." Ph.D. diss., Columbia University, 1978.

_____. "The Implications of Jewish Economic Activities for Christian-Jewish Relations in the Polish Commonwealth." In *The Jews in Poland.* Edited by Chimen Abramsky, et al. Oxford: Blackwell, 1986, pp. 55–63.

_____. *The Jews in a Polish Private Town.* Baltimore: Johns Hopkins University Press, 1992.

_____. "The Role of the Jews in Commerce in Early Modern Poland-Lithuania." *The Journal of European Economic History* 16.2 (Fall 1987): 245–75.

Jordan, William. *Women and Credit in Pre-Industrial and Developing Societies.* Philadelphia: University of Pennsylvania Press, 1993.

Kahana, Yizhaq Z. *Sefer ha-'agunot.* Jerusalem: Mossad Harav Kook, 1954.

Kapisch-Zuber, Christiane. *Women, Family, and Ritual in Renaissance Italy.* Translated by Lydia Cochrane. Chicago: University of Chicago Press, 1985.

Katz, Jacob. "Beyn TaTN"U le-Ta"Ḥ ve-Ta"Ṭ." In *Sefer ha-yobel le-Yiẓḥaq Baer.* Edited by Salo Baron, et al. Jerusalem: Historical Society of Israel, 1961, pp. 318–37.

_____. *Beyn Yehudim le-goyim.* Jerusalem: Mossad Bialik, 1960.

_____. *Goy shel Shabbat.* Jerusalem: Zalman Shazar Center, 1984.

_____. "Hirhurim 'al ha-yaḥas beyn dat le-kalkalah." *Tarbiz* 60 (1991): 99–111.

_____. "Ma'arib be-zemano ve-she-lo' be-zemano." *Zion* 35 (1970): 35–60.

_____. *Masoret u-mashber.* Jerusalem: Mossad Bialik, 1958.

_____. "Nisu'im ve-ḥayyey ishut be-moẓa'ey yemey ha-beynayyim." *Zion* 10.1–2 (1945): 21–54.

_____. "Soblanut datit be-shiṭato shel Rabbi Menaḥem ha-Me'iri be-halakah u-be-filosofyah." *Zion* 18 (1953): 15–30.

Kula, Witold. *An Economic Theory of the Feudal System: Towards a Model of the Polish Economy 1500–1800.* Translated by Lawrence Garner. London: NLB, 1976.

Kutrzeba, Stanisław. *Historja źródeł dawnego prawa polskiego.* 2 vols. 1925?-1926?; Reprint, Cracow: Krajowa Agencja Wydawnicza, 1987.

Levine, Hillel. *Economic Origins of Antisemitism.* New Haven: Yale University Press, 1991.

Levinthal, Louis Edward. "The Early History of Bankruptcy Law." *University of Pennsylvania Law Review* 66 (April 1918): 223–50.

Lewin, Isaac. *Demuyyot ve-eyru'im hisṭoriyim.* Jerusalem: Mossad ha-Rav Kook, 1988.

———. "Le-she'elat ha-'geṭ me-Vina'.'" In *Me-boqer le-'ereb.* Jerusalem: Mossad Harav Kook, 1981, pp. 115–26.

Lichtenstein, Aharon. "Kabod ha-beriyyot." *Maḥanayim* 5 (1993):8–15.

Link-Lenczowski, Andrzej. "Lucność Żydowska w świetle uchwał sejmikowych XVI-XVIII w." In *Żydzi w dawnej Rzeczypolitej.* Edited by Andrzej Link-Lenczowski. Wrocław: Ossolineum, 1991, pp. 154–61.

Maciszewski, Jarema. *Szlachta polska i jej państwo.* 2nd edition. Warsaw: Wiedza Powszechna, 1986.

Małecki, Jan. *Studia nad rynkiem regionalnym Krakowa w XVI wieku.* Warsaw: Państwowe Wydawnictwo Naukowe, 1963.

———. "Żydzi w życiu gospodarczym Krakowa w XVI i pierwszej połowie XVII wieku." *Krzysztofory* 15 (1988):14–18.

Malkiel, David. *A Separate Republic.* Jerusalem: Magnes, 1991.

Malowist, M. "The Economic and Social Development of the Baltic Countries from the Fifteenth to the Seventeenth Centuries." *The Economic History Review*, 2nd series, 12, no. 2 (1959): 177–89.

Mandelsberg-Schildkraut, Bella. *Meḥqarim le-toledot Yehudey Lublin.* Tel Aviv: Circle of Friends of the Late Bella Mandelsberg-Schildkraut, 1965.

Margoliouth, Reuben. "Margaliyyot ha-yam." *Qol Torah* 2.2 (Fall 1947): 9–10.

Mełen, A. "Ordynacje w dawnej Polsce." *Pamiętnik Historyczno-Prawny* 7.2 (1929): 40–60.

Mevorakh, Baruch. Review of '*Im ḥilufey tequfot*, by Ezriel Shochat. In *Kirjath Sepher* 37.2 (March 1962): 150–55.

Morell, Samuel. *Precedent and Judicial Discretion: The Case of Joseph Ibn Lev.* South Florida Studies in the History of Judaism, no. 26. Atlanta: Scholars Press, 1991.

———. "The Constitutional Limits of Communal Government in Rabbinic Law." *Jewish Social Studies* 33.2–3 (April–July 1971): 87–119.

Morgensztern, Janina. "Żydzi w Zamośćiu na przełomie XVI i XVII w." *BZIH* 43–44 (July–December 1962): 3–17.

Munro, John. "Die Anfänge der Übertragbarkeit: Einige Kreditinnovationen im Englisch-Flämischen Handel des Spätmittelalters (1360–1540)." In *Kredit im Spätmittelalterlichen und Frühneuzeitlichen Europa.* Edited by Michael North. Köln: Bohlau, 1991, pp. 39–69.

———. "The International Law Merchant and the Evolution of Negotiable Credit in Late-Medieval England and the Low Countries." In *Banchi pubblici, banci privati e monti di pietà nell'Europa Preindustriale* Atti della Società Ligure di Storia Patria, nuova ser., vol. 31. Genova: Società Ligure di Storia Patria, 1991, pp. 49–80.

Nadav, Mordechai. "Ma'aseh allimut hadadiyyim beyn Yehudim le-lo' Yehudim be-Liṭa' lifney 1648." *Gal-Ed* 7–8 (1985): 41–56.

Nadel-Golobic, Eleonora. "Armenians and Jews in Medieval Lvov: Their Role in Oriental Trade 1400–1600." *Cahiers du Monde Russe et Soviétique* 20.3–4 (July–December 1979): 345–88.

Nadelmann, Kurt H. "Bankruptcy Treaties." *University of Pennsylvania Law Review* 93 (September 1944): 58–97.

Nemoy, Leon. Review of *Jews of Arab Lands* by Norman Stillman. In *Jewish Quarterly Review* 71 (October 1980): 123–25.

Neuman, Abraham A. *The Jews in Spain.* 2 vols. Philadelphia: Jewish Publication Society, 1942.

Noonan, John T., Jr. *The Scholastic Analysis of Usury.* Cambridge, Mass.: Harvard University Press, 1957.

North, Michael. "Banking and Credit in Northern Germany in the Fifteenth and Sixteenth Centuries." In *Banchi pubblici, banci privati e monti di pietà nell'Europa preindustriale.* Atti della Società Ligure di Storia Patria, nuova ser., vol. 31. Genova: Società Ligure di Storia Patria, 1991, pp. 811–26.

Papers Relating to the Scots in Poland 1576–1793. Edited with an Introduction by A. Francis Steuart. Edinburgh: T. and A. Constable, 1915.

Passamaneck, Stephen. *Insurance in Rabbinic Law.* Edinburgh: Edinburgh University Press, 1974.

Pelc, Juljan. *Ceny w Krakowie w latach 1369–1600.* Lvov: J. Mianowski, 1935.

Pennington, Kenneth. *Pope and Bishops.* Philadelphia: University of Pennsylvania Press, 1984.

Pennington, Robert R. "Retention of Title to the Sale of Goods under European Law." *International and Comparative Law Quarterly* 27 (1978): 277–318.

Polski słownik biograficzny. Edited by Władysław Konopczynski et al. 32 volumes to date. Cracow: Nakład Polskiej Akademii Umiejętnośći, 1935– .

Postan, M. M. "Private Financial Instruments in Medieval England." *Vierteljahrschrift für Sozial- und Wirtschafts-Geschichte* 23 (1930): 26–75.

Radžius, Aleksandras. "Cash Flow in Medieval Lithuania." *The Knight* 12.5 (March–April 1990): 1–2, 4–5, 8; 14.1 (September–October 1991): 2, 4–7.

Raffeld, Meir. "Ha-Maharshal ve-'Ha-yam shel Shelomoh.'" Ph.D. diss. Bar-Ilan University, 1990.

Redlich, Fritz. *Die deutsche Inflation des frühen siebzehnten Jahrhunderts in der zeitgenössischen Literature: Die Kipper und Wipper.* Köln: Böhlau, 1972.

Riesenfeld, Stefan A. "The Evolution of Modern Bankruptcy Law." *Minnesota Law Review* 31.5 (April 1947): 401–55.

Rivkind, Isaac. "Diqduqey-soferim." In *Sefer ha-yobel le-kebod Alekkesander Ma'rks.* 2 vols. Edited by Saul Lieberman. New York: Jewish Theological Seminary, 1950, pp. 391–432.

Rosenthal, Judah M. "Marcin Czechowic and Jacob of Bełżyce Arian-Jewish Encounters in 16th Century Poland." *PAAJR* 34 (1966): 77–97.

Rosman, M. J. *The Lord's Jews.* Cambridge, Mass.: Harvard University Press, 1990.

_____. "Dimmuyav shel beyt Yisra'el be-Polin ke-merkaz Torah aḥarey gezerot Ta"Ḥ—Ta"Ṭ." *Zion* 51.4 (1986): 435–48.

_____. "Jewish Perceptions of Insecurity and Powerlessness in Sixteenth-Eighteenth Century Poland." *Polin* 1 (1986):19–27.

_____. "Reflections on the State of Polish-Jewish Historical Study." *Jewish History* 3.2 (Fall 1988): 115–30.

_____. "Samkuto shel va'ad arba' araẓot mi-ḥuẓ le-Polin." *Annual of Bar Ilan University* 24–25 (1989): 11–30.

Ross, Arnold, ed. *European Bankruptcy Laws.* Chicago?: Section of International Law, American Bar Association, 1974.

Rutkowski, Jan. *Histoire économique de la Pologne avant les partages.* Paris: Champion, 1927.

Schiper, Ignacy. *Dzieje handlu żydowskiego na ziemiach polskich.* 1937; Reprint, Cracow: Krajowa Agencja Wydanicza, 1990.

Segal, Agnes Romer. "Yiddish Works on Women's Commandments in the Sixteenth Century." In *Studies in Yiddish Literature and Folklore.* Research Projects of the Institute of Jewish Studies. Monograph Series 7. Jerusalem: Hebrew University, 1986, pp. 37–59.

Shmeruk, Chone. "Baḥurim me-Ashkenaz be-yeshibot Polin." In *Sefer ha-yobel le-Yizḥaq Baer.* Edited by Salo Baron, et al. Jerusalem: Historical Society of Israel, 1960, pp. 304–17.

_____. "Qavvim le-demutah shel sifrut Yiddish be-Polin u-be-Liṭa' 'ad gezerot Ta"Ḥ ve-Ta"Ṭ." *Tarbiz* 46 (1977): 258–314.

Shmuelevitz, Aryeh. *The Jews of the Ottoman Empire in the Late Fifteenth and the Sixteenth Centuries.* Leiden: Brill, 1984.

Shulman, Nisson. *Authority and Community.* Hoboken, N.J.: Ktav, 1986.

Shulvass, Moses. *From East to West.* Detroit: Wayne State University Press, 1971.

Siekanowicz, Peter. *Legal Sources and Bibliography of Poland.* Praeger Publications in Russian History and World Communism, no. 22. New York: Praeger, 1964.

Słownik geograficzny królestwa polskiego i innych krajów slowianskich. Edited by F. Sulimierski, et al. 15 volumes. Warsaw: F. Sulimierski, 1880–1904.

Słownik polszczyzny XVI wieku. Edited by Maria Renata Mayenowa. 21 volumes to date. Wrocław: Zakład Narodowy im. Ossolinskich, 1966– .

Soloveitchik, Haym. "Can Halakhic Texts Talk History?" *AJS Review* 3 (1978): 152–96.

_____. *Halakah, kalkalah, ve-dimmuy 'aẓmi.* Jerusalem: Magnes, 1985.

_____. "Pawnbroking A Study in *Ribbit* and of the Halakah in Exile." *Proceedings of the American Academy for Jewish Research* 1970–1971 (38–39): 203–68.

_____. "Religious Law and Change: The Medieval Ashkenazic Example." *AJS Review* 12.2 (Fall 1987): 205–21.

_____. *Shu"t ke-meqor hisṭori.* Jerusalem: Zalman Shazar Center, 1990.

Soroka, Wacław. "Main Institutions of the Polish Private Law, 1400–1795." In *Polish Law Throughout the Ages.* Edited by Wenceslas Wagner. Stanford: Hoover Institution Press, 1970, pp. 73–95.

Spiegel, Jacob. "Derek qeẓarah bi-lshon tanna'im ve-'al peshaṭ ve-derash ba-mishnah." *Asufot* 4 (1990): 9–26.

Strayer, Joseph, ed. *Dictionary of the Middle Ages.* New York: Scribner, 1982–1989.

Sysyn, Frank. "A Curse on Both their Houses: Catholic Attitudes toward the Jews and Eastern Orthodox during the Khmel'nyts'kyi Uprising in Father Pawel Ruszel's Fawor nibieski." In *Israel and the Nations Essays Presented in Honor of Shmuel Ettinger.* Edited by Shmuel Almog, et al. Jerusalem: Historical Society of Israel, 1987, pp. xi-xxiv.

Szewczyk, Roman. *Ludność lublina w latach 1583–1650.* Lublin: KUL, 1947.

Ta-Shma, Israel. "Le-toledot ha-yehudim be-Polin be-me'ot ha-12—ha-13." *Zion* 53 (1988): 347–69.

Taubenschłag, Rafal. "Skrypty dłuzne z klauzula 'na zlecenie' i 'na okaziciela' w średniowiecznem prawie polskiem." *Czasopismo prawnicze i ekonomiczne* 30 (1936): 84–92.

Tazbir, Janusz. "Images of the Jew in the Polish Commonwealth." *Polin* 4 (1989): 18–30.

_____. "La tolérance religieuse en Pologne aux XVIe et XVIIe siècles." In *La Pologne au XIIe congres international des sciences historiques a Vienne.* Warsaw: Państwowe Wydawnicza Naukowe, 1965, pp. 31–48.

_____. *Reformacja w Polsce. Szkice o ludziach i doktrynie.* Warsaw: Książka i Wiedza, 1993.

Thirsk, Joan. "The European Debate on Customs of Inheritance, 1500–1700." In *Family and Inheritance: Rural Society in Western Europe, 1200–1800.* Edited by Jack Goody,

Joan Thirsk, and E.P. Thompson. Cambridge: Cambridge University Press, 1976, pp. 177–91.

Tollet, Daniel. "La place faite aux juifs dans la société Polonaise (fin du XVIe s., XVIIe s.): Representation social et aspects juridiques." *Revue des études juives* 138 (July–December 1979): 533–46.

_____. "Les Juifs et le trésor royal polonais sous les règnes des Wasa, de 1588 à 1668." In *The Jews in Poland.* Volume 1. Edited by Andrzej Paluch. Cracow: Research Center on Jewish History and Culture in Poland, 1992, pp. 51–65.

_____. "Les manifestations anti-Juives dans la Pologne des Wasa (1588–1668)." *Revue d'histoire moderne et contemporaine* 33 (July–September 1986): 427–39.

_____. "Marchands et hommes d'affaires juifs dans la Pologne des Wasa (1588–1668)." Ph.D. diss., Université de Paris, 1985.

_____. "Merchants and Businessmen in Poznań and Cracow, 1588–1668." In *The Jews in Poland.* Edited by Chimen Abramsky, et al. Oxford: Blackwell, 1986, pp. 22–30.

Topolski, Jerzy. "La régression économique en Pologne du XVIe au XVIIe siècle." *Acta Poloniae Historica* 7 (1962): 28–49.

_____. "On the Role of the Jews in the Urbanization of Poland in the Early Modern Period." In *The Jews in Poland.* Volume 1. Edited by Andrzej Paluch. Cracow: Research Center on Jewish History and Culture in Poland, 1992, pp.45–50.

_____. "Sixteenth-Century Poland and the Turning Point in European Economic Development." In *A Republic of Nobles.* Edited and translated by J. K. Fedorowicz. Cambridge, 1982, pp. 74–90.

_____. "Wpływ wojen połowy XVII wieku na sytuacje ekonomiczna Podlasia." In *Studia historica w 35–lecie pracy naukowej Henryka Łowmianskiego.* Edited by Aleksander Gieysztor. Warsaw: Państwowe Wydawnictwo Naukowe, 1958, pp. 309–49.

Treiman, Israel. "Majority Control in Compositions: Its Historical Origins and Development." *Virginia Law Review* 24.5 (March 1938): 507–27.

Udovitch, Abraham. *Partnership and Profit in Medieval Islam.* Princeton: Princeton University Press, 1970.

Urbach, Ephraim. *Ba'aley ha-tosafot.* 4th edition. 2 vols. Jerusalem: Mossad Bialik, 1980.

Usher, Abbott Payson. *The Early History of Deposit Banking in Mediterranean Europe.* Cambridge, Mass.: Harvard University Press, 1943.

Van der Wee, Herman. "Monetary, Credit and Banking Systems." In *The Cambridge Economic History of Europe,* vol. 5. Edited by E. E. Rich and C. H. Wilson. Cambridge: Cambridge University Press, 1977, pp. 290–393.

_____. "The Medieval and Early Modern Origins of European Banking," in *Banchi pubblici, banci privati e monti di pietà nell'Europa preindustriale,* Atti della Società Ligure di Storia Patria, nuova ser., vol. 31. Genova: Società Ligure di Storia Patria, 1991, pp. 1159–73.

Van Horn, William Dwight III. "Suburban Development, Rural Exchange, and the Manorial Economy in Royal Prussia 1570–1700." Ph.D. diss., Columbia University, 1987.

Vinogradoff, Paul. *Roman Law in Medieval Europe.* 3d edition. With a Preface by F. de Zueleta. Oxford: Clarendon Press, 1961.

W.B.[Wacław Borowy] *Scots in Old Poland.* Edinburgh: Oliver and Boyd, 1941.

Węgrzynek, Hanna. "*Czarna legenda*" *Żydów.* Warsaw: Wydawnictwo Bellona, 1995.

Weinryb, Bernard. "The Beginnings of East European Jewry in Legend and Historiography."

In *Studies and Essays in Honor of Abraham A. Neuman.* Edited by Meir Ben-Horin, et al. Leiden: Brill, 1962, pp. 445–502.

———. *The Jews of Poland.* Philadelphia: Jewish Publication Society, 1976.

Weissler, Chava. "The Religion of Traditional Ashkenazic Women: Some Methodological Issues." *AJS Review* 12.1 (Spring 1987): 73–94.

Wischnitzer, Mark. *A History of Jewish Crafts.* With a Foreword by Salo W. Baron. New York: Jonathan David, 1965.

Wójcik, Zbigniew. "Poland and Russia in the 17th Century: Problems of Internal Development." In *Poland at the 14th International Congress of Historical Sciences in San Francisco.* Edited by Bronisław Geremek and Antoni Mączak. Wrocław: Ossolineum, 1975, pp. 113–33.

Wyczanski, Andrzej. *La consommation alimentaire en Pologne aux XVIe et XVIIe siècles.* Paris: Institut d'études slaves, 1985.

Wyrobisz, Andrzej. "Economic Landscapes: Poland from the Fourteenth to the Seventeenth Century." In *East-Central Europe in Transition.* Edited by Antoni Mączak, Henryk Samsonowicz, and Peter Burke. Cambridge: Cambridge University Press, 1985, pp. 36–46.

———. "Rola miast prywatnych w Polsce w XVI i XVII wieku." *Przegląd Historyczny* 65 (1974): 19–46.

———. "Small Towns in 16th and 17th-Century Poland." *Acta Poloniae Historica* 34 (1976): 153–64.

Wyrozumska, Bożena. "Did King Jan Olbracht Banish the Jews from Cracow?" In *The Jews in Poland.* Volume 1. Edited by Andrzej Paluch. Cracow: Research Center on Jewish History and Culture in Poland, 1992, pp. 27–37.

Yuval, Israel Jacob. *Ḥakamim be-doram.* Jerusalem: Magnes, 1988.

———. "Ha-hesderim ha-kaspiyyim shel ha-nisu'im be-Ashkenaz be-yemey ha-beynayyim." In *Dat ve-kalkalah.* Edited by Menahem Ben-Sasson. Jerusalem: Shazar Center, 1995, pp. 191–207.

Ziegler, Joseph. "Reflections on the Jewry Oath in the Middle Ages." In *Christianity and Judaism.* Studies in Church History, no. 29. Edited by Diana Wood. Oxford: Blackwell, 1992, pp. 209–20.

Zinberg, Israel. *A History of Jewish Literature.* Volume 7. Translated and edited by Bernard Martin. Cleveland: Press of Case Western Reserve University, 1975.

Zulueta, Francis de. *The Roman Law of Sale.* Oxford: Clarendon Press, 1945.

Zunz, Mattahias Jehiel. *'Ir ha-ẓedeq.* Lvov, 1874.

General Index

Adultery, 51–52,53
Agriculture: Jews in, 27–28
Agunah, 67
Alcholic beverages, 27 n.58; non–kosher wine and Moravian wine trade, 95–105; beer, 99 n.107
Arenda: definition, 26 n.55; encroachment on leasing, 108–28
Asher ben Yehi'el (ca. 1250–1327), 71,98 n.105,141
Ashkenazi, Abraham, 58
Ashkenazi, Me'ir ha–Kohen (fl. 1630–1645), 29,32
Ashkenazi, Menaem, 48 n.3,101 n.113,104–105

Bankruptcy: division of assets, 138–43; reputations of potential bankrupts, 148; in halakhah, 149–50; collection from debtors, 151–57; ketubbah vs. other creditors, 157–59; death of debtor, 159–60; in non–Jewish society, 160–61
Berechiah Berak ben Isaac Eiziq, 27
Bezalel ben Solomon the Preacher, 61 n.57
Bills payable to bearers: origins, 129–31; in Poland (membrany), 131–33; in halakhah, 133–38
Boleslaw the Pious, 25
Bona Sforza, Queen, 109,110
Brest Litovsk, 121
Burial: 69; refusal of to debtors, 159–60

Censorship, 8 n.22
Chmielnicki massacres, 61 n.57
Clothing, 30 n.70
Collective responsibility for debtors, 147–48
Colon, Joseph, 79–80,124
Council of Four Lands, 42–46,42 n.17,119,153, 155
Cracow, 19 n.19,22 n.33,33,39 n.6,52,54 n.22,55,102
Czopowe, 121 n.45

David ben Samuel ha–Levi, 102
Death of debtor, 159–60

Dina' de-malkuta' dina', 115–18
Division of assets, 138–43

Economic and social conditions: general, 18; for Jews, 19–23,26–28; crisis of early 17th cent. 144–46; impact on Jews, 146–48
Edels, Samuel, 57
Egypt, 46,46 n.36,83,83 n.54
Eliezer ben Joel ha-Levi, 122 n.48
Eliezer ben Nathan of Mainz (ca. 1090–1170), 79
Ephraim of Łęczyca (1550–1619), 48 n.2
Ethnic and religious diversity in Poland, 16–18
Excommunication, 149 n.25,154

Falk, Joshua (d. 1614), 45,136,137–38,154
Franco-German Jewry: 3; qahal, 40–41; taqqanot, 46; and female inheritance, 81 n.46,82–84

Gdansk, 19
Gold coins, value of, 86 n.64
Gombin, 33
Government in Poland, 23–24
Grain trade, 106–107
Guilds, 38 n.3

Halakhah: authority of, 2–3; easing the difficulty of observance, 67–69,105; *dina' de-malkuta' dina'* and economic practice, 117; and membrany, 133–38; on insolvency, 149–50,155–57,159–62; in commerce 162–63
Halakhah and popular norms & current conditions: 2,4–5,36–37,76,78–95; current practice used to support halakhah, 74; authority in face of popular behavior, 104; vs. public values on insolvency, 160–62; commerce in general, 163
Halakhah and taqqanot: in Franco–German Jewry, 46; on arenda, 123,126–28; membrany, 137–38, 143; on

insolvency, 149–50, 155, 156–57, 159; in commerce 162–63
Half a male's portion contract, 86–94
Handel, Manoa ben Shemariyah (d. 1612), 55
Hanover, Nathan, 60–61
Hanukkah candles, 68
Hasidey Ashkenaz, 3,16,56
Hayyim ben Bezalel of Friedberg, 20 n.24
Hazzan, 73,73 n.18
Head-covering, 50
Heller, Yom Tob Lipman, 57,57 n.35
Hermeneutics, 3
Horowitz, Isaac, 8 n.21
Host desecration, 33 n.85

Imprisonment of debtors, 153–55,154 n.42; Polish law, 155
Inflation, 144–45
Inheritance contract: 82; in Poland, 85–86
Inheritance in Poland, 84–85
Isaac of Evreux (first half 13th cent.), 114
Isaac ben Bezalel (d. 1576), 110–12,116
Isaac ben Moses of Vienna (ca. 1180–ca. 1250), 117
Isaac ben Samuel of Dampierre (d.ca. 1185), 97–98
Isserles, Moses (d. 1572): 5,22; Sabbath marriage case, 69–76; female inheritance, 85 n.61; and expectancies, 90; non–kosher wine and Moravian Jewish wine trade, 95–99,105; and bankruptcy, 153,159–60

Jacob ben Asher (d. 1340), 71,93 n.90,98 n.105,137,153
Jacob ben Me'ir Tam (d. 1170): 71 ff.,75 n.25,97–98,113,117
Jaffe, Mordecai (ca. 1535–1612), 44,78,135–136,136 n.30,153–54
Jewish-Christian relations, 17–18,28–36; stealing from non–Jews, 54–55
Johanan ben Zakka'y, 97
Joseph Tub Ellem, 113
Joshua Höschel, 58,105
Judah ben Nathan (11th cent.–12th cent.), 97
Judging alone, 111–12

Kabod ha–beriyyot, 67–68
Kalisz, 33
Karo, Joseph, 153
Katz, Joseph (d. 1591): 43,45–46; and female inheritance, 91–94; and judging alone, 116–17
Katz, Yehuda' Leb ben Jacob, 101 n.113
Kazimierz, 21,22 n.33
Ketubbah, 157–59
Krochmal, Menaem Mendel (d. 1661): 53; on division of assets, 139–43; on insolvency, 151–56; and collection of debts, 156–57; ketubbah and other creditors, 157–59

Languages used by Polish Jewry, 29
Łęczyca, 33
Legal status of Jews in Poland, 24–26
Lithuanian Jewish Council, 42–43,119–20
Local vs. distant creditors, 156–57
Löw, Judah (ca. 1525–1609), 32
Lublin: 19 n.19,21,33,42 n.19; fairs, 29,42
Lubmol, 22
Luria, Solomon (ca. 1510–1574): 5,22,49,57,153; philosophy of interpretation, 10–11; on headcovering, 50; women in the marketplace, 77–78; women as husbands' business agents, 79–81; and Moravian Jewish wine merchants, 99–101; witnesses to kashrut of wine, 102; and encroachment on arenda leasing, 111–20
Luzzatto, Simone (ca. 1582–1663), 50 n.9
Lvov, 21,33,44

Ma'arufia, 113–114, 114 n.25
Mainz, 46
Male children marriage contract, 81–82
Manuscripts as sources, 8–9
Me'ir ben Baruch of Rothenburg, 59 n.51,82–83,117
Me'ir ben Gedaliah of Lublin (1558–1616): 55,103; stam yeynam, 102; enroachment of arenda, 123–25
Membrany. *See* Bills payable to bearers
Mezuzah, 34 n.93
Mintz, Moses, 94
Moravia: half a male's portion contract, 87 n.68; Jewish wine trade, 96–105; collection of debts, 156–57
Mordecai ben Hillel ha–Kohen, 113
Murder, 59–60

Nahmanides, Moses, 136
Nissim ben Reuben Gerondi, 100 n.112
Non–Jews: residence among Jews, 22–23; stealing from by Jews, 54–55

Oaths, 62 n.61,100–101
Ottoman Jewry, 162 n.67

Penance, 62–63
Perfet, Isaac ben Sheshet, 156 n.46

Personal piety: lay values, 51–56; popular desire for, 60–63; rabbinic vs. popular concepts, 63–64
Płock, 33
Polish Jewry: origins, 15–16
Pollak, Jacob (1460/70–after 1522), 5
Popular norms: 7; vs. rabbinic values, 48–59,63–64
Poznań, 21–22,32,33,39 n.6
Primogeniture: Jews, 84 n.57; Europe, 84 n.58
Printing: impact on Jewish knowlege, 6–7; errors, 7–8
Przemyśl, 31 n.77,33

Qahal: general, 38–41; leadership, 39–40
Qolonimos, 114

Rab, 97
Rabbis: scholarship in Poland, 5–6; as interpreters of halakhah, 3–5,7,10–12; communal duties, 11–12; and qahal, 40–41; and Council of Four Lands, 43–46; and taqqanot, 46; influence on personal piety, 48–51; corruption among, 56– 59; as viewed by laymen, 58–59; concepts of piety as opposed to lay, 63–64; only ones concerned with gap between law and practice, 81; and membrany, 134–37; and taqqanot in Moravia, 157
Rapoport, Abraham (1584–1651), 44
Rashi, 71,97,113,155
Regional councils, 41–42
Responsa as sources, 7–10
Rymanów: and kosher wine trade, 102–105

Sabbath laws, 60
Sabbath marriage, 69–76
Salonika, 39–40, 40 n.9
Samuel (the amora'), 97
Samuel of Przemyśl, 103–104
Samuel ben Isaac ha–Sardi (1185/90–1255/6), 93 n.89
Samuel ben Me'ir (ca. 1080/85–ca. 1174), 89–90,113
Sandomierz, 9 n.26,22,23 n.37,33
Scots in Poland, 17 n.7
Secular court records as sources, 10
Sexual mores, 51–54
Shakna, Shalom (d. 1558), 5
Simeon ben Gamli'el, 68–69
Sirkes, Joel (1561–1640): philosophy of interpretation, 3; 49; and Sabbath marriage, 75; Jewish men and non-Jewish women, 78; and Moravian wine merchants, 101; 103,104; encroachment of arenda, 120,122–23; and membrany, 136–37,139; on insolvency, 151–56
Slonik, Benjamin: encroachment of arenda, 125–28
Solomon the Doctor, 124, 124 n.53
Solomon ben Judah Leybush, 101,103
Spain, 24–25,46,46 n.36,156 n.46
Speyer, 46
Stam yeynam, 98–99,100–105
Stealing: in general, 55–56; from non–Jews, 54–55,55 n.28
Sulkes, Isaac, 47 n.40,55–56

Taqqanot: as sources, 10; general, 38–47; basis of authority, 40–41; Council of Four Lands, 45; and halakhah in Franco–German Jewry, 46; on arenda bidding, 118–19; vs. halakhah, 123,125–28; and membrany, 137–38; division of assets, 139,143; vs halakhah on insolvency, 149–50,155,156–57,159; in commerce 162–63
Taxes, 38 n.1
Tosafists, 46

Ukraine, 20 n.25
Usury, 133

Venice, 44,44 n.27
Volhynia, 42

Warsaw, 19

Wealthy in qahal leadership, 39–40,39 n.8
Wine of gentiles, 95–105
Włodzimierz, 27,42,58
Women and inheritance: in ancient and medieval times, 81–84; in Poland, 84–85; among Jews, 85–95
Women in the marketplace: physical presence, 76–78; as husbands' agents, 78–81
Women's Books, 50 n.8
Worms, 46

Yeshivot, 5–6
Yeyn nesek, 97–98

Zak, Me'ir ben Abraham, 54,54 n.22
Zamość, 20
Żółkiew, 39 n.7,87 n.68

Index of Medieval and Pre-Modern Rabbinic Sources Cited

Adarbi, Isaac (ca. 1510–1584). *She'elot u-teshubot dibrey ribot, no. 124,* 40 n.9

Asher ben Yehi'el (ca. 1250–1327). *Commentary on Baba' Mezi'a', chapt. 5, no. 38, n. 2,* 156 n.47; *She'elot u-teshubot le-Rabbeynu Asher ben Yehi'el, no. 36.6,* 82 n.51, *no. 54.1,* 159 n.54, *no. 65.1,* 134 n.22

Ashkenazi, Abraham. *Sam ayyim,* 58 n.42

Ashkenazi, Eliezer. *Damaseq Eli'ezer, vol. 1, p. 88b–89a,* 49 n.6; *Ma'asey Mizrayim,* 28 n.64; *Seliot u-pizmonim,* 34 n.91

Avron, *Pinqas ha-kesherim, nos. 391,591,631,* 132 n.15

Berechiah Berak ben Isaac Eiziq. *Zera' berak,* 27 n.57, 30 n.70, *vol. 2,* 57 n.37,61 n.57

Colon, Joseph. *She'elot u–teshubot ha–Mahariq, no. 8,* 84 n.57, *no. 14,* 122 n.48, *no. 78,* 85 n.61, *no. 118,* 113 n.23, *no. 132,* 124 n.51, *no. 193,* 80 n.41

David ben Menasseh ha-Darshan. *Shir ha-ma'alot le-David. p. 12a,* 76 n.29, *p. 15a,* 28, n.64,59 n.49

David ben Samuel ha-Levi. *Magen David, 566.2,* 46 n.38; *Turey zahab, Yoreh de'ah 119,n.2,* 102 n.118, *246,n.7,* 49 n.6, *265.5,* 34 n.93

De Medina, Samuel. *She'elot u–teshubot Maharshdam, Yoreh de'ah, no. 152,* 40 n.9

Delmedigo, Joseph Solomon. *Sefer eylam,* 47 n.40; *Sefer ma'yan gannim,* 47 n.40

Edels, Samuel. *iddushey aggadot, Baba' Batra 73b,* 57 n.37, *Ketubbot 67b,* 54 n.23, *Sanhedrin 7b,* 57 n.37, *Shabbat 119b,* 49 n.4,55 n.25, *Sotah 40a,* 39 n.8,57 n.37

Eleazar ben Judah. *Sefer ha-roqea ha-gadol, no. 28,* 111 n.16

Eliezer ben Nathan of Mainz (ca. 1090–1170). *Sefer Ra'aban, pt. 1, no. 115,* 79 n.39, *pt. 2, p. 195b,* 80 n.44

Falk, Joshua (d. 1614). *Derishah, Eben ha-'ezer 21 n.3,* 78 n.34; *Quneres me-ha-Sema', pp. 2b–3a,* 45 n.29,45 n.30,102 n.117, *p. 10b,* 30 n.70,n.73,36 n.103, *p. 51,* 27 n.56; *Sefer me'irat 'eynayim, 34 n.10,* 49 n.7, *45 n.5,* 138 n.36, *48 n.1,* 136 n.31, *107 n.10,* 154 n.39,160 n.58

Gershom ben Judah. *Teshubot Rabbenu Gershom me'or ha-golah, no. 70,* 114 n.25

Gombiner, Jacob. *Sefer shalom bayit, no. 157,* 30 n.70

Hagahot Maymoniyyot, 6.8, 114 n.25

Hayyim ben Bezalel of Friedberg. *Sefer ha-ayyim,* 30 n.71

Horowitz, Abraham. *Yesh no.halim,* 30 n.73

Isaac of Evreux (first half 13th cent.). *Tosafot, Qiddushin 59a,* 114 n.27

Isaac ben Abraham of Poznań. *Responsa, no. 44,* 28 n.60, *no. 85,* 162 n.66, *no. 119,* 43 n.24

Isaac ben Eliakum of Poznań. *Leb ṭob,* 60 n.51

Isaac ben Moses of Vienna (ca. 1180–ca. 1250). *Sefer or zaru'a. Vol. 1, no. 113,* 15 n.2

Isaac ben Samuel ha-Levi. *She'elot u-teshubot R. Yiaq ha-Levi, no. 7,* 9 n.26, *no. 40,* 53 n.16

Ishbili, Yom Tob ben Abraham. *Ḥiddushey ha-Riyṭba', Maseket Qiddushin,* 77 n.30

Isserlein, Israel. *Sefer terumat ha–deshen, no. 331,* 137 n.34

Isserles, Moses (d. 1572). *Darkey Mosheh*

ha-shalem oshen mishpaṭ, 97, 153 n.37, *vol. 2, 281,* 86 n.63; *Darkey Mosheh me-Tur Yoreh de'ah, no. 119.1,* 101 n.114; *Darkey Mosheh eben ha-'ezer, 108.2,* 85 n.61, *no. 113.5,* 88 n.71; *She'elot u–teshubot ha–Rama', no. 3,* 90 n.79,81, *no. 4,* 26 n.53,88 n.71,90 n.80, *no. 8,* 90 n.80, *no. 29,* 22 n.34, *no. 61,* 22 n.33, *no. 63,* 34 n.90, *no. 69,* 43 n.20, *no. 71,* 90 n.80, *no. 73,* 41 n.14,15,42 n.20,45 n.33, *no. 75,* 43 n.20, *no. 87,* 28 n.60, *no. 95,* 34 n.89, *no. 123, n.1,* 56 n.32, *no. 123,* 56 n.34, *no. 124,* 8 n.22,96 n.97,99 n.109, *no. 125,* 70 n.10,73 n.22, *no. 132,* 22 n.34,23 n.39; *Shulḥan 'arukh, Eben ha-'ezer 21.5,* 78 n.34, *no. 90.1,* 88 n.71, *no. 108.3,* 88 n.70, *no. 113.2,* 88 n.71, *Ḥoshen mishpaṭ 2.1,* 41 n.14, *34.4,* 96 n.99, *42.15,* 138 n.36, *53.1,* 143 n.51, *97.15,30,* 153 n.38, *107.2,* 159–60, *281.7,* 88 n.69, *Oraḥ ḥayyim 193.3,* 31 n.74, *Yoreh de'ah 123.1 and 133.1,* 102 n.122

Jacob ben Asher (d. 1340). *Ṭur, Ḥoshen mishpaṭ, 66,* 134 n.24, *70.1,* 134 n.25, *104.11,* 138 n.39, *119,* 141 n.47

Jaffe, Mordecai (ca. 1535–1612). *Lebush 'ir Shushan, 48,* 132 n.14,135 n.28, *97.15,* 154 n.39, *128.1,* 148 n.21; *Sefer lebush ha-ḥur, Minhagim 36,* 78 n.33

Joseph ben Elijah of Zaslaw. *Sefer rekeb Eliyyahu,* 26 n.54, *p. 2a,* 34 n.89, *p. 12b,* 147 n.16, *p. 18b,* 50 n.8, *p. 22a,* 60 n.55; *Sefer yesod Yosef, 2.2, p. 17a,* 58 n.44

Joshua Höschel. *She'elot u–teshubot peney Yehoshu'a. Pt. 1, Eben ha–'ezer, no. 1,* 53 n.18, *Ḥoshen mishpaṭ no. 10,* 139 n.43,140 n.45,142 n.49, *Oraḥ ḥayyim no. 7,* 62 n.59, *no. 14,* 30 n.72, *Yoreh de'ah 16,* 99 n.110,105 n.131, *Pt. 2, no. 25,* 36 n.103, *no. 26,* 101 n.113, *no. 35,* 27 n.58, *no. 39,* 62 n.58, *no. 62,* 56 n.31, *no. 94,* 22 n.34, *no. 97,* 9 n.25,23 n.37,148 n.19

Judah of Worms. *Sefer ha–roqeaḥ, no. 28,* 118 n.40

Kahana, Natan. *Sefer she'elot u-teshubot dibrey renanah, no. 49,* 88 n.69,71

Katz, Joseph (d. 1591). *She'elot u-teshubot she'erit Yosef, no. 1,* 88 n.73,89 n.76,91 n.82–83, *no. 2,* 87 n.66,89 n.74, *no. 8,* 89 n.75,92 n.87,94 n.91, *no. 16–17,* 80 n.41, *no. 17,* 116 n.31,32,117 n.34, *no. 18,* 39 n.8,59 n.47, *no. 19,* 56 n.33,34, no. 24, 28 n.60, no. 37, 88 n.69, no. 42, 43 n.22, no. 58, 46 n.35, no. 62, 144 n.1, no. 66, 59 n.51, no. 74, 87 n.68,92 n.86, no. 75, 144 n.1, no. 78, 55 n.27,59 n.45

Katzenellenbogen, Me'ir. *She'elot u-teshubot Maharam Paduv'ah, nos. 45,51,* 86 n.66

Krochmal, Menaḥem Mendel (d. 1661). *She'elot u-teshubot ẓemaḥ ẓedeq, no. 2,* 39 n.8,40 n.10,59 n.47, *no. 10,* 134 n.26, *no. 15,* 138 n.40,139 n.42,43, *no. 55,* 54 n.20, *no. 95,* 87 n.66,68, *no. 96,* 87 n.66,68, *no. 108,* 151 n.29, *no. 109,* 157 n.51, *no. 111,* 35 n.96, *no. 114,* 87 n.66,68,88 n.72, *no. 117,* 152 n.34, *no. 118,* 156 n.48

Löw, Judah (ca. 1525–1609). *Derek ḥayyim,* 32 n.81

Luria, Solomon (ca. 1510–1574). *She'elot u–teshubot ha–Maharshal, no. 1,* 111 n.17, *no. 15,* 111 n.17, *no. 17,* 22 n.33, *no. 33,* 54 n.23,55 n.27, *no. 35,* 110 n.14, *no. 36,* 112 n.20,115 n.29, *no. 49,* 90 n.80, *no. 65,* 43 n.23, *no. 69,* 59 n.51, *no. 72,* 30 n.73,31 n.74,50 n.10,101 n.115, *no. 89,* 108 n.10,113 n.24,118 n.38, *no. 91,* 28 n.60, *no. 94,* 31 n.76, *no. 99,* 79 n.38; *Yam shel Shelomoh, Baba' Qamma' 1.20,* 26 n.53,148 n.20, *3.21,* 59 n.51, *6.26,* 33 n.87, *8.28,* 79 n.38, *8.29,* 79 n.38,40,80 n.42,43,44, *8.31,* 31 n.78, *8.58,* 11 n.31,56 n.33,58 n.39,43, *8.72,* 80 n.41, *10.18,* 115 n.29, *10.20,* 54 n.21, *10.59,* 80 n.43, *Beyẓah 3.25,* 60 n.55, *5.6,* 28 n.60, *Giṭṭin Introduction,* 11 n.30, *1.18,* 77 n.31, *Ḥullin 1.6,* 100 n.111, *1.36,* 102 n.119, *5.11,* 62 n.58, *8.22,* 31 n.76, *8.42,* 58 n.41, *8.44,* 31 n.76, *Ketubbot 1.8,* 36 n.101, *1.12,* 36 n.101, *1.20,*

78 n.32, *1.22*, 35 n.94, *2.25*, 134 n.25, *2.42*, 49 n.5, *Qiddushin 1.28*, 54 n.22, *2.19*, 57 n.38, *3.2*, 113 n.22, *4.21*, 31 n.76, *4.25* cf. *4.4*, 77 n.30, *4.25*, 78 n.34, *Yebamot 4.49*, 35 n.98, *6.40*, 36 n.101

Me'ir ben Baruch of Rothenburg. *Teshubot R. Me'ir me-Rotenburg, no. 248*, 82 n.51, *no. 588*, 15 n.2, *no. 815*, 114 n.25

Me'ir ben Gedaliah of Lublin (1558–1616). *She'elot u-teshubot Me'ir me-Lublin, no. 11*, 149 n.22, *no. 12*, 148 n.20, *no. 13*, 8 n.23, *no. 14*, 92 n.85, *no. 16*, 52 n.13, *no. 22*, 135 n.27, *no. 24*, 54 n.22, *no. 25*, 55 n.24, *no. 26*, 151 n.31, *no. 47*, 149 n.21, *no. 50*, 102 n.121,103 n.124, *no. 52*, 52 n.13, *no. 62*, 123 n.49, *no. 79*, 43 n.23, *no. 80*, 52 n.15, *no. 81*, 55 n.27, *no. 88*, 41 n.16, *no. 111*, 124 n.53, *no. 125*, 44 n. 28, *no. 138*, 35 n.96,60 n.52

Meth, Moses. *Sefer mateh Mosheh, no. 150*, 31 n.74

Mintz, Moses. *She'elot u-teshubot rabbenu Mosheh Minz, no. 22*, 86 n.63,88 n.69, *no. 45*, 84 n.56, *no. 47*, 94 n.93, *no. 47b*, 83 n.55

Molin, Jacob. *She'elot u-teshubot ha-Maharil, no. 88*, 85 n.61,62; *Shu"t Maharil ha–ḥadashot, no. 155*, 86 n.63,65,87 n.67, *no. 164*, 85 n.61,86 n.65,88 n.71

Mordecai ben Hillel ha-Kohen. *Sefer Morddekhay, Baba' Batra' 464*, 117 n.36, *481–482*, 122 n.48, *515*, 114 n.25, *599*, 88 n.71, *Baba' Mei'a' 366*, 117 n.37, *Baba' Qamma' 89*, 79 n.40

Moses of Coucy. *Sefer mizvot gadol, positive commandment no. 97*, 112 n.18

Perfet, Isaac ben Sheshet. *She'elot u-teshubot ha–Ribash, no. 484*, 155 n.45

Pinqas ha-medinah o pinqas shel va'ad ha-qehillot ha-ro'shiyyot be-medinat Liṭa', nos. 21–31,33,117,148,250, 149 n.24

Pinqas va'ad arba' ara.zot no. i, 42 n.19,121 n.45, *no. 16*, 45 n.31, *no. 32*, 119 n.42,120 n.44, *no. 89*, 44 n.25, *no. 91*, 44 n.26, *no. 96–97*, 44 n.25, *no. 104*, 41 n.15, *no. 112*, 147 n.15,154 n.41, *no. 128*, 160 n.59, *no. 129*, 148 n.19, *no. 137*, 151 n.33, *no. 138*, 150 n.28,156 n.48, *no. 169*, 150 n.28, *no. 176*, 57 n.35, *no. 178*, 44 n.25,57 n.35, *no. 179*, 57 n.35, *nos. 401, 403*, 44 n.26, *no. 852*, 103 n.124

Rapoport, Abraham (1584–1651). *She'elot u-teshubot eytan ha-ezraḥi, no. 9*, 148 n.19, *no. 43*, 59 n.51, *no. 45*, 54 n.22,23

Samuel ben David ha-Levi. *Naalat shib'ah, no. 21*, 87 n.66,88 n.71,95 n.96

Samuel ben Me'ir (ca. 1080/85–ca. 1174). *Shulḥan 'aruk, Ḥoshen mishpaṭ 231.25*, 107 n.5

Shabbatay ben Me'ir ha-kohen. *Megillat 'eyfah* 61 n.57; *Sefer geburat anashim, no. 1*, 29 n.67,32 n.82, *no. 9*, 29 n.67, *no. 10*, 62 n.58; *Siftey kohen, Ḥoshen mishpaṭ 42 n. 36*, 138 n.36, *50 n. 7*, 133 n.21, *69 n. 17*, 136 n.32, *237*, 113 n.22, *Yoreh de'ah 246 n. 20*, 49 n.6

She'elot u-teshubot ha-ge'onim batra'ey, 8 n.21; *no. 13*, 101 n.113,105 n.130, *no. 19*, 59 n.48, *no. 24*, 27 n.60, *no. 26*, 59 n.50, *no. 48*, 58 n.40

She'elot u-teshubot harrey qedem, no. 15, 103 n.127

Sirkes, Joel (1561–1640). *Bayit adash, Eben ha-'ezer 21*, 78 n.34, *62*, 78 n.33, *Ḥoshen mishpaṭ 34.7*, 49 n.7, *48*, 136 n.32,138 n.37, *69 n. 9*, 138 n.37, *96, n. 23*, 152 n.35, *97 n. 28*, 155 n. 45, *99.9*, 156 n. 49, *104.2*, 156 n. 49, *108.7*, 152, n.35, *280.1*, 152, n.35, *Oraḥ ḥayyim 339*, 75 n.25, *Yoreh de'ah 246*, 49 n.6, *293.3*, 36 n.99; *She'elot u-teshubot ha-bayit ḥadash no. 4*, 22 n.36,28 n.60,62 n.60, *no. 12*, 55 n.27, *no. 13*, 148 n.19, *no. 18*, 23 n.38, *no. 27*, 28 n.60, *no. 32*, 134 n.22,137 n.35, *no. 35*, 139 n.41, *no. 38*, 144 n.1, *no. 44*, 148 n.19, *no. 50*, 76 n.29, *no. 51*, 58 n.40, *no. 52*, 49 n.6, *no. 60*, 41 n.14,45 n.33,120 n.43–44,122 n.47, *no. 61*, 121 n.45, *no. 78*, 76 n.29, *no. 79*, 3 n.6, *no. 82*, 29 n.67,

nos. 85–87, 7 n.18, *no. 91*, 43 n.24, *no. 94*, 151 n.30, *no. 95*, 151 n.30, *no. 97*, 9 n.26, *no. 98*, 52 n.12, *no. 99*, 53 n.15, *no. 100*, 52, 52 n.14, *no. 104*, 9 n.25, *no. 110*, 3 n.6, *no. 127*, 32 n.79, *no. 139*, 3 n.6; *She'elot u-teshubot ha-bayit ḥadash ha- ḥadashot, no. 29*, 26 n.54,48 n.3,101 n.113,104 n.128, *no. 30*, 101 n.113,103 n.126, *no. 32*, 3 n.6, *no. 42*, 75 n.25, *no. 43*, 3 n.6,7 n.19,45 n.32, *no. 51*, 3 n.6, *no. 52*, 35 n.96, *no. 55*, 78 n.33, *nos. 56–57*, 52 n.14, *no. 79*, 9 n.26, *no. 84*, 59 n.50, *no. 89*, 3 n.6, *no. 94*, 9 n.24, *no. 146*, 26 n.54

Slonik, Benjamin. *She'elot u-teshubot masa'at Benyamin, no. 3*, 33 n.88, *no.6*, 32 n.79, *no. 27*, 24 n.44,31 n.75,126 n.58,127 n.60, *no. 28*, 125 n.55, *no. 29*, 8 n.22, *no. 32*, 149 n.22, *no. 33*, 45 n.32, *no. 43*, 27 n.57, *no. 51*, 55 n.27, *no. 86*, 8 n.22,28 n.64,31 n.78, *no. 105*, 60 n.53

Solomon ben Judah Leybush. *Sefer pisqey u-she'elot u-teshubot Maharash me-Lublin, no. 58*, 23 n.40,35 n.95, *no. 88*, 35 n.96, *no. 139*, 101 n.116,103 n.123

Taqqanot medinat Ma'hareyn, nos. 228–336, 149 n.24, *no. 229*, 156 n.48, *no. 235*, 157 n.51, *no. 292*, 45 n.33, *p. 76 n. 4*, 151 n.32

Teshubot ḥakmey Ẓarfat ve-Lotir, no. 94, 81 n.46

Teshubot Maymoniyyot, Nashim, no. 26, 82 n.51

Weil, Jacob. *Dinim ve-halakhot, 16, 27*, 85 n.61; *She'elot u-teshubot Mahar"i Vveyil, no. 109*, 85 n.61